MW01227619

The Lost Casket

THE LOST CASKET

TRANSLATED FROM

"*LA MAIN COUPÉE*"

OF

F. DE BOISGOBEY

BY

S. LEE

NEW YORK

G. P. PUTNAM'S SONS

1881

80006B

CONTENTS.

THE LOST CASKET.

CHAPTER I.

THE LOST CASKET.

IT is not beautiful, certainly, the Boulevard de la
Madeleine, on a November evening, when a violent wind is driving before it, over the flag-stones, the
leaves that line the sombre alley that runs along the Rue
Basse-du-Rempart. The fog is extending its gray vail,
which the yellowish light of the gas jets is scarcely able
to penetrate, while the trees bend and moan under the
blasts of the damp westerly wind. Promenaders have
disappeared. The Paris, which circulates so freely of a
summer night, has sought refuge in clubs and cafés. An
occasional hackney-coach rolls noiselessly over the muddy
street. Only afar off may be heard the murmur, which
is as the breath of the great city of Paris. The season
has come when, toward ten o'clock, solitude begins at
the corner of Rue Scribe.

But when one is twenty-five, has gaiety in his heart, and
louis in his pocket enough and to spare, he mocks at

autumn mists, and walks straight on heedless of threatening showers.

Thus there were two young men who, on such an evening, launched out into this desert region. They were tall, well made, and elegantly dressed. Side by side they walked, their hands in their pockets, their overcoat collars turned up over their ears, talking loud and punctuating their discourse with peals of laughter. A passer-by might have supposed them brothers so much alike were they in height and carriage ; but here the resemblance ceased. One was dark, the other fair. One had irregular features, eyes dark and piercing, a bold, expressive physiognomy, quick gestures and abrupt manner ; he might have been taken for an officer of hussars fresh from Saumur. The other had regular features, blue eyes, a mild expression, and the quiet, dignified deportment of an English gentleman.

"My boy," one of them said, striking the heels of his polished boots on the asphaltum, "you must be the devil himself to undertake a walk to Rue de Luresnes in such weather as this."

"Bah ! we are not so far from your uncle's ; we shall get there before the rain sets in."

"And shall have saved forty sous in hack hire. There are no such things as small economies. I admire you, Jules, and predict that you will be enormously rich."

"I hope so ; and I venture to prophesy that, at the

present rate, you will soon come to the end of your fortune."

"So my uncle tells me every day."

"And much you heed his admonitions. You are wrong. M. Dorgères is devoted to you, and if you would take life in earnest and go to work in his counting room, you might aspire to the hand of your cousin Alice."

"Thank you. Alice is charming, I grant, but I have no idea of marrying. Moreover, I fancy my uncle's design for her is an aristocratic marriage."

"I would lay a wager, on the contrary, that he means to make of his son-in-law his partner and successor."

"Then he could not make a happier choice than my friend, Jules Vignory, model cashier and accomplished gentleman, equally capable of directing vast financial operations or leading a cotillon."

"You are insane. I am not so aspiring."

"Why not? You have already a high place in my uncle's regard, and are not, I am sure, displeasing to my cousin Alice."

"But I have no desire to get into difficulties with Robert."

"Robert de Carnoël, my uncle's secretary! You believe him to be in love with her?"

"I am sure of it."

"Now you speak of it, I remember he did look at her very often the other day at table. *Ma foi!* since you put yourself out of the lists, I should not object to his

marrying her. He is not rich but is well born, and has
heart and intelligence. You know him well, do you
not?"

"Intimately."

"Then he must have confided to you his love
affairs?"

"No ; but he has allowed me to guess them. He is
madly in love with Mlle. Alice, and I should not be surprised if he brought matters to a crisis pretty soon. I
should be glad to know of his success—but I have my
doubts."

"And I likewise. However, if Alice wishes it, my
uncle is not the man to drive her to despair."

·They had reached, whilst talking, the Rue de Suresnes,
and were in sight of the gateway leading to the beautiful
residence recently built by M. Dorgères.

The financier was a widower with an only daughter.
He was no lover of society, and never gave fêtes, but
every Wednesday there was a reunion at his house of a
small number of friends, amongst whom he made a point
of including his nephew, though said nephew, it must be
owned, derived very little amusement from them. His
cashier, Jules Vignory, and secretary, Robert de Carnoël,
were always among the guests, and had wellnigh come
to class their presence on those occasions among their
official duties.

It was time, for the rain was coming down in earnest
and pelting their faces. Jules was about to pull the bell,

when Maxime, who was a little in the rear, stopped him, saying in a low tone :

"Strange—there is a light in the safe-room. Can it be that the clerks work now till eleven o'clock in the evening ?"

"Not that I know of," replied Vignory, retreating a little to look at the window his friend pointed out.

The main building in which the banker resided was at the further end of the court-yard, and his offices composed the ground floor of a building bordering on the Rue de Suresnes. The openings to this separate building were protected by gratings, and through the closed shutters of the window nearest them could be seen the faint glimmering of the light which had attracted the attention of M. Dorgères' nephew.

"It is nothing," said Jules, after an instant's reflection. "Probably the watch who is making his round before going to bed. Make yourself easy ; the safe is protected in such a way that woe betide the unfortunate who should attempt to force it ! "

"Yes ; my uncle told me his safe was fortified with murderous engines, and if a thief should trifle with the lock he would be killed instantly."

"Your uncle was jesting ; but the truth is, he would be caught in a trap like a wolf. An ingenious mechanism would seize him by the wrist, and I would defy him to disengage it."

"That is first-rate. Ring and let us go in."

The cashier sounded the bell, the door opened, and Maxime passed in first. They came in collision with two persons who seemed waiting impatiently for the porter to draw the cord, for they were pressed close against the inside of the gate and went out precipitately, without apology or salutation.

One was tall, the other, of medium height, leaned on his companion's arm. Both wore hats pulled down over their eyes, and ample comforters.

"*Diable!*" said Maxime, as he closed the gate on them. "The guests are leaving as we arrive. We shall have a sorry reception. My uncle is not disposed to jest on the subject of punctuality."

"See!" he added, after a glance into the porter's lodge. "Father Denlevant is as fast asleep in his arm-chair as a dormouse in his hole."

"That is his habit, and if it depended on him to guard the house—— "

"It would be poorly guarded, to be sure. But the faithful Malicome sleeps in the office. The crowns are safe, and that is the main point."

"Malicome doesn't return till midnight. He is a drunken fellow, and I place no reliance on his watchfulness, and am going to take a look at the safe. Go up to the salon."

"No ; I prefer to go with you."

"Then you shall help me to face the storm."·

Vignory turned quickly to the right instead of toward

the front door. Maxime followed, humming a fragment of a hunting song.

"See !" said the cashier, "the door is half open."

They passed first into a room appropriated to the use of the public who came to draw or deposit money. It communicated with that in which the safe was by another door, which was likewise open. Passing on quickly they found the safe-room empty, but a lamp burning upon a table revealed the rows of portfolios, closed gratings, counters filled with balance-sheets and stamps. In a dark corner was a monumental closet of polished steel.

"Who can have been at work here at such an hour !" exclaimed Vignory.

"M. Dorgères alone has the key."

"Ah ! well, *parbleu !* it is he."

"You forget he receives this evening. Besides, he would not have failed to put out the light and lock the door. It is all very strange ; but I believe the safe is untouched."

"Are you sure?" asked Maxime, approaching it. "Eh ! you are mistaken. They have so well operated that the thief-trap has acted."

"What !"

"Look ! these two arms terminating in something like pincers which cover the lock—— "

"If they are united it must be because some one has attempted to pick it," stammered the bewildered Vignory.

"But how can the thief have escaped ? The mechanism must be worthless."

"On the contrary, it is only too effective ! " exclaimed Maxime, bending over that he might examine the trap. "It has not caught the thief, but has cut off his hand ! "

"Impossible ! "

"Bring the lamp closer and you will see. The hand remains caught in the vice, and what is strangest of all, it is a woman's hand ! "

"A woman's hand ! " repeated Vignory. He was so agitated that in taking up the lamp he nearly let it fall. Bringing it close to the safe, he soon saw that his friend was right. The branches of the ingenious contrivance had suddenly approached and seized the audacious hand that attempted the lock.

"*Diable!*" exclaimed Maxime. "I call that going too far. To stop any one in opening the safe were well done ; to mutilate the thief is too much, and useless, moreover, since it does not prevent his escape."

"But," muttered the cashier, "these arms were made to seize, not to cut. That is proved by the hand remaining in them."

"You are right. If the hand had been amputated by the machinery it would have fallen instead of being caught in the vice. It is inexplicable, unless—yes, it must be so—the hand has been cut off by a sword or hatchet."

"Cut off ! By whom ?"

"By the thief herself. Sooner than be taken she has sacrificed her hand."

"It is incredible!"

"On the part of an ordinary thief, yes; but women are capable of anything, and this was certainly a woman's hand. A fashionable lady's too. See the slender fingers, the almond-shaped nails. Look! she wore a ring, which she had the *sang froid* to draw off after the operation, and which has left a mark in the flesh. Being unable to extricate her hand, she has taken off the ring that might have betrayed her."

"But how could she leave the room after such an operation! She must have fainted, and the hemorrhage would have killed her. There is a pool of blood on the floor."

"Yes, and it is tracked along toward the table. We must see where the track stops. Hold the light."

Vignory obeyed mechanically and almost unconsciously. Maxime, on the contrary, was quite self-possessed, and acted with as much coolness as a veteran commissary of police.

"Good!" exclaimed Maxime, after his friend had replaced the lamp on the table. "I have it—the thief had an accomplice, and it was the accomplice who performed the operation. To amputate one's own hand would be almost too heroic; besides it would have been impossible without assistance to prevent the consequences of such a mutilation. Her companion has seen to that. This ball of twine has furnished the means of tying up the arm to stop the flow of blood, which was first stanched with this sponge borrowed from your inkstand. He has tied up the wound with one of the napkins used by you after handling money, and then led away the wounded, who perhaps was still able to walk, or he carried her in his arms."

"Now I think of it, perhaps we met them,—that couple who were crouching in the gateway when we arrived."

"Impossible, my dear fellow. We saw only two men. The thief and her accomplice had decamped before Father Doulevant opened to us. We may spare ourselves the trouble of following! They are already far from here."

"But the woman must have been barely able to stand."

"They would take a hack. These are, I repeat, no common thieves; and, to tell you my real mind, they are persons who are familiar with my uncle's household. The day and hour they chose indicate that. They knew he received Wednesdays, that the servants were occupied, that the porter would not observe them, that the watch returns late enough——"

"Who knows if some one in the house has not been in league with them? I must inform M. Dorgères immediately."

"You will act as you think best, but were I in your

place, I would say nothing to my uncle or to any-one."

"What! you would keep silent concerning an attempt at theft which may be repeated to-morrow. You forget that I am responsible for the safe."

"It is precisely because you are responsible that I ad-vise you not to mention this singular adventure. My uncle is not always just, and would, I believe, accuse you of negligence. He would be wrong, for you cannot pass your life mounting guard over his crowns ; but you would be reproached nevertheless."

"I prefer being exposed to that rather than by my si-lence secure impunity to rogues."

"You fancy then that they will be arrested if you tell your story ?"

"I hope so, at least."

"You are mistaken. The police will get on the wrong scent. All Paris will be talking of the severed hand, and our rogues, being warned, will take good care not to be found. Believe me when I tell you this is not an affair the police agents can unravel."

"You think you can show them how it is to be done ?"

"In this particular case, yes. But the secret must rest between us two. Be so good as to shut the door of the waiting-room."

"And the guard, who will soon be here——"

"At twelve o'clock. It is now two minutes past

eleven. We have time to talk. First show me how you can open the safe without accident."

"It is very simple. It is necessary to have the key and to know the word, which must be formed with the movable buttons on the door. If the five letters are not in place, the key will not enter. I have a key, your uncle has one, and only we two know the word. The contrivance is not altogether new, but we have an improvement in the cranks that have just acted. Every evening before going out I touch a spring which retains them, and am relieved from all anxiety, knowing that no one can touch the lock without being caught by the wrist. When I arrive in the morning I push the arrest crank, the iron arms can no longer come together, and I open it without difficulty."

"Good! But suppose you forgot this precaution, and my uncle should come to the safe during the night?"

"M. Dorgères never opens it without first arranging the mechanism; but in case it should be overlooked, he would only be subjected to a disagreeable pressure."

"Suppose some one without the key or the word should attempt to pick the lock?"

"He would be caught inevitably."

"I only require now to know how the operation was performed a while ago."

"With a picklock or crowbar, *parbleu!* Your uncle keeps his key in his pocket; mine never leaves me. It is impossible there could be a third."

" Before deciding that question I should like to examine
the safe more thoroughly. Give me the light once
more."

The cashier obeyed. His companion's confidence had
subdued him.

The two returned together to the safe, and Maxime began a minute inspection.

" My boy," he said, " I have never seen a picklock, but
fancy it must be a longer implement than a key. Had
one been employed it would have remained in the safe,
for there would have been no means of withdrawing it.
The hand nearly touches the lock, but between the end
of the fingers and the lock there is room for a small key
—a key which the accomplice perhaps has been able to
remove. What say the movable buttons? To form the
word, each letter must be brought under the indicating
arrow that is placed above each circular alphabet, must it
not ?"

" You are right."

" Well, the first letter is M, the second I, the third D,
the fourth A, the fifth S. Total Midas.

" Is that your word ?"

" Precisely."

" Then I recommend you to change it, for the thief
knows it. To return to this hand. It might be that of a
princess truly. Ah ! it is the left. There we have something significant. She is left-handed or rather was, for
henceforth she must make the right serve her. Now be

kind enough to manœuvre the spring which puts the apparatus in place."

"You will not touch those bloody remains, surely?"

"Certainly, otherwise everybody must know what took place here this evening."

There was no denying this. The cashier bent down and pressed upon a bar of metal concealed in the lower part of the safe. In an instant the hand fell to the floor.

"A bracelet!" exclaimed Maxime. It was a circle of gold with a setting of turquoise and diamonds. The brilliancy of the diamonds contrasted fearfully with the redness of the wound and the dazzling whiteness of the hand, from which all the blood had flowed.

Maxime had coolness enough to pick up the hand and throw it upon the table.

"When one prefers losing a hand to going before the Court of Assizes," he said, "it must be that there is a reputation at stake. An ordinary thief would not sacrifice the end of his little finger to avoid condemnation. The heroine of this adventure is not of that sort, and I am persuaded she has accomplices in my uncle's household."

"But M. Dorgères and I are the only ones who know the word, and I change it frequently. It so happens it was changed at six o'clock to-day. I do not suppose he has entrusted to any one the secret of the new word."

"The thief, however, could not guess it. Some one must have revealed it to her. My uncle may have committed some indiscretion that has come near costing him dear. On the other hand, it seems clear that the thief, well informed on one point, had no knowledge of the existence of the mechanical trap, since she suffered herself to be caught."

" None of the employés know of it; it is the first time the contrivance has acted. It is, as you see, skilfully concealed by the projecting framework of the safe. No one enters this room but the two clerks who work under me, and the three messengers; and these do not remain. Besides these, there is Malicome, who sweeps in the morning, and sleeps in a room communicating with this by a glass door. None of them have ever touched the spring. I come in before and leave after them."

" Then there is the urchin in groom's livery, whom my uncle took in out of charity."

" Oh ! he never sets foot here ; I have relegated him to the waiting-room, and it is seldom enough he is to be found there when wanted ; and as soon as the gratings are closed he is off."

" Then he doesn't sleep in the house ? "

" No, he lives with his mother at Montmartre or Batignolles, I forget which."

" I must question him."

" You persist in your idea of opening an inquest and conducting it alone? It will come to nothing. It is

folly.   And if M. Dorgères should learn that an attempt
has been made on the safe, he will be greatly displeased
that I did not tell him of it."

"But he will never know it.   Or if by any chance it
should reach his ears, I will take on myself the whole
responsibility."

"What of this blood—and this hand?"

"The blood?   I will see that it does not remain here
as a witness; and for the hand, I am going immediately
to throw it into the Seine.   I scarcely feel equal to em-
balming and keeping it by me to aid my search.   I must
confess it is revolting to look at, and still more to touch.
The bracelet I shall keep till I have found its owner.
She will scarcely inquire for it at the Lost Office, and
some day I intend to return it to her."

"Then you mean to give your life up to this search?"

"Why not?   My uncle reproaches me every day with
being good for nothing.   I mean to prove the contrary;
for when I have succeded I shall tell him the whole
story.   Instead of continuing on the race to ruin, I shall
spend my time usefully, economically and agreeably."

"Agreeably!" growled Vignory.   "There's no ac-
counting for tastes.   What pleasure can you get from
tracking a knave of a woman?"

"I have always had a passion for rebuses, enigmas,
problems.   I am a devotee to hunting; therefore am I
born for a police agent, and now that the opportunity
presents itself for following the right path, I seize upon

it. But do you not think it would be prudent to change the word, in case of a new attempt on the part of these rogues who have unaccountably surprised the secret of the combination ?"

"What shall we substitute ?"

"The first that occurs to us. For example, the name of my cousin Alice."

Vignory substituted for the word Midas the proper name of M. Dorgères' daughter.

"It is understood that you are not to breathe a word of this to my uncle ?"

"It is, if you are bent on carrying out your design."

Maxime returned quickly to the table and entered upon his self-appointed task. It was not the work of a moment. He had to wipe up with a sponge the blood that was on the floor, and then to detach the bracelet which still adhered to the wrist.

"You have no nerves ?" asked Vignory.

"*Ma foi* ! no ; and then who wishes the end must wish the means. You have the key of the two doors? Good. Put out the light and follow me."

They met no one in the court. The porter, who was still half asleep, opened to them without rousing to see who they were.

"Now, my dear Jules," said Maxime, when they found themselves on the sidewalk of the Rue de Suresnes, "go home, try to sleep well, and when you wake in the morning fancy all this has been a dream."

"I wish, indeed, it were," murmured Vignory. He augured no good from the strange adventure his careless companion treated so lightly, but he was far enough from foreseeing the stranger consequences which were to follow.

CHAPTER II.

M. CLAUDE JUSTUS DORGÈRES was born in a hamlet of the Gatinâes, where he had been a shepherd boy. His father was too poor to send him to school, and the future financier had perhaps never learned to read, if the village curé had not taught him out of charity. He profited so well by the instructions of the good priest, that in a year he was in a position to gain his livelihood by other than manual labor. He departed to Paris on foot, with three hundred sous, the fruit of his hard-earned savings, and a recommendation from the curé to a rich merchant of Rue du Sentier. Claude began by sweeping out the store, but his patron was not long in discerning that the little peasant would make an excellent clerk. He was not mistaken.

The boy was gifted with extraordinary energy and an exceptional capacity for business which, placed at the service of the house in which his career had begun so humbly, contributed so largely to its success, that his chief ended by making him his associate and successor.

19

Twenty years later, the shepherd boy of the Gatinâes is a great and prosperous man.   His youngest brother he brought to Paris, associated with his business, and he had married a rich wife.

But into the most prosperous lives adversity must enter, and in the course of a few months M. Dorgères lost his brother, his sister-in-law, and his wife, and was left with only an infant daughter, and a nephew, not seven years old.

This nephew, now grown to manhood, possessed none of the qualities of his race.   He was neither industrious nor prudent ; but he had ease, good taste, courage, and perfect rectitude of character.   He was incapable of a base action, and was beloved even by those who condemned his follies.   His uncle had given up preaching as utterly useless, and seldom saw him except on such Wednesdays as it pleased the nephew to present himself. How should they meet? . Maxime frequented the world, the races, clubs and theatres.   He retired usually at the hour M. Dorgères rose.

The life of M. Dorgères was regulated like the clock of the Bourse.   Letters to read, orders to stockbrokers' clerks, audiences to important clients, absorbed the morning.   The afternoon was spent in visits to financiers, signing letters, and a thousand little matters.

But the hour arrived when this indefatigable worker forgot all these cares to think only of his daughter.

At twelve o'clock precisely, breakfast was served in a room adjoining his own.

Alice appeared fresh and bright, and passing her father, took a seat opposite him at a small round table. This was the best moment of the banker's existence. Dinner was a formal meal in the grand dining-room, where, if no strangers were present, there were always the respectable female companion who had been entrusted with Alice's education, and the young secretary of M. Dorgères. The juvenile confidences and paternal scoldings must be reserved for breakfast time.

On the morning after the soirée when the safe made so narrow an escape, both father and daughter were in their liveliest mood. Since the early morning, the banker had been engaged in important financial concerns, which seemed all progressing to his wishes. Not a cloud on the financial horizon, and nothing to mar his domestic happiness.

To Alice everything was rose-colored ; not for similar reasons, for the tides of business and commercial crises concerned her little enough. Her life was calm and transparent as the waters of a clear fountain ; her heaven was always cloudless.

But, whatever the cause, it might be read plainly in her clear blue eyes, that she had never been so happy as to-day.

She flung herself into M. Dorgères arms, and after embracing him, led him to his seat, and fastened his napkin herself.

"Suppose you take your seat now, mademoiselle," said M. Dorgères. "Will you never be anything but a playful child? Remember you were nineteen years old three days ago."

"True, papa. It is well you reminded me. I was about to climb up on your knee."

"What folly, at your time of life!"

"I am going, papa. And I mean to be straight as a gate post and wise as an image. Oh, I know how to play the young lady when I choose!"

"A pretty cause for boasting at your age. Do you know that you are old enough to be getting married?"

This time Alice made no reply. She was seated already opposite her father. Taking up an egg, she lent an unusual amount of serious attention to the operation of breaking the shell. It might have been remarked that this allusion to marriage had clipped the wings of her gaiety.

M. Dorgères, surprised at this sudden change, looked up and observed that she colored deeply.

"It is time to be thinking of it," he said. "You have not, I suppose, taken a vow to be an old maid?"

"I have taken a vow never to leave you," she said, without raising her eyes.

"And who said anything about leaving me? Do you suppose I would select a son-in-law who would take you away from Paris?"

"I sincerely hope not."

"There are foreigners, however, who would be brilliant matches," the banker went on a little maliciously. "What would you think of a Russian, a millionaire several times over. Col. Borisoff is rich, of great consideration in his own country, is still young and good-looking, and never fails to enquire for you when I meet him. I am quite confident he would esteem himself a happy man could he marry you."

"And for me, I am confident, should you force me to do so, I should die."

"Really?" said the banker, with a smile. "Don't be uneasy. I should never marry you against your will, and have never dreamed of giving my little Alice to this Muscovite, who would carry her away to that ugly country of snow. I should not even give her to a husband from the country, because he would take her from me."

"Thanks, papa," exclaimed Alice, raising her head.

"So that is understood. When any one asks your hand, I have my own conditions to make. This house is large enough to accommodate a young household, and my son-in-law must live with me."

"Ah! papa, how happy I should be!"

"You are not averse to marrying, then?"

"That depends."

"I understand. You wish to choose a husband that pleases you."

"And you, papa."

"Very well; it is only necessary to find him. I have

my programme; we must know yours. If we agree as to the necessary qualifications, all will go well. Come, explain yourself."

"I prefer to have you begin, papa."

"So be it. We will say this husband of yours must be young."

"Not too young."

"From twenty-five to thirty? Agreed. We will not dispute as to age. He must be handsome."

"It is only necessary he should have the bearing and manners of a gentleman who has intelligence and heart."

"Approved. There remains the question of money."

"I should not require him to be rich."

"Nor I. But that he shall be capable of becoming so."

"What do you mean?"

"Listen to me, little one. When I married your dear and lamented mother, I had nothing, and she brought me a large dowry; but she knew that I was a worker, and should one day achieve an independent position. I was poor then. To-day I am possessed of a large fortune, which I owe only to myself."

"Can you think it possible I should want a lazy husband?"

"No, for if you could love a useless man you would not be of my blood. You would not, then, refuse a young man whom I had trained to business, and might one day associate with myself?"

"I should be too happy," the girl murmured, in some agitation.

"Ah! then we both know this young man," said the banker, with a smile of approbation. "Since he has been in my employ he has rendered me important service, and I have absolute confidence in him. Do I need to mention his name?"

"Robert!" exclaimed the young girl, in a transport of joy. Then, recovering herself, "M. de Carnoël, your secretary?"

The banker knit his brows.

"Why do you suppose I allude to M. de Carnoël?" he asked.

"Is he not your private secretary, and have I not frequently heard you say he had your entire confidence? Is he not such as you were at his age,—poor, industrious and proud?"

The banker winced a little.

"True," he said, "he is all this; but I am astonished you could have so mistaken my meaning. How could you suppose I had thought of him for partner—and son-in-law?"

"And how could I suppose you would jest on this subject which so nearly concerns the happiness of your daughter?"

"I am not jesting."

"Then of whom do you speak?"

"Of another, perhaps. But listen to me. You know

the circumstances under which M. de Carnoël came to
me. His father had just died, having squandered an immense fortune. Moved by the situation of young Robert,
I made him the offer of a modest employment, which he
accepted, although up to that time he had moved in a
world into which the thought of earning one's livelihood
never enters. I am glad to say, that the more I have
tested him the more I have learned to know his value ;
but he will never succeed in business."

"Why ?" his daughter asked, timidly.

"Because he was born a great lord, and such he will
remain. The instinct of trade, don't you see, is in the
blood. It is in mine, because I come of the people ; because my father and grandfather were peddlers, and sold
handkerchiefs and cotton at fair-time. And then life began for me with suffering and privation. I was hungry
and cold. I came to Paris with bare feet, and the loft
where I lodged as a store-boy seemed to me a palace.
Robert was reared in luxury, and learned only too late
what it was to want money, if indeed he has known it at
all."

" He deserves only the more credit for going to work
to retrieve his fortunes," Alice interrupted, with an earnestness which left no further doubt on the banker's
mind as to the nature of her feelings toward M. de
Carnoël.

"I grant it," he said, " but this merit will never make
him rich. Robert makes a first-rate secretary. He has a

good mind, writes an admirable hand, and I can trust him to reply to letters from men of fashion, or to receive them when they present themselves. But I should not care to trust him with a great financial operation ; not that I want confidence in him, but men of his rank know nothing of these things."

Alice said nothing, but the tears would force themselves into her eyes. M. Dorgères, more moved than he chose to appear, suddenly changed the subject.

"What has become of your usually fine appetite?" he asked, with an attempt at gaiety. "You have eaten nothing this morning."

"I am not hungry, that is all."

"It is my fault. I should not have spoken to you of marriage, for all your bright humor fled as soon as I approached this solemn subject. Let me tell you only once more in closing that I should be grieved to see you marry a nobleman. I want no mésalliance for my little plebeian. The son-in-law I picture to myself is a tradesman, son of a tradesman. Robert de Carnoël, I believe, is a marquis. Between him and me the distance is too great. And after passing this sentence, which I promise you is my last word on the subject, I hope you will recover your pretty smile and try these grapes."

Alice could contain herself no longer, and her pent-up feelings were about to burst forth, when a light noise made her turn her head.

The door had just opened, and M. de Carnoël entered.

It needed something of unusually serious importance to occasion this interruption of the tête-a-téte between father and daughter.

Evidently it concerned only the banker, and Alice, as he approached her father, gave him a quick glance, which said plainly, " All is lost ! "

The young man stopped, and turned pale. He was tall, dark, with features altogether wanting in anything like regularity. The last of the Carnoëls had even been ugly but for his eyes ; dark eyes, full of fire ; eyes that spoke. He had a large, well-shaped forehead, and a countenance full of expression ; all that might be necessary to win the regard of a bright, sensible woman, and to escape the notice of a frivolous one. Elegant withal, with that elegance which is nature's gift and not to be bought of fashionable tailors. Reserved in manner and speech, with a spice perhaps of disdain, the young secretary represented a class whose tendency is to decrease, and M. Dorgères could hardly have been far wrong in assuming that the young man of family was not born to win a fortune.

"What is the matter, monsieur?" asked the severe financier, dryly.

The unaccustomed "monsieur" showed the young man clearly the new situation which some unguarded expression on the part of the banker's daughter had created.

"Col. Borisoff is here," replied the lover, trying to suppress all signs of emotion.

"Well, let him wait. I am not ready to see him."

"So I have just had the honor to say to him, but he insisted so positively on seeing you that I took the liberty of informing you."

This firm and unabashed reply recalled to M. Dorgères that his secretary had never suffered himself to be treated with hauteur.

"Excuse me, my friend," he said, "it is not your fault if this Russian intrudes on my breakfast hour. Moreover, I have finished," he added, throwing his napkin on the table. "Be so good as to say to the colonel that I will be at his service in a moment."

The young man bowed and went out.

Left alone with his daughter, M. Dorgères said, as he bent over and kissed her :

"Be yourself once more, my dear child. A little reflection will calm your mind, and you will see that your old father wishes only your happiness."

Alice left the room without a word. She was choking.

"Hum !" growled the banker, "I do not regret bringing up the subject of this marriage I owe to this chance conversation having surprised a secret which I might have discovered too late. Alice dotes on this country squire, but it shall be my aim to nip this childish caprice in the bud."

With this resolution briefly expressed but firmly taken, M. Dorgères passed into his office, a large room furnished with simple luxury, and separated by a tapestried door from a smaller one appropriated to his secretary. Of the probity and discretion of the latter M. Dorgères had not a doubt. He knew there was no danger that chance information, gathered from financial conversations that went on in his hearing, would be made use of at the Bourse. Still less did he believe him capable of eavesdropping.

The young man had already resumed his place in his· office when M. Dorgères passed into his, and pretty soon Col. Borisoff entered alone.

This foreigner was a handsome man, and had quite an imposing air which, with his broad shoulders and somewhat abrupt manner, made him a compound of the great lord and the soldier ; and his heavy moustache, military whiskers, and forehead marked with a scar, completed this appearance.

"Good-morning," he said, extending his two hands to greet the banker. "May I first be allowed to enquire for your charming daughter, and to offer my apologies for this intrusion on your breakfast hour. I should be inconsolable to think I was so unfortunate as to displease her."

He spoke in the caressing tone which may be recognized as peculiarly Russian, and his voice was musical in its well-modulated tones.

"Thanks, sir," replied the father of Alice, quite coldly. "My daughter will be very sensible of your kind remembrance. May I ask to what I am indebted for the honor of your visit?"

"To an unforeseen occurrence. I have just received a dispatch which obliges me to leave Paris to-morrow. I have some funds with you, and——"

"You wish to withdraw them. Nothing more simple, monsieur, though it is not customary to call in, without previous notice, a deposit of this importance."

"It is not for that I came, monsieur, and I regret to have been misunderstood. I deposited in your safe a casket containing family papers and notes payable to the bearer. I wish to regain possession of this casket. That is all."

"Very well. I will have it brought, and you may assure yourself that the seals are intact."

"Not at present. I am pressed for time to-day. I shall call to-morrow at the hour your office opens. Perhaps I may require also a few thousand louis."

"You have, monsieur, more than fourteen hundred thousand francs to your credit, and, as I have just said, the entire sum is at your disposal. Ordinarily we keep here only the money required for current purposes, but I had placed in bank this morning three millions for the payment of a dividend that will fall due. These three millions are now in my safe."

Just as the banker mentioned this imposing sum, Robert de Carnoël entered with a file of papers in his hand, which he was about to deposit on the table according to his daily custom at a certain hour.

He was so pale that the colonel asked, in a low tone :

"What is the matter with the young man? He seems agitated."

M. Dorgères did not reply, and Col. Borisoff, who was standing, saw there was nothing for him but to take leave. The banker showed him to the door, and then turning to Robert, said :

"A word with you now, M. Secretary."

The young man, who was about going to his office, paused and waited for the communication, of whose nature he felt a presentiment.

"You have been with me two years, have you not?" the banker asked abruptly.

"Two years lacking one month," answered Robert, surprised at this beginning.

"In that time have I given you any reason to complain of me?"

"Never, sir. I can only say that I fully appreciate all the kindness and delicacy of your conduct toward me."

"Very well. Is it to thank me for having treated you less as subaltern than as friend that you pay your court to my daughter?"

Robert was unprepared for this direct attack, and he made a gesture which M. Dorgères took for denial.

"You need deny nothing," he said. "Alice has told me all."

There was a short silence. The father waited with the coolness of an examining judge for the accused to justify himself. He little knew the last of the Carnoëls.

"Sir," replied Robert, "I have nothing to conceal, since I have nothing to reproach myself with."

"Speak frankly. You love Alice?"

"It is true," replied Robert, without hesitation.

'Sir,' said the banker, after a moment's reflection, "I might ask why you have deferred acquainting me with a state of affairs which I had a right to know ; but I deem it useless to animadvert on the past. I prefer to show you my views of the situation, and the course I have resolved upon in order to bring it to an end. I acknowledge that I ought to have foreseen what has come to pass. My daughter is young and pretty. You had everything that was calculated to please her. I should have been more prudent. You are, I know, incapable of seeking Alice for her fortune. You love her sincerely, and would love her though she had not a sou for her dowry. My esteem and regard for you are undiminished, but I owe you the truth. M. de Carnoël cannot marry Alice Dorgères for reasons which in no way touch his honor, and which Alice has acknowledged. I convinced her with some difficulty, I confess, but she was convinced at last that her happiness consisted in choosing a husband who was her equal in social condition if not in fortune. I am only a merchant. It were folly for my daughter to become a marchioness."

"Then, monsieur, if I had not inherited a title which I have voluntarily relinquished, you would have had no repugnance to accept me as son-in-law?"

" I have not said that, for I think you lack an essential qualification—commercial aptitude, the instinct of business. You possess many others ; but that is one not to be acquired, and without which it is impossible to direct a house like mine. Now, the truth is, it would be a great trial to me to have a stranger for my successor. I am growing old, and hope before I die to see my place filled by Alice's husband. Excuse me for repeating to you what I have just said to my daughter, and let me hope you will not entertain any hard thoughts of me if my frankness has seemed somewhat rough. And now there only remains to ask how I can serve you. I have important relations with Egypt. It is a country where your intelligence and energy might do you good service. Would it suit you to represent me there ? "

Robert de Carnoël roused himself at this question from the depression which each successive sentence of the banker's had occasioned, and replied with cold politeness :

" I thank you, monsieur, for your care of my future. The offer you make is very flattering. Permit me, however, to reflect before deciding."

" At your leisure. And whatever may be your decision, count on my aiding you with my influence and my purse. I am and shall remain your friend. Time will efface the cloud that has risen up between us, and the day will come when you will thank me for having opened up to you a different career."

"May I ask if you have any further need of me to-day?"

"No, no; I give you your discharge for to-day. You are free to dispose even of your evening, for ·I dine in town."

The young man bowed and went out.

"Poor fellow!" murmured M. Dorgères, "he is disconsolate. I have been a little abrupt, but the longer I deferred the operation the harder it would have been. He suffers, but will get over it. The most important thing was to send him off. I shall not, however, speak to Alice any more of my candidate. After a while, she will accustom herself to the idea of becoming Madame Vignory."

While the banker was felicitating himself on having regulated an affair of the heart as quickly as if it had been a current account, Robert de Carnoël went out from him with despair in his soul. ·His dream had vanished, for it did not seem that Alice had even made any protest when this inflexible father signified to her his will.

Everything seemed crumbling in pieces under him. He walked, however, with head erect, and his pale face expressed invincible resolution, for this last scion of a fallen house had a courage that nothing could subdue, and a pride that could not be brought low. ·

·He had known how to bend, without complaining, to his altered circumstances, and to love passionately and in silence. He felt strong now to bear everything except humiliation.

The only friend to whom he could recount his misfortunes and confide his projects, was Jules Vignory. The two had been college mates, and subsequently found themselves associated at the Rue de Suresnes banking house, where their mode of life brought them in frequent contact.

On parting with M. Dorgères, his first thought was to seek his friend. He took a stairway communicating with the offices on the ground-floor. The waiting-room was nearly empty. Two clerks were figuring up some accounts, and an urchin in dark green livery, flat cap, and vest with three rows of buttons, was seated on a bench amusing himself, till his services were called for, by manufacturing bits of paper into different shapes.

He rose quickly on perceiving M. de Carnoël, planted himself against the wall, and made the military salute.

Robert passed on to the open grating and called to Vignory, who was buried in figures.

" Come," he said shortly, " I want to speak with you."

Vignory complied, not without locking the safe and withdrawing the key.

" What is it ? " he asked.

" I came to say good-bye. I am going away."

" Going away ! M. Dorgères has, then, given you a mission ? I heard him say he wanted some one to represent him in Egypt."

" I am not going to Egypt."

" Where then ? "

" I do not know ? "

" Going away, and you do not know where ! What does that mean ? "

" It means that I no longer belong to the house."

" What ! you are dismissed ? "

" No, it is I who leave it."

" Why ? "

" If you want to know come with me into the yard. I do not wish to be overheard, and that youngster is listening."

" Georget ! he is not thinking about us. He is amusing himself with nothing more important than catching at the gnats. But no matter. Let us go. I can give you five minutes, though I have work to-day,"

" Jules," began Robert, after he had led the cashier into a secure corner. " You are the only one who has guessed that I love Mlle. Dorgères."

" And I do not doubt that she loves you. Moreover, you have my sincere congratulations."

This was said in a light, careless tone, very different from the serious attention with which he had listened at the beginning.

" I believed she loved me. I was deceived."

" Can it be possible ! Have you not spoken to her ? Has she not made you promises—vows even ? "

" Yes," said Robert, " the vow of a young girl. I was

a fool to trust to it. Her father had only to speak and it was forgotten. He has just signified his opposition to our marriage, and added that Mlle. Dorgères understood his motives and approved them."

" It is incredible. And what are they ? "

" First, I am guilty of having a *de* before my name. Moreover, I have no vocation for business, and shall never be able to direct a banking house. M. Dorgères wants his son-in-law to succeed him, and his daughter is preparing to accept this husband, whether he pleases her or not."

" Mlle. Alice has accepted these conditions ? "

" Yes ; since she authorized her father to say so to me. He has done it in all due form ; has offered me a position in Egypt, and even money."

" Why not accept his proposition ? Why not prove to him that he is mistaken, and that you are as capable of business as any one ? Who knows if this is not a kind of test he has imposed on you ? "

" I have resolved never to see M. or Mlle. Dorgères again, and to quit France, never to return."

" Quit France ! And where would you go ? "

" To America, Australia, Japan ; what matters, provided I hear no more of her who has betrayed me. What I seek is to forget."

" What folly ! You would expatriate yourself, give up the future that awaits you, run the risk of ending miserably in some unknown quarter of the globe, and all because your patron makes difficulties about according you the hand of Mlle. Alice. I see no reason for being disheartened before an obstacle that might have been foreseen."

"I did not foresee that Alice would be wanting in good faith; that she would yield to her father's first refusal. I do not complain. It was I who was wrong to take in earnest a mere childish càprice; but I have suffered, and I wish to suffer no more. You see, then, that I am right to go."

"My dear Robert," said Jules, after a pause, "you are too much agitated for me to hope at the moment to bring you to calmer views. Besides, I cannot leave the safe longer, as I have a large deposit to receive and verify. Let us postpone this talk till to-morrow."

"To-morrow I shall be no longer in Paris."

"Once more; you cannot take a journey like this beyond the seas without money. What I have is at your disposal, but it is not in my pocket nor even at my house."

"Thanks. I should not be too proud to accept it from you, but I do not need it. When I am far from here I shall write to you. But I do not wish to leave without passing a few hours with you. Where can I meet you this evening?"

"I can hardly say. I have promised to dine with Maxime Dorgères, who is coming for me at nine, and should not care to have him present at our meeting.

Suppose I call to see you early in the morning in your room ?"

"You would run the risk of not finding me. But if I should not see you again, I shall always remember our friendship. Give me your hand before we part."

"Where are you going?" asked Jules, retaining the hand that was held out to him.

"Don't be uneasy. I am not going to kill myself. Suicide is cowardice. I give you my word of honor you shall hear from me. Now let me go. I am impatient to get away from this house."

Vignory made no further effort to detain him, and disengaged his hand ; he turned quickly away.

He returned to his office, but had no heart for work. With so much to preoccupy his mind, it may well be supposed there were now and then errors made in his accounts; but we must do him the justice to say his thoughts dwelt more upon his friend's troubles than upon the incident of the previous evening.

The time allotted for business seemed long, and it was with great satisfaction that he heard the hour strike for closing the gratings. The millions brought from the Bank of France were safely deposited. M. Dorgères had gone himself to advise his cashier of the intention of M. Borisoff to withdraw his casket and a sum of money next morning.

The door opened suddenly and Maxime's joyous voice cried out :

"What ! you have not yet finished your shutting up ? Make haste, the weather is delightful, and I want a stroll on the boulevard before dinner."

"Here I am," answered the cashier, putting on his overcoat.

"Wait, the groom is still there. You had better get out of the way, youngster."

Georget was off with the speed of a hare. Vignory turned, surprised to see him there at that hour, and then followed Maxime who, putting his hand in his arm, whispered in his ear :

"I have news."

"What have you discovered ? "

"Wait till we get in the street. I always fancy some one is listening."

The young cashier turned back involuntarily, but saw no one.

"Speak !" he said, when they were on the sidewalk.

"Well, yesterday evening, on leaving you, I went directly to the Seine. On returning from my nocturnal expedition some one followed me as far as the Madeleine, and would have followed me to my door if I had not chanced to meet a hack with a good horse. I jumped in and rode to Rue Châteaudun, and so the spy was distanced."

"Who was it ? "

"A man who stood leaning against the parapet of the wharf. I passed first without remarking him, threw my wretched package in the river, and was hastening back when I observed him in the same spot. He followed on after me at a little distance."

"What does that prove?"

"That he saw me throw the object in the river and wanted to know who I was."

"If you have nothing more than that to tell—"

"But that is not all. Come under this gas reflection while I read you an interesting article. Listen," he said, unfolding a newspaper.

"This morning a bargeman fishing in the Seine caught in his net a woman's hand. Is this melancholy capture the result of a crime? Everything seems to point that way. The hand has been carried to the Commissary of Police. It is said it will be submitted to a certain process in order to preserve it, and exhibited at the morgue. We shall keep our readers advised of the result of this mysterious affair."

"What do you think of that?" asked Maxime, "after all I have done to keep the police from meddling with this affair."

"You see I was right in advising you to let it alone."

"Bah! There is nothing to regret. The severed hand will be talked of for a week and forgotten with the next crime. A scamp might chop his wife into mince-meat, and Paris would very soon forget to talk about him. My uncle knows nothing, I hope?"

"No; besides he has other things to think about just

now. He has found out that Robert loves your cousin
and that your cousin wants to marry him, and is much
vexed about it. I do not know what he said to his
daughter, but he has dismissed his secretary, offering, by
way of compensation, a position in Egypt."

" And M. de Carnoël has accepted ? "

" You do not know him. He would starve sooner
than accept what he considered a humiliation. He has
resigned his place and is going away."

" *Ma foi !* he is a brave fellow, and has my sympa-
thies. I admire his independence. He was right to
fling to the winds my uncle and his charities. At his
age and with his rank he might do better things. The
world swarms with heiresses who would be delighted to
marry a marquis."

" You forget he is engaged to Mlle. Dorgères."

" Alice is a child, and it would be folly to trust to her
vows. My cousin will grieve for him about a month.
The next month she will say M. de Carnoël cared very
little for her, since he crossed the seas rather than stay
in Paris, where he might sometimes see her driving out
in an open barouche. In the third she will listen patiently to her father's reasonings in favor of a rational
choice. In the sixth she will suffer herself to be led by
him to the altar. My opinion is that this sudden departure opens the way to you ; that the situation is now most
favorable to you as the candidate for Alice's hand."

" Without mentioning any other impossibility, what

would you think of my trying to supplant an unfortunate friend ? "

"That has nothing to do with it. M. de Carnoël abandons the field. He goes to the antipodes and you remain. Alice is certainly not going to enter a convent. You will see her every day. If she should find out that your merit is equal to that of her old lover, you would have nothing to reproach yourself with, if her father offered you her hand."

"That will never happen," murmured Vignory.

"Everything happens, my dear fellow. My cousin would be a phenomenon to keep her heart for a lover whom she will never see again. There are women, however, whose love is increased by a forced separation from the beloved object."

"Mlle. Dorgères is one of·those."

"Perhaps. But in the case of a separation like this, while it sometimes throws a romantic halo around a lover, it frequently happens that some chance, or simply reflection robs him of half his prestige. If rich she will begin to suspect some day that the object of her preference cared only for her money, and gave her up for the sake of seeking his fortunes elsewhere. The slightest circumstance will tend to strengthen and confirm this idea, and when once it takes possession of the mind, her illusions ·have vanished and the absent is definitively wrong."

Vignory made no effort to dispute this application of a

well-known proverb. He was visibly moved, but made
no revelation of the state of his feelings, and the conversation took another turn.

Maxime reverted to his plans for the campaign, which
interested him more than M. de Carnoël's mishaps.

Vignory gave him only half an ear. He had little faith
in Maxime's predictions, but could not but admit to himself that he would be fortunate if the time should come
when Mlle. Dorgères could see that he too thought her
charming. He tried to banish these thoughts for fear he
should come to wish for the ruin of his friend's hopes.
The promenade had no enlivening effect, and the dinner
seemed stupid and dull. He allowed himself to be led
to the theatre, where he heard not a word of the perform-
ance, and returned past midnight to his little room in
Rue d'Aguesseau. He found a letter awaiting him, and
recognizing the handwriting of Robert de Carnoël, tore
it open hastily.

It contained only two lines :

" Do not expèct me. I leave to-night, and to-morrow
shall be far from here. Pity and forgive me."

This singular farewell threw the young cashier into a
state of indescribable agitation. He read it over ten
times, and thought of nothing else during his sleepless
night. This sudden departure seemed to decide his destiny, and when the day broke he was still asking himself
whether he should follow the ambitious counsels of Maxime Dorgères.

CHAPTER III.

THE SECOND ATTEMPT.

IN the Claude Dorgères house the office was opened precisely at ten, and exact punctuality was rigorously exacted. Jules Vignory carried this virtue to excess, for he arrived always before the regulation minute, and prolonged his stay beyond the appointed limits.

On the morning following the evening he had passed with Maxime Dorgères, there were good reasons for not being behind time, for, unable to sleep, he had risen at daybreak. Nevertheless, when Col. Borisoff presented himself in the waiting-room he found the grating closed. Just as he entered, the office clock struck the hour of ten. One does not serve in the Russian army without learning habits of military precision. Georget, the groom, was already at his post and following the noble stranger with his eyes with a curiosity he was at no pains to conceal. Evidently the height and broad shoulders of the Muscovite inspired the urchin with the liveliest admiration, for he eyed him from head to foot as if taking his measure.

M. Borisoff consulted his watch.

"Then there is no one here? This is very extraordinary. What time do the clerks arrive?"

"Oh! they are not far off," Georget replied. "In three minutes, three minutes and a half, you will see them all. One of them must be there now, for I hear moving. Strike on the grating."

"I believe this little dog is making fun of me. I am sorry I haven't time to pull his ears."

But he contented himself with following the advice to make known his presence.

At the first knocks the shutter remained closed; but as they were redoubled, a face appeared at the grating, so pale and agitated that the colonel failed to recognize it, though he had several times seen it there before.

"I am Col. Borisoff," he said. "M. Dorgères must have told you that I should be here at this hour to——"

"To draw some money; yes, sir, I know," interrupted Jules Vignory, in a stifled voice. "Pardon me for having made you wait, and for begging you to wait yet longer."

"What is the matter?" asked the stranger haughtily.

"I have just found that the safe was open. I locked it myself yesterday, and no one had occasion to enter last night. I fear a theft has been committed. I must inform M. Dorgères. I can do nothing until he arrives."

"Then be good enough to send for him, for I am much hurried."

"Georget!" cried Vignory.

The groom was not far off. He **was** behind the colonel, almost under his heels.

"Close the door of the waiting-room, and go quickly and beg your master to come down without losing a minute. Then go into the court and tell all who come that the office will not be open till eleven."

"And if they ask why ?"

"Tell them there has been a fire—an explosion of gas—anything you choose. But run—the door first."

The urchin ran to lock the door, and then darted toward the stairway that led to the banker's room.

"Monsieur," stammered Vignory, walking toward the door as he perceived his patron approaching, "I fear a misfortune has befallen us."

"To the safe, no doubt," said M. Dorgères, coolly. "Let us see. Come, Colonel, you are not *de trop*."

The door of the safe was wide open.

"I found it just as you see, when I arrived this morning," murmured Vignory.

"That cannot be," replied the banker. "No one has a key but you and myself."

"My key has not left me, monsieur. Here it is."

"And here is mine."

"There is a third," said the Russian, "and that remains in the lock."

"You are right," said M. Dorgères. "The strangest thing is, they have not robbed us ; there are the rolls of gold on the first shelf. Where do you put the notes, Vignory ?"

" In this portfolio, monsieur—there, to the right."

" What was the sum total of your safe yesterday ? "

" Three hundred and sixty-six thousand and eighty-nine francs, besides the three millions received from the bank, which I put in the middle drawer."

" See if they are there," said the banker with stoical calmness.

Vignory opened with a trembling hand the steel drawer which was, as the donjon of this fortress, filled with treasures.

" They are here ! " he exclaimed, showing the precious papers piled up in ten packages of three hundred thousand francs each.

" Count," said M. Dorgères.

Vignory counted them over rapidly.

" Not one is missing," he said with a sigh of relief.

" God be praised ! I am not ruined. It is very extraordinary. There is no appearance of anything having been disturbed. Verify now the rest of the contents."

Vignory hastened to obey. The work was quickly done, for he had arranged all with his own hands the evening before, and knew where everything ought to be as well as a bibliophile knows the spot in which he has put each book ; so many rolls of a thousand on the left, so many notes in the portfolio to the right, so many piles of crowns on the third shelf.

" The rolls are all complete," he said, after having run over them with his finger, and then passed to the inspec-

tion of the portfolio; "the notes, too," he added after a
little longer examination.

"Then nothing is lost," exclaimed the banker.

"No, sir, nothing—that is—"

Vignory turned visibly paler.

"Fifty thousand francs which I had left open to pay a
draft that was to be presented this morning—and—they
have disappeared."

"A strange thief," observed M. Borisoff, who might
have stolen a fortune and contents himself with a pit-
tance."

"Very strange indeed," replied the banker; "but I
must not forget that you have no time to lose. My
cashier will place in your hands the sum you want and
your casket."

The cashier had hardly strength to reply: "It is not
here."

".What! the casket gone! You must be mistaken.
Who would have taken that and left these three millions?"

"I begin to understand," muttered the colonel.

"Then I hope you will explain the mystery," said the
banker, brusquely.

M. Borisoff was pale but retained his self-possession.

"Monsieur," he began, "I might have the right to
complain, and to ask why you have not more carefully
guarded the deposit I entrusted to you, but recrimina-
tions are useless, and I content myself with requesting
that you—"

"That I should reimburse you for your losses. There shall be no difficulty between us on that point. You are a man of honor—that is enough."

"I am flattered by your compliment," said the Russian with ironical politeness, "but permit me to remind you that my casket contained papers of the greatest importance to me which it is not in your power to restore."

"I may at least discover the thief, and I shall set all the police on his track. The rogue will try to negotiate the paper and will undoubtedly be caught."

"I doubt it. My papers are payable to the bearer, and I have not kept the numbers."

"It is truly unfortunate ; but I repeat, monsieur, that I intend to restore to you the amount of your loss. I should not have accepted this sealed deposit, but having done so I feel myself responsible and—"

"Once more, monsieur, your generosity cannot restore to me my papers, and the rest matters little. I am able to bear the loss of the money. All I ask is, that you should not mix the police up with my affairs. I do not wish to have Paris and all Europe know that I have been robbed. I prefer to act myself, alone, or in concert with you if you choose to aid me."

"To act—how ?"

"By opening a private inquest amongst all the people we know, who could have been interested in committing so extraordinary a theft. You admit that an ordinary thief would not have been contented with carrying off the casket when your safe was filled with gold."

"You forget the fifty thousand francs."

"That was a mere accessory. The thief probably needed this money to secure the stolen papers by getting out of the country ; but the papers were all he wanted."

"I begin to believe you are right," said M. Dorgères.

"I am sure of it," replied the colonel. "I have enemies, as have all who exercise political functions, and have been charged with several secret missions by my government. I am, then, forced to believe that this blow, directed against you, was designed for me."

"But I have spoken to no one of this deposit."

"It was known you were my banker. It was natural to suppose that, having entrusted you with a large part of my fortune, I had deposited with you my important papers also. Besides, there must be some around you who were aware of your having received this deposit, and that it belonged to me."

"Two only," said M. Dorgères, after a moment's reflection. "My cashier whom you see, and my secretary, the young man whom you met yesterday morning in my office."

"I remember. He came in just as you told me that the casket and money would be at my disposition this morning. I even remarked his extreme paleness and apparent embarrassment."

"I had just informed him of the necessity for withdrawing from the service."

"Ah ! he is no longer with you ?"

" He has not left my house, but will leave in a few days."

" May I ask his name ? "

" Robert de Carnoël."

" Carnoël ? There was formerly, at St. Petersburg' an attaché of the French embassy of that name."

" His father ; he died ruined in fortune, but he kept up, I believe, some relations with Russia."

" It is likely that the son also has some acquaintances among my compatriots."

" Not that I know of. He is not in a condition to frequent fashionable society, and goes very little into the world."

" Could you present me to him ? "

" Certainly, I have not seen him to-day, which is natural enough, since I relieved him of his duties yesterday ; but he stays in the house and must be somewhere about. Vignory, will you be kind enough to look for him ? "

" I doubt if he is here, sir," replied the cashier. ' He wrote me yesterday that he was going to leave—to quit Paris."

" Pshaw ! he cannot have left Paris in a day. Go up to his room, and if you find him bring him down."

Vignory was in no haste to comply. He thought of the singular farewell letter he had received the evening before.

" May I remind you, monsieur, that it is half-past ten, and that the office should have been opened at ten. I have had the outer door locked to prevent the clerks and callers from entering. It is not worth while to let the public know—"

"That there has been a robbery. You are right. They can wait till eleven. Go, and return quickly."

The cashier bowed and went out.

"You are sure of this young man?" asked the colonel.

"As of myself," replied M. Dorgères. "So much so that I propose some day to take him into partnership."

"What kind of life does he lead in Paris?"

"That of an orderly, industrious young man. He thinks of little besides his work, and has few acquaintances."

"Oh, I do not accuse him. I only wish to get all possible information since you enter into my plan."

"Yes, I agree with you that it is just as well this affair should be kept quiet. My cashier is discretion itself, and I have no fear that my secretary would noise the story abroad."

"I should like to ask him a few questions without referring to the casket. Probably, however, your nephew will speak to him of it."

At this moment, Vignory returned in evident agitation.

"Well?" asked M. Dorgères.

"I have not found Robert," he murmured.

"He has gone out. No doubt he will return before long."

"He will never return."

"What! he has left Paris?"

"At half-past eleven last night, your porter saw him pass with a satchel in his hand. He left nearly all his clothes in his room."

"That is a leave-taking that looks very much like a flight," observed M. Borisoff dryly.

"It is one! The rascal has escaped after robbing me! But he has not had time to pass the frontier. Set the telegraph to work—he shall be arrested—"

M. Dorgères was beside himself.

"Dear sir," said the colonel, who had lost nothing of his marvelous *sang-froid*, "before taking such a step you would do well to calculate the consequences. We have just agreed that the police are not to be mixed up with this affair. To whom would you telegraph to procure the arrest of M. de Carnoël? Besides, it is not certain that your secretary is guilty. Appearances are sometimes deceptive."

"You did not hear, then, he has fled—left the house secretly, at the very time the theft was committed."

"The time—that we must find out first. Your cashier may assist us on this point."

"Monsieur," said Vignory, "I know only one thing. Yesterday, when I closed the safe, it was intact."

"Does any one keep watch during the night?"

"There is a man who occupies the room adjoining this. He must have returned as usual at twelve."

"At twelve!" exclaimed M. Dorgères. "Malicome returns at twelve! I shall send him off."

"Not before questioning him, I hope?"

"No, though I do not suspect him. He is an old servant who has been in my house twenty-five years, and I
answer for his honesty. But his negligence is unpardonable, and you, Vignory, have been very wrong not to
speak of this."

Vignory said nothing. His fault was greater than the
banker knew, for he had been silent concerning the first
attempt at theft, and had taken no extra precautions.

He regretted bitterly having followed the advice of the
insane Maxime, and felt tempted to confess all to his
patron. But he dared not.

The colonel resumed:

"Since we are sure of this man we must admit that
the theft was committed before he came to his post and
after the departure of your employés."

"Between six and twelve, and my knave of a secretary
made off at half-past eleven."

"It is an indication but not a proof. Which way
would he come in?"

"He could have passed down an inner stairway and
through a corridor that ends in the waiting-room."

"But the office door was locked, I believe, and has not
been forced. How could he open it?"

"He had, no doubt, a false key—unless he stole that
of the watch."

"It seems scarcely probable; and the safe key, where
could that have been obtained?"

M. Dorgères withdrew it from the lock and examined it.

"It is new, and the maker of it was a skilful workman, for it is perfect. It could not have been made without a model."

"For your secretary to have furnished this model, he must have obtained possession either of your key or of the cashier's."

"He has never had mine," asserted Vignory quickly, seizing the occasion to come to the aid of his friend.

"Mine has been sometimes left on my table," said the banker, "where Robert might have seen—have handled it."

"But he must have taken it away, and that you would have discovered. Is not some word necessary in order to open the safe?"

"Yes," said M. Dorgères. "Vignory, did you tell Robert the word?"

"No, sir. I changed it yesterday. No one knew it."

"Not even I in that case. Why did you change it without letting me know?"

"I did not think—I forgot to tell you," stammered Vignory.

"Did Robert come in after the change was made?"

"No, sir—that is—I made the change day before yesterday evening, and he came here yesterday morning with a note from you. He remained only a moment, and I do not think stopped near the safe."

"You do not think, but you are not certain. And the two arms that meet when any one attempts the lock, why have they not acted?"

"I—I do not know," muttered Vignory.

"I have the answer. Robert de Carnoël knew the secret. I have several times spoken to him of it. He knew it was only necessary to move a spring to prevent it from acting, and has taken this precaution. I can doubt no longer. It is he."

"But, sir—"

"It is useless to insist; for if it is not he, it is you or I, since we three only know the mechanism."

This peremptory reply cut short the objections the cashier was about to make in the effort to vindicate his friend. It was clear it must rest between Robert de Carnoël and Jules Vignory.

There was but one way out of this dilemma—to confess that it was the second attempt to open the safe, and thereby prove Robert's innocence, since the evening before he had not left M. Dorgères' salon. Even that might not suffice, as it might be supposed he had accomplices. Vignory concluded to wait rather than compromise himself uselessly. Time might throw some light on the mystery, and he would do nothing without consulting Maxime. He had placed himself in a false position, and lacking decision and energy, remained there.

"It is neither you nor I, is it?" repeated M. Dorgères, with his pitiless logic. "Then it must be Robert."

"I begin to believe it," said the colonel. "The thing is to determine what course to pursue. If you will yield the affair into my hands, I will undertake to find the thief on condition that I am to act alone. I can manage the case better than your French police. I am personally interested, and one is never so well served as by himself. Whom did M. de Carnoël know in Paris?"

"Scarcely any one. During the two years he has spent with me he did not go out at all."

"His family live in the country?"

"He has neither family nor lands. His father left him only an old ruined castle in the heart of Brittany. But it is not there he has gone, I warrant you. He took the midnight train and embarked for America or England."

"Or some other country—Russia, for instance."

"It would be repugnant to me to have the young man brought before the Court of Assizes. He has been for two years an inmate of my house. Act, then, as you think best. I give the case up to you."

"It is well, sir. Justice shall be done without scandal or publicity. I leave this evening to be absent for a month or two. My casket I shall not be able to take, but you have sustained but a slight loss, and I may draw the thirty thousand francs I came for."

"My cashier will place it in your hands. Now let me say good-morning. It is time to open the door. The public has been kept waiting too long already. You understand, Vignory? Not a word to any one."

M. Dorgères made his adieux to the colonel and hastened out. He was impatient to see his daughter. He
had controlled himself reasonably well in the presence of
M. Bòrisoff, but the catastrophe had irritated him ex-
cessively; not on account of the loss of the money,
though he was not insensible to that, but at the idea that
his daughter had allowed her affections to be engaged
by a thief.

For he had not the slightest doubt of the guilt of M. de
Carnoël. Every thing tended to convince him of the
guilt of the unfortunate young man, even to the moderate
amount of the sum abstracted.

Any other thief would have carried off millions. He
alone would have conceived the idea of making this sort
of forced loan upon his patron, to be returned later should
he succeed in his foreign enterprises. Besides, suspicion
must rest on either Robert or Vignory. Vignory had not
disappeared; Vignory had no interest in possessing himself of the fifty thousand francs. His situation was excellent, his future assured. He would hardly risk at one
stroke his position and the hope of marrying an heiress.
What this mysterious casket contained he could not guess.
He doubted the existence of the certificates and stocks
which M. Borisoff spoke of. M. Borisoff knew well
enough that a banker only answers for such deposits as
are made in a regular manner, and was not a man to de-
prive himself by negligence or stupidity of a valuable
guarantee.

His mind dwelt on the necessity for making the event known to Alice, and he foresaw a stormy interview. Determined as he was to enlighten her without delay on the moral value of M. de Carnoël, he wished to gain some information first.

As soon as he reached his apartment he rang for his valet, an old servant who possessed and who deserved his entire confidence. The old man guessed the purpose for which he was summoned, and M. Dorgères hardly needed to question him before he ascertained that all the servants about the house were aware of the departure of M. de Carnoël. The porter had seen him return at ten, and go out at half-past eleven. Had he passed that hour and a half in his room, was a question no one could answer.

M. Dorgères was especially desirous of being enlightened on a somewhat delicate point. He had dined in town the evening before, and Alice had not accompanied him.

Had she seen Robert before he left the house, was what he wished to ascertain, but could not bring himself to question the servant.

Finally the valet was disposed to be communicative, and mentioned, without being asked, that Mlle. Dorgères, after dining with only Madame Martineau, had retired to her own room.

To restrain the gossip of the servants, M. Dorgères gave out that M. de Carnoël had gone away for the purpose of attending to business abroad of a pressing nature.

He was very careful to make no allusion to what had happened to the safe, but after dismissing the faithful Joseph, he sent for Malicome, and upbraided him roundly for his carelessness.

" There has been no attempt to rob me so far," he said, " designedly, but there doubtless will be if you continue to neglect your duties. At nine o'clock I require you to be at your post, and shall dismiss you the first time I know you to fail."

The poor devil acknowledged his delinquencies, but protested it was impossible for any one to enter the offices during his absence, as he invariably carried the keys with him. This was just what the banker wished to ascertain. Nothing now remained but to have an explanation with his daughter.

On going to her room he found her writing a letter. She looked pale, and her eyes were red. Instead of springing into his arms as usual, she simply offered her forehead to be kissed. He took both her hands.

"You have been weeping," he said; "what is the matter?"

"It is true," said Alice, resolutely. "I have done nothing else since yesterday—and you are the cause."

M. Dorgères was not prepared for this frank declaration, and he foresaw that the scene would be more painful than he had anticipated.

"You are displeased because I talked reason to you. You owe me thanks, rather; but I do not ask that. I came to speak to you of this marriage. When you know all you will recognize its impossibility."

The girl shook her head, but made no reply.

"It is M. de Carnoël himself who has rendered it impossible," he went on, trying to prepare her for the fearful blow that was to come.

Still there was no reply.

"To whom are you writing?" he asked, pointing to the letter which lay on the table.

"To him," replied Alice, without hesitation.

"What! you write to this man? And you do not hesitate to say so to me?"

"Why should I hide it? I have promised to marry him, and mean to keep my word. I may well write to my betrothed."

"So you have become engaged, and without consulting me? Ah, well, your punishment will be equal to your fault! Would you know what he has done, this pretty gentleman whom you call your betrothed?"

"Nothing that is unworthy of the name he bears—I swear it."

"He has stolen."

"It is not true."

"He has *stolen*," repeated M. Dorgères, emphasizing the word. "Yesterday I told him what I thought of his pretensions, signified my intention to remove him from his present position, and made him an offer to represent me abroad. He refused."

"He did right."

"Let me finish. You may defend him, if you can, when you have heard his story.   He refused the place I offered him, and went out haughtily from my presence. I saw him no more ; but he returned in the evening, opened the safe with a false key, and took fifty thousand francs and a casket belonging to Col. Borisoff."

"You mean that he is accused of this infamy, but you do not believe it.   Question him ; he will easily vindicate himself."

"He has gone—he has fled like the thief that he is. I shall not pursue him. It is sufficient that my house is well rid of him."

"Gone !" murmured the young girl, "without a word —without telling me why !" and she fainted in her father's arms.

CHAPTER IV.

MAXIME'S THEORIES.

"WHERE are you taking me?" asked Jules Vignory of his friend Maxime who, on meeting him on the boulevard, took his arm and was leading him toward Rue de la Chaussée d' Antin.

It was a few days after the theft, one evening toward ten o'clock, and Maxime had no doubt dined satisfactorily, judging by his high spirits and flow of talk.

"Where we can find amusement, and where you have never set foot before, I venture to say."

"I am in no humor for being amused."

"*Parbleu!* you are never in the humor. Since last week you are always in the dumps."

"Truly I have nothing to be merry about."

"I know; the hand, the colonel's casket, and the fifty thousand francs. But what of them? My uncle does not suspect you."

"Certainly not, but——"

"And he does not know that the mechanism of his safe has amputated a woman's hand."

"That is precisely what I am disturbed about. The

silence I have been compelled to keep weighs on me, especially now that they have accused Robert."

"And they are right."

"Then you consider him guilty?"

"I do not believe he would otherwise have decamped as he has done; and I also believe any ordinary thief would have made a clean sweep. This gentleman was content to go off with the few notes of a thousand that he needed, and hoped to return some day."

"But what could he want with the casket?"

"To answer that I should need to know what this Muscovite box contained. A woman's secret most likely; some woman connected with Col. Borisoff. That being so the case would seem quite clear. She first tried to operate herself, and her failure cost her her hand. *Ma foi!* a pretty hand too. Carnoël then undertook it for her, and finished it successfully; gave the casket into the hands of the interested party, and kept the money to build his fortunes on in America or elsewhere."

"That is all a romance and a most unlikely one. Carnoël had no liaisons."

"How do you know?"

"He was and still is madly in love with your cousin."

"That proves nothing. He may have loved some one before he knew her, and she may still preserve some empire over him."

"To the extent of dishonoring himself to please her?"

" My dear boy, I don't undertake to explain everything. But tell me something about Alice. How has the dear child taken this sorrowful adventure of the man of her choice ? "

" Very much to heart as might be expected. She has been ill, and has not yet recovered from the shock she received. I have scarcely dared to enquire for her of M. Dorgères."

" That is just like you. Timid as a school-boy. You must dare, my dear fellow ; you must dare. My uncle has designs on you ; and my cousin will find out in the end that you are well worth M. de Carnoël, who has been led into buying a forced loan upon the safe. They are not the kind of levities a young girl readily pardons. If his innocence should be proved now, the case would be quite different. But that has not come to pass yet. Carnoël has fled ; the place is free. Try and take possession of it. Help yourself, and fortune will help you. And by way of beginning, never miss a single Wednesday. To-morrow I will come to watch over and sustain you. These little feasts are not very gay, but there is nothing I cannot do for the sake of friendship. Tell me, will this Russian colonel be there ? I shouldn't be sorry to meet the boyar."

· " The colonel left the day the casket was stolen. I suppose he is engaged in the pursuit after Robert."

" Ah ! ah ! he, too, wishes to act the policeman, the good colonel ! I am not surprised, for I fancy that is his

profession. Let him pursue Carnoël. I shall follow after the one-handed ; it is more certain."

"If you can find her and vindicate poor Robert, you
will do a truly noble act."

"Which will give the death-blow to your hopes, for
Alice would return to her first love. But this consideration shall not stop me, for I am no partisan."

"What a fine judge you would make ! You have become solemn as a magistrate. If you would only change
your mode of life now, the transformation would be complete; but I suppose you have given up neither baccarat
nor betting, nor the company of *demoiselles à la mode.*"

" Faith, no ! If I gave them up I should give up my
best chance. It is not by remaining in a chimney corner that I shall find out the owner of the bracelet."

" Ah, yes ! the bracelet—what have you done with it ?"

" I carried it to my jeweller, who recognized it immediately as one that had been brought to him, to replace a
missing diamond, by a woman, young and pretty, and
whom he believed to belong to the demi-monde. He
said he had never seen her before, and thought she was
a stranger in Paris. As I told you, the bracelet is of
foreign manufacture."

"You have it still ?"

" On my arm. First I kept it in a secretary, but
was afraid it would be stolen. Rosewood furniture, is
more easily forced than a safe, so I concluded to wear
it."

"You will be laughed at."

"Oh, it will not be seen unless I choose to show it. The women will say I am in love ; that this is a souvenir of my adored one. This sort of foolishness will do me no harm with them. If my little cousin learns that I am becoming sentimental, I shall go up many degrees in her esteem."

"All this doesn't explain to me where you are going this evening."

"Haven't you made out, at least, why I wear this bracelet ? Don't you see that I am searching for its owner at theatres, balls, and wherever ladies are to be met ? "

"You are insane. After such an operation how can she frequent theatres and balls ? She must at least be in bed if she has not died of her wound."

"It is not she whom I hope to find at the Rink this evening."

"The Rink ! You don't say you are going there ? "

"I don't intend to take you there by force," laughed Maxime. "You have the right, if you please, to prefer your chimney corner to a reunion of pretty women. Besides, if my uncle knew you frequented pleasure resorts he might tell his daughter, and it might displease the charming Alice. You are right to take care of the future ; while I, who have no reputation, and who mean never to marry, am going to the Rink where I shall not waste my time. Now let me explain to you in a few words my plan. I expect to exhibit the bracelet to all the ladies I meet this

evening. It is more than likely that one of them will
have seen it on the arm of some acquaintance, and will
exclaim on finding it in my possession. Then we will
have a talk, and I answer for it we do not part till I have
found out the name of this friend. Now do you understand ? "

"A little ; but I feel no confidence in your method.
Suppose the thief to belong to the *demi-monde.* There
are thousands of such in Paris. It would be the merest
chance if you should meet with one of her friends."

"To meet with her the first time would be a mere accident ; but I shall try again, and the oftener I make the
experiment the greater will be my chances of success.
Has it ever occurred to you what the jade and her accomplice must think of the consequences of their adventure ? They must have expected to see in the papers that
this attempt at theft had been made and an active pursuit
set on foot. Nothing of the kind. The papers simply
announce that a hand had been thrown into the Seine, no
one knew by whom. They concluded that M. Dorgères
had not chosen to lodge a complaint, and had the audacity to return to the attack. After this second expedition, the same silence. The police continue to be occupied with the hand, but they have on their mind a crime
of a different description, for there is no question of safes
or traps or caskets. Nevertheless, they are not perfectly
reassured. They want to know what has become of the
bracelet. And if they hear of a *viveur* sporting a tur-

quoise and diamond bracelet, such a report would not pass unnoticed by them, would it ? "

" Probably not," said Vignory, who had listened with marked impatience. " But assuredly they will not come to you and say : ' The bracelet is ours ; restore it to us.' "

" No, but they would try to establish some intercourse between said hair-brained féllow and themselves by sending an emissary, a *cocotte*, for instance, who would try to seduce me for the purpose of obtaining the bracelet as a gift, or at least finding out where I got it. I, on my part, should profit by the situation to ascertain who sent the embassadress,"

" You are engaging in a perilous enterprise, and coming in conflict with rascals. Beware ! "

" Come ! I am no child. I'm afraid of nobody. Let them try to serve me a trick ; they will soon see whether they have their match. It is freezing cold here, and I am impatient to begin the campaign, so good-evening."

Vignory grasped the hand held out to him, and then resumed his melancholy route to his lodgings, while his friend walked with rapid step up the slope of Rue Blanche.

The blaze of light from the gas jets at the entrance of the Rink was visible from afar, directing the vehicles, which formed one long aisle in the middle of the street, toward this beacon-light of pleasure.

Women elegantly dressed—late comers—were passing

in quickly, not to miss the hour when the entertainment was at its height.

The placards announced a new pantomime, and the crowd was great in the robing-room. The evening gave promise of being a brilliant one.

Maxime got his ticket and passed on without wasting time on the bagatelles of the vestibule, which afforded no opportunity for talking. At the same moment he felt his arm grazed, and turning quickly saw only the back of an urchin, who immediately disappeared.

" I must keep my eyes open here," he said, feeling to see that the golden circle was safe in its place and the clasp firm.

The Rink was becoming crowded to excess. The blinding lights flooded the two square halls and the space appropriated to' promenaders. A cloud of warm vapor rose to the high ceiling, and became a canopy of smoke above the spectators seated before the theatre, which occupies the central point in this fantastical arrangement.

The Rink is an establishment adapted to various purposes. Designed at first for the use of skaters, little by little it has changed its character. It is a theatre, a café, and a promenade. Nor is skating altogether overlooked. A long arena is dedicated to the lovers of this sport, which the Parisians seldom have an opportunity to practise in the open air. Elbowing his way through the crowd that blocked up the space where the two halls met, and passing to the right, Maxime took the gallery that runs along the café concert. His progress was slow, but Maxime was not pressed for time so he passed on step by step, his nose in the air, taking careful note of the pedestrians who crossed his path, and passing in review the sitters enthroned in the boxes.

Around the tables where the habitués of both sexes were wont to refresh themselves with drinks not too cooling, there was a medley of noises which, though by no means agreeable, rendered the place propitious for private and familiar talk. Above the pattering of feet, the murmur of voices, the striking of glasses, and the incessant grinding of skates on rollers, there was little danger of being overheard by one's neighbors.

In a box toward the middle of the promenade he recognized three of his acquaintances who were without cavaliers, and seemed to be amusing themselves by watching the débutantes and country people. It needed no importunity to bring him to their box, where he soon established himself, his hands resting upon its front that he might exhibit his prize.

"Why is it we do not see you now?" asked a tall blonde named Delphine, who affected English manners. "For the last week I have not once met you in the Bois. Have you parted with your chestnut who paced so well?"

"Max, my good friend, you were not at the Variétés, Friday," said the brunette Cora.

"Do not look for me, ladies," replied Maxime. "I am nowhere to be seen, because I am in love."

" Come now ! "

" Madly in love, my dear friends."

" Ah ! " said the little Bertha, " it is really true. He is over head and ears in love—no, above his wrist ; see, he has a souvenir of his adored one on his arm."

He made a pretense of trying to disengage his wrist, as the delicately gloved fingers passed over the tell-tale jewel.

" It is superb ! " exclaimed Cora, derisively. " The lady has made you an ugly present. The diamonds are yellow and the turquoise pale. That is always the way with the *femmes du monde ;* they have no taste."

" You know nothing about her," said Maxime, trying to put on an aggrieved air. " She is a stranger, and her diamonds are all family diamonds."

" For my part, I am certain I have met that bracelet somewhere at a supper."

" Really ! you would do me a favor to tell me whom you saw wearing it."

" I have forgotten now, but it will come to me. You think I am romancing. You are wrong, my little Max, and I shall prove to you some day that I know your princess."

Maxime was about to protest. He thought she would end by letting fall some useful hint, but this first inquest was not destined to progress further.

Delphine observed, lackadaisically :

" Look ! here comes the most agreeable of doctors."

Maxime turned, and found himself face to face with a gentleman whom he met every evening at his club, a Hungarian physician, who was a great chess player and a master of all games. He was surprised to encounter this sober gentleman at the Rink, and still more so, at being interrupted by him in the midst of this interesting conversation. But he accepted the interruption with a good grace, promising himself to resume it so soon as the *mal-à-propos* physician had passed on his way. This gentleman bore very little resemblance to a physician. He wore an immense moustache and whiskers; and would have made a very good figure at the head of a troop of cavalry. It was, indeed, impossible to look at him without wondering why he was without gimp on his shoulders and spurs to his boots. He was, however, a real doctor, loaded with diplomas from various universities, German and Polish. He did not practise his profession, having no need of it, but gave his attention gratuitously, and was much in vogue with ladies of the *demi-monde*, though he had not been known to enter into any irregular liaison during the few years he had resided in Paris.

"Good-afternoon, doctor. You come to look after your patients at the Rink? That is well. Do tell me a remedy for headache."

M. Villagos had already given Maxime a warm shake of the hand, and after exchanging a few words with the girls, took his arm, saying in his ear:

"Come, sir, let me show you something marvellous."

He had never before treated Maxime so familiarly, and
he was about to disengage himself politely, but reflecting
that he could join these ladies later, he suffered himself
to be led away.

" Something marvellous ? that is rare here."

" You will admit that I do not exaggerate when I have
shown you this woman."

"Ah!" said Maxime, "it is a woman. So much the
better, for in the way of marvels I like pretty faces, and
also that they should be new. Now, I come here frequently and have seen all the habitués of the place."

"So have I, and if it were a question of a Cora, a
Delphine, or a Bertha, I should not have disturbed
you."

They had reached the spot where the promenade turns
at a right angle, and where the hall reserved for the skaters
begins, a long arena, extending toward the Rue de Clichy.
Ordinarily it is less frequented than the café, where one
may gargle his throat with music whilst swallowing beer.

The skating of the establishment is only a pretext, a
diversion imposed by the name of the place, and those
who engage in it wear the appearance of having been paid
to train their casters on the wax floor that is substituted
for the lakes of the Bois de Boulogne. The fair sex is
but poorly represented there ; and these are chiefly foreigners who, coming from lands where there is freezing
every winter, hope to find here their national amusement.
Leaning his hands on the balustrade which separates the

passage way appropriated to promenaders from the hall of the skaters, the doctor observed :

" It is here this marvel is to be seen.   Just now she is on the other side, but will soon come this way."

Maxime smiled, distrusting the doctor's admiration, and prepared to combat it.   A Parisian's enthusiasm is not easily aroused.

He kept a lookout for the person who had attracted the notice of M. Villagos, and saw from afar a woman turning on her skates with wonderful ease and rapidity. Groups had formed themselves at the end of the promenade, trying to follow her movements.

" It is quite curious," said Maxime, ironically, " and this young woman might have great success in le Prophéte where there is skating on the scene ; but for my part I know nothing about it, and am hardly capable of appreciating her merit."

" It is not her skill, but her person that I wished to call your attention to.   Wait before you decide that I had no reason to be carried away.   She is coming toward us."

In truth, the artist skater had suddenly changed her tactics.   Abandoning circles and complicated figures she darted forward in a straight line.   Rapidly as a bird flies, grazing the wooden wall in front of the arena, she passed close to Maxime.

She was a brunette, with a complexion of reflected gold ; but Maxime saw only her eyes,—great dark eyes, burning with an intense light.   She turned toward him, but before hé had recovered himself, was lost in the distance.

"Well, what do you say?" asked M. Villagos.

"I say that you are right," exclaimed Maxime. "She is a real marvel, and I cannot tell why I have never seen her. If she had shown herself anywhere in Paris she would have been heard of. It is an event—such an apparition as that."

"Bah! you Frenchmen take no note of women who are not classified and numbered. Some would think her ugly because she is not known."

"I am not one of them, you may rest assured. I felt when she looked at me as if I had been struck by lightning. And her figure! See her swaying like a reed; not an effort, not an ungraceful movement! But tell me who can this unknown beauty be? Spanish? Italian? Creole? One thing is certain—she is not Parisian."

"Who knows? We have every type in this country. However, I would willingly believe her to be one of my compatriots. We have at Pesth some, even among the great ladies, who resemble her; but they do not frequent the Rink."

"*Parbleu!* I don't take this one for a duchess, in proof of which I mean to make advances to her immediately."

"All right. Let me know the result," said the Hungarian, pressing the hand of Maxime, who made no effort to detain him. His thoughts were fixed entirely upon this

marvel, forgetting the object of his expedition and even
his bracelet. Had his friend Vignory been present he
would have laughed to see him abandon his great enterprise to attach himself to this princess of skating. She
was dressed in perfect taste, elegant without excessive
care, in a costume designed expressly for skating : fur
cap, tight-fitting corsage, short skirt, and fawn-colored
leather boots. In this costume, completed by a sable
coat and muff, she might have skated on the Neva.

Maxime became more and more satisfied that the lady
with the burning eyes was a foreigner, and that in seeking to enter into conversation with her he must use some
forms.

"Provided she speaks, or, above all, understands
French," he said to himself, as he walked slowly toward
the end of the hall, where he knew she would put off her
skates.

Had she remarked him ?

He almost hoped so.

More than once as he followed her rapid movements
their eyes had met.

"*Ma foi !* if I cannot speak to her I feel in the humor
to follow and see where she lives. I can give myself a
few hours' respite from looking up the owner of the bracelet. To-morrow I can go to see Bertha Verrier and resume the conversation M. Villagos interrupted."

These sage reflections occupied his mind as he took his
position at the point where the skaters made their egress.

He had been there a few moments, never losing sight of the lady who continued to glide over the floor, when he heard a voice behind him say :

"Good-evening, M. Maxime."

"What, you !" he exclaimed, on perceiving Georget, the little groom of his uncle's office, whom he little expected to find there.

"Yes, M. Maxime ; haven't you observed a gentleman with a frock coat and red moustache? He has been watching you ever since you came."

During the colloquy Maxime had not remarked that the man with the formidable moustache had approached the skater and whispered a word in her ear.

The unknown took off her skates and walked quickly toward the opening. At the same moment Maxime turned and saw her.

Advancing hastily to meet her, determined not to let the opportunity pass, he bowed, and without further preamble offered his arm.

Not at all abashed apparently by this abrupt offer, she quietly accepted it.

The Hungarian, who had watched this little scene, nodded to Maxime just as the unknown entered the robing-room.

"What an original !" thought Maxime, as he returned from afar the bow of M. Villagos. "He discovers a marvel, and contents himself with pointing her out to me as a lover of the beautiful."

The marvel had left in the robing-room her sable cloak and muff ; the cloak of an excellent cut, and the muff a tiny one, into which she hastily thrust her hands daintily gloved with Swedish skin.

"I am ready for you, monsieur," she said, with a bantering air.

He advanced with *empressement* and offered his arm, which she took without hesitation.

Maxime was beside himself. He walked on without observing any one ; he saw only the stairs, and did not perceive Georget, who was striking his feet on the sidewalk of the Rue de Clichy.

"You are going to walk?" he asked of the brunette, who leaned daintily on his arm.

"Certainly. It is one of the conditions which you have accepted, and I count upon your observing them all."

"Then you must be guide, as I do not know where we are going."

"You will know in a half hour."

"So soon?"

"Let us take the Rue de Tivoli, please."

Maxime yielded to the gentle pressure of the hand on his arm, and followed the route it indicated. He was wondering where this nocturnal ramble was to lead. To a superb mansion of the Boulevard Malesherbes, or some modest dwelling of the Rue Mosnier? It mattered little, however, for the brunette had eyes that could turn the head though they inhabited a garret.· At the end of Rue Tivoli she made him cross Rue Amsterdam into Rue de Londres. It was late, and between eleven and twelve passers-by were not many in these parts. Lovers might talk without any fear of being remarked, still less over-heard.

Nevertheless, after the first trifling gallantries the con-versation came to a sudden halt.

Maxime was thinking of the strangeness of this adven-ture and that he would like to study the ground before advancing farther. He was being gradually possessed by a fear that is truly Parisian, the fear of being hoaxed.

The unknown passed Rue Mosnier without entering it, and led him toward the Place de l'Europe, but did not stop there.

Leaning on the parapet were three men, who appeared to be observing the evolutions of a locomotive, and who turned as the pair passed near them.

"Would you not have been afraid of these men had you returned alone?" he asked, by way of renewing the conversation.

"No, for I should have taken a carriage. I am no coward, but at night my neighborhood is nearly de-serted."

"Where do you live? You may as well tell me since we are going there."

"Rue Jouffroy, near Place Wagram. It is a long dis-tance, and I should have told you, but I wanted to impose this task on you to teach you not to insist upon escorting a lady when you do not know where she is going."

"A charming punishment. I am sorry you do not live beyond the fortifications."

"Compliments again. Since you insist upon ignoring our agreement, I may be a little indiscreet, too, and ask if you wear a coat of mail like the chevaliers of the middle ages. I feel something under my hand which rubs the skin through my glove."

This was an unexpected question, but he saw no reason for hiding the truth from her, and replied :

"It is a bracelet."

"A bracelet ! a love token ! Then we shall be on better terms hereafter."

"You believed me, then, incapable of loving ?"

"Not exactly. The verb to love can be understood in more ways than one. I did not imagine you to be sentimental."

"When you will allow me I shall be glad to prove the contrary. Have I not already proved it ? Is it not enough that for fear of displeasing you I content myself with such a walk as this ? "

" Cold as it is, your conduct is meritorious, I confess, and I beg you to let me warm the hand that is resting on your bracelet in my muff ; not that I withdraw my confidence," added the unknown, as she disengaged her hand, " but my fingers are numb."

The walk was drawing to a close, and there was not much time to lose if the adventure was not to end at the lady's door.

"You speak of confidence," he said, "and you have not even told me who you are."

"It seems to me it is your place to begin," retorted the lady ; "I do not even know your name."

"Nor I yours."

"I told you that mine was Justine."

"And mine Maxime.   Is that exchange of prefixes sufficient ?"

"I understand.   Before giving me your family name, you must know mine.   It is not elegant, I warn you; it is Sergent—Justine Sergent.   You will no longer, I suppose, take me for a Russian or a Spaniard.   Now for yours."

"Maxime Dorgères, without an apostrophe after the D, 99 Rue de Châteaudun."

"That is equal to having your visiting card."

"Twenty-five years old, unmarried, independent position, excellent character—"

"No more, I beg.   To answer a description so complete, I should need to tell you many things not the least interesting to you."

"Concerning yourself, everything interests me."

"To the extent of making you forget the one who enchained you with that bracelet ?"

"Why not ?"

ↆ "Such are men—always ready to deny the absent and to deceive her who has inspired him with a passing fancy. You love her, this woman,- or you have loved her, and you scarcely know me."

" I swear to you that I speak the truth, and that this is not a love-token."

" I should like to put your sincerity to the test."

" Try me."

" If I asked for this bracelet, would you give it to me ? "

This question fell like a shower of cold water on the ardent flame of Maxime. He was ready to do everything to win the favor of this matchless creature—everything except what she had just asked. To yield the bracelet were to renounce forever the hope of finding the woman who had lost a hand, and the enterprise was too near his heart to be given up on the first occasion that presented itself.

And then the proposition came so suddenly, it flashed into his mind that Madame Sergent might be nothing more than an adventuress.

The question was asked near one of the candelabra that light the Avenue de Villiers, and the beauty of the Rink might have read in the face of her chance cavalier a doubt which wounded her, for she said, dryly :

" Spare yourself the trouble of refusing. I simply wished to prove you. I ought to have remembered that this bracelet had an intrinsic value, and that you might mistake the proof I was putting you to for a wish to possess it for its own sake."

"I protest," exclaimed Maxime, "that such an idea has not entered my mind, and if this bracelet were not a family relic—"

"Let us say no more about it, I beg, but since you have been kind enough to accompany me so far, go with me to the end. I have never returned on foot so late, and was not aware the street was so deserted."

"Fear nothing, mademoiselle," said Maxime, anxious to make her forget, by dint of politeness, the bad impression his hesitation had produced. "I am not dreaming of leaving you, but there is not the least danger."

"You will laugh at me, but since we passed the boulevard I have imagined we were pursued."

Maxime turned but saw no one. "I wish," he said, laughing, "some opportunity would occur to defend you. Unfortunately, I do not believe we shall be attacked. The neighborhood is not much frequented, it is true, but we are not in the forest of Bondy, and the men I see at a distance do not appear to be coming this way. Will you take my arm again?"

"No, thank you. Your bracelet hurts me."

"This bracelet evidently weighs on your mind. You would not allow it to do so if you knew why I attach a special value to it."

"I do not desire to know."

"Not more than you desire to see me again. Is not

that it ? In five minutes you will wish me good-evening, and all will be said. My romance will end on the first page."

"The shortest stories are the best."

"They must have a commencement though."

"This walk you count for nothing ? "

"It is not a commencement ; it is a preface."

"The preface is often worth more than the book. But I still fancy I hear steps approaching. Let us hasten."

Maxime began to think the lady was leading him very far. The localities were becoming unfamiliar, and he lost the points of the compass in these solitary pathways. He smiled a little at the prospect of returning alone on foot, for there seemed little likelihood that he would find a carriage, and he thought he should not care to re-count to Dr. Villagos the termination of his romantic adventure.

"At last," murmured the unknown, "we have arrived without accident ; here is the street I live on, and it only remains for me to thank you for your protection. You have rendered me a real service, for—it is foolish, I confess—but this evening I am timid."

"Your street is long," said Maxime, "and if you live at the other end—"

"No, monsieur ; the house is but a few steps off. I see it from here."

"You do not forbid me to escort you to your door ? "

The lady hesitated. "I should refuse with an ill grace, having brought you so far. Come."

Maxime followed. The unknown stopped before a basement door and drew a key from her muff, which she introduced into the lock.

"Must I pass in that way when you do me the honor to receive me?" asked Maxime.

"I have not said that I would receive you."

"No, but I hope you would not drive me to despair by refusing to allow me to visit you."

"When?"

"To-morrow."

"To-morrow I shall leave Paris. You would not see me."

"Forever?"

"No; for a fortnight."

"It is long, but I resign myself to wait, if you promise that on your return—"

"On my return you will think no more of me, or if the contrary were possible you would do well not to follow after an illusion. Come, though, if you will, but not till the end of a fortnight."

"For whom shall I ask?"

"Madame Sergent. Good-evening, sir." And she disappeared quickly and silently, the key turning noiselessly in the lock. The adventure was cut short, but Maxime did not acknowledge that it was ended. The beauty had put him off for a fortnight, and what is merely postponed is not lost. He compensated himself for the delay by the hope of getting some information concerning this enigmatical creature, and began by examining her dwelling. It was two stories high without counting the basement floor, right on the street, with a garden in the rear.

Whilst he was making this inspection, a light noise of footsteps caught his ear, and looking in the direction whence the sound came, he saw distinctly three men walking in the Avenue de Villiers, and he saw indistinctly another form advancing toward him, close to the walls, in Rue Jouffroy.

The ideas of Maxime immediately took another direction. It came into his mind, all of a sudden, that it was past midnight, and that the inhabitants of this elegant but peaceful quarter went to bed early; that he was without arms or any hope of aid should he be attacked. Now these men had every appearance of being on the watch for him.

"Oh!" he exclaimed, "can it be that the marvel brought me here that I might fall into an ambush? That would be quite serious, for I have nothing to defend myself with, and should have to deal with three or four rascals. I would willingly part with the few louis I have with me, but would be devilishly vexed to be robbed of my bracelet. But perhaps I am mistaken. They are not coming this way. It seems to me I see one creeping along in the shadow. They may have sent him to reconnoitre."

Maxime was brave, and these reflections, though not reassuring, did not determine him to retreat before the enemy.

On the contrary, he resolved to put an end to this painful uncertainty by going to meet this scout. He had not taken three steps, when he heard these words spoken in a low voice :

" Do not budge, M. Maxime. It is I."

" Who are you ? " he asked, greatly surprised at being addressed by his name.

There was no reply, but soon he caught sight of a triple row of brass buttons gleaming in the light of the gas reflector.

" Georget ! " he cried, " ah, little imp ! under my feet, as usual."

" Not so loud, I beg you, sir," muttered the groom.

" What do you mean ? "

" I mean they are watching for you down there, to do you an ill turn."

" How do you know ? "

" I heard them talking. They are three men who would rob a passer-by or even murder him, as they would quaff a glass of absinthe."

" You know them, then ? "

" By sight, yes. They lounge every day around the Barriere de Courcelles, and I live in this neighborhood."

" Bah ! if they meant to attack me they would be on me already, and you see they are not stirring."

"Because on Rue Jouffroy there are too many houses and people; if attacked, you need only sound a bell or give the alarm, and persons would come to your assistance. On the Avenue de Villiers, the street is wide and the houses few. That is why they wait for you there."

"Then what am I to do? I have no fancy for spending the night here, and if I start for the other end of the street I shall be pursued."

"They will follow, but will do you no harm while I am with you."

"Ha! ha! you fancy they would be afraid of a little gnat like you?"

"No, but they will think that if they come too near I would spin off to a café not far from here, which keeps open till two o'clock. But let us go, I beg."

"All right. We will see what those scoundrels who are mounting guard there propose to do. March, little one."

Without waiting for a second order—for he was evidently impatient—Georget moved on, pattering his feet like a horse that is held in and is impatient to be let off on a gallop. But instead of going in advance, he kept close to Maxime, who gave a last glance, as he turned away, toward the residence of the lady.

"Her room doesn't look on the street or there would be some light visible," thought the incorrigible young man, the danger which threatened him being unable to drive altogether from his mind the recollection of his adventure.

"I guessed right," cried the boy, "they are setting off."

Maxime turned and saw the three men entering, but without haste, Rue Jouffroy. This discreet mode of following after a man whom they meant to rifle seemed to him singular. But everything was unusual to-night.

"We have only one dangerous place to pass," said the boy. "We will turn to the right into the Boulevard Malesherbes—don't you see that is like the Avenue de Villiers?—but we will soon reach Rue Cardinet; the café where I have friends is at the entrance, and grandmother stops a little farther on."

"You live with her?"

"Yes, M. Maxime. She keeps the lodge and I sleep above in the loft, so if you've a mind you can come in and wait, while I look for a hack."

"That is a good idea. Only your grandmother must have retired before this."

"No danger; she waits for me. She must be uneasy now, for I am not often out so late. I leave the Rink every evening at half-past eleven, and twenty minutes after am at home."

"Then to-day you went out of your way to follow me. Why was that?"

"I was just going, M. Maxime, when you came out with a lady. You passed on without observing me, and took Rue de Tivoli and Rue de Londres, which was my route—"

· "Do you know the lady who was with me?"

"I didn't look at her but I think not—and when you passed the Place de l'Europe, the three men who were seated there got up and followed, which I thought queer. I ran and caught up with them, and I heard one of them say, 'we must wait till he is alone'—but here we are at the Boulevard. Have you good legs? Ah, well, let us make for Rue Cardinet; it seems to me they are already on our heels." Maxime turned, and saw the men approaching rapidly. But he was sufficiently in advance to hope to distance them. They had reached the point of intersection of Rue Jouffroy and the interminable Boulevard Malesherbes. Turning to the right they started at full speed.

"Do you hear?" said Maxime. "They are running too.".

"As I expected," answered the boy. "But I am not afraid of them now."

"It seems to me they are gaining on us."

"Make yourself easy. Do you see those two lights ahead in the middle of the street? Ho! coachman, a hundred sous 'extra for a drink!"

At this cry the coachman whipped up his horses and led them in the twinkling of an eye to the sidewalk. Georget opened the door leisurely.

"Get in with me," said Maxime. "I can't leave you alone in face of these scoundrels."

"Never fear. They are not concerned about me. See,

they are turning off !   They understand that the game is up.   You are going home ?"

"Yes, 99 Rue de Châteaudu   Thanks, little one. You have done me great service, for I have had a narrow escape."

" And the bracelet too," he added, under his breath.

CHAPTER V.

M. DORGÈRES' RECREATIONS.

THE Wednesday soirées at M. Dorgères were never extremely gay. A few old friends of the banker, with their wives and daughters, and the attachés of the house very nearly completed the personnel of these weekly reunions. From time to time two or three gentlemen of the financial world dropped in, attracted by the beautiful eyes and still more the dowry of Mlle. Dorgères.

They were kindly welcomed, but received no encouragement in their pretensions, and soon tired of listening to duet sonatas, and playing baccarat.

But there were two or three young habitués of this quiet salon who seemed to accommodate themselves to the innocent amusements they found there. Robert de Carnoël never failed, and Jules Vignory seldom; but Robert had disappeared, and seemed to have carried with him all the charm of these private feasts of which he was the soul.

Alice had lost her spirits; her father was preoccupied; Vignory more serious and thoughtful than ever. Maxime

alone was unchanged, but Maxime had not arrived when
the seven or eight guests of M. Dorgères passed from the
dining-room to the salon, the evening after his adventure.

Jules Vignory had been invited to dinner and given a
place by the side of Alice. It was the first time the favor
had been accorded him, and he did his best to justify it;
but he was naturally timid, and the memory of his unfortunate friend came up between him and the girl he
wished to please to such an extent that conversation lan-
guished.

Her father, who wished to make him appear to advantage, questioned him on matters with which he knew he
was thoroughly conversant, but questions of finance had
little interest for Alice; and the stratagem met with no
success. The governess, a respectable and well-informed
widow, was without vivacity, and added no element of
gaiety to this solemn assembly. The other guests were
all fashioned after the same model—old merchants who
had amassed a great fortune, but had not had time to
learn how to talk. They discussed business and their
wives' toilets. The least tiresome of them was M. Camaret, who had travelled a good deal in the interests of his
business, and could relate stories of South America or
Cochin China.

It was matter of some astonishment that M. Dorgères
attached himself to a society so little recreative. Par-
venus, enriched by some financial or commercial stroke,

animadverted upon his want of polish. He laughed at them, and continued to enjoy himself in his own fashion.

But he had not been able to do so during the past week, for he lived only for his daughter, and he saw that his daughter was wounded to the heart. The common-place maxim that time heals all wounds failed to reassure him with regard to her. Moreover, he could not but feel that the sudden departure of Robert had thrown a veil of sadness and gloom around the whole house. He fought against this feeling of regret, being firmly convinced of his guilt; but there were moments when there came over him a feeling of pity and of regret that he should have driven him to crime by so downright a refusal.

Not at all sorry that he had refrained from delivering him to the officers of justice, he felt a secret wish also that he might escape the pursuit of this Russian, who did not inspire him with any great sympathy.

M. Camaret's narratives were not found sufficient to restore the loss of gaiety occasioned by Robert's absence, or to prevent anybody from being relieved when the hour came to pass into the salon for coffee. Groups formed, the ladies surrounding the fire-place, the gentlemen talking politics with M. Dorgères, while Vignory, ashamed of the part he had played at table, held himself aloof from all.

The coffee was served by Mlle. Dorgères. When he saw her approach with a cup in her hand, he trembled lest, instead of the polite pleasantry with which he would like to greet her, he should be guilty of some awkward blunder. But all this feeling vanished when, instead of inquiring whether he would have one or two lumps of sugar, she pronounced the name of Carnoël.

"Is it true that he has not written to you?" she began.

"No, mademoiselle. At least not since he left."

"And before he left?"

"He sent me a few words of farewell. He was in despair. He had just had a conversation with M. Dorgères."

"Who had forbidden him to think of marrying me. You must know as you were his friend. He told you all, did he not?"

"Mademoiselle," murmured Vignory. "I fear to distress you if I say that Robert—"

"Go on."

"Thought you approved of your father's refusal."

"In other words, he thought I loved him no longer, and had failed of my promise. That is why he left without seeing me again?"

Vignory made a sign of affirmation.

"I thank you, monsieur, for your frankness," said Alice with earnestness, "and have only one more question to ask. Do you believe he is guilty of the act of which he is accused?"

"No, a thousand times no," cried the young cashier. "There is a mystery in this sad affair, which the future

will no doubt explain. The guilty will be discovered,
and then—"

" Will you help me to discover him ? "

" Will I ? Ah, mademoiselle, dispose of me ! I shall
be too happy to serve you, and desire nothing more than
to prove the innocence of my best friend."

Alice looked at Vignory attentively. At this passionate declaration tears came into her eyes, and it was with
difficulty she found voice to say :

" Thank you once more from the depths of my heart.
I had some prepossessions against you. With a word
you have dispelled them, and from this moment we are
joined in one purpose."

" What are you plotting there ? " said the banker,
rubbing his hands, delighted to find his daughter engaged in friendly talk with the husband he designed for
her.

" M. Maxime Dorgères," announced a servant in
brown livery.

Maxime's appearance in the salon always caused a sen-
sation, for they knew he had a stock of gaiety on hand,
and news enough from the Parisian world to supply the
habitués with conversation for a week. But this evening
he had a warmer welcome than usual. Vignory was not
sorry to see the friend who had promised him his support with Mlle. Dorgères. Alice received him smilingly,
and M. Dorgères laid aside the frown with which he
usually greeted this scapegrace of a nephew.

Maxime entered the circle with his habitual careless ease, distributing bows and hand-shakes around, with a few pleasant words for the ladies, and an affectionate greeting for Alice.

" Here you are, you good-for-nothing fellow," said the banker. " What chance brings you here so early as this ? "

" Remorse, my dear uncle, remorse for not having been here last Wednesday, for which I am in haste to sue for pardon."

" Really ? I know you, you pretended saint. Say rather that you had nothing better to do to-day."

" I beg your pardon. I had a première at the Variétés."

" And you gave it up to come here ? I shall never be astonished again. Should I even be told you were reforming and meant to set to work, I might come to believe it."

" But I am leading the most orderly and industrious life in the world. I rise and retire always at the same hour."

" Yes, go to bed at daybreak, and get up at mid-day."

" If I should tell you what I did yesterday, you would think I deserved the prize of virtue. I passed the afternoon at my own fireside, reading a serious book, then I dined alone and afterward walked."

" On the boulevards, no doubt."

" No, I felt the necessity of walking for my health, and

took to the most out-of-the-way districts. I have just missed being murdered."

"Good! there is the wisdom and sobriety you boast of—picking quarrels in the street!"

"You are mistaken. I was pursued by fellows who wanted to rob me, and if Providence had not sent on my path your little groom Georget, you would perhaps have had to deplore my sad fate, my dear uncle."

"Ah, you are laughing at us! What help could a child thirteen years old give you?"

"He gave me warning that the rogues were following to attack me, and pointed out the means of escaping them."

"Your story has a likely air. What time was it?"

"A little after twelve. On Rue Jouffroy."

"And this mischievous little scamp was racing the streets after twelve? I shall send him off. But you will hardly convince me they waylay people within a few steps of the Boulevard Malesherbes."

"It is a fact, though, that I had a narrow escape last night, and that your groom did me good service; and I ask you to promote him."

"I second my cousin's petition, papa," said Alice. "He seems so good-natured and bright, I am sure he deserves it."

'All this doesn't make him of any account in my service. Ask Vignory."

"I have nothing to complain of, sir," said Vignory,

hastily, unwilling to accuse the protégé of Mlle. Dorgères.

"Enough," said the banker, "if this youngster should
play me some ill turn, I should get only what I deserve,
for I took him without sufficient recommendation."

"May I ask who this lady is who interested herself in
my preserver?"

"Some one whom you must know by sight if you do
not visit her, for she receives all Paris, and fellows like
yourself by preference,—the Countess Yalta."

"She who has the beautiful residence on the Avenue
de Friedland?"

"They tell wonderful tales of the life she leads," said
M. Camaret.   'It is said she goes about the streets
dressed like a man; that she loses enormous sums at play,
and practises arms.   You laugh?   It is not the first time
a woman has been known to draw a sword.   At Monte
Video—"

"Is it true," asked an elderly lady, "that she takes her
baths in a gold bathing tub ornamented with precious
stones?"

"I am disposed to think they exaggerate," laughed
Maxime, "but it is certain that this countess is enormously rich."

"She has a large sum of money with me," said the
banker.   "It was in that way she chanced to beg that I
would take this Georget into my service.   I took the liberty of remarking that she might take him into her own.

Dor-

)uld

rve,

in

do

ke

e

l

Where there are equipages and horses there is always room for a groom. She replied that she resided in Paris only occasionally, and that the child could not follow her abroad because he lived with his old grandmother. The reason did not seem to amount to much, but I yielded at last."

"By the way, why did she take such an interest in him ? They say she is Greek, American, or something like that, and it is only two years since she came to France."

"She told me some story to explain her protection of the boy. It seems that the father of Georget was sergeant of Zouaves in the Crimean campaign, was taken prisoner by the Russians and carried off to a village in the heart of Russia which belonged to the father of the countess. It chanced that the sergeant saved the life of Madame Yalta's father, in a bear chase, I believe ; the noble rewarded him handsomely, and on his return to Paris he left the service to enter a bank. They gave an excellent account of him at the bank. That was what decided me to take the child, for I had not much faith in the assurances of a giddy sort of woman. And that is how I happen to have in my service this little monkey who is of no use to me."

"Is she pretty ?" asked the governess.

"She is a very slender blonde," replied M. Camaret, "with a papier-maché complexion, and a figure that could be enclosed within the ten fingers. I have seen her often in the Champs-Elysées driving herself with a brisk team, and she is not at all my type. She wants roundness, and looks like a snow woman. Talk to me of the beauties of cold countries! In India now—"

"Is she married?"

She is a widow," said the banker; "mistress consequently of herself and her fortune. There is a *parti* for a fellow who has already devoured the half of his. Advice to monsieur, my nephew."

"A first-rate idea," said Maxime, "I shall get myself presented to her."

"Calm this beautiful ardor. She has gone off on a journey."

"For long?"

"For a fortnight, I believe. Last week she sent her steward with an order for fifty thousand francs which she wanted for a little excursion to Monaco or Nice, and I remitted the sum to her."

"It is astonishing how all the women travel nowadays. One would say the prettiest of them had all agreed to leave Paris at once."

"They would also say, young man, that you were regretting somebody's absence," said M. Camaret.

"I? Not at all! I am free as air and have no desire to sacrifice my liberty."

"Then take care. They say the countess turns all heads; I don't know why, I am sure. She is so very spare—"

"Alice, dear," said Madame Martineau, "will you be kind enough to play us a waltz ; the Wave, for example ; that is my favorite ?"

Alice, besides being a skilful performer on the piano, had the passionate love of music which touches hearts as well as charms ears. But she was not inclined to exhibit her talents for the benefit of the profane, and yielded to such solicitations chiefly to gratify her father.

This evening she assented without hesitation, though the waltz called up sad memories. It was the last she had played for Robert de Carnoël, who never wearied of listening to it.

Robert was an excellent musician, and their love had dated from one of Schübert's melodies.

She had seen tears in Robert's eyes ; Robert had read the language of hers ; and Robert was no longer there.

M. Dorgères, who had recognized rather late the dangers of this German music, and knowing that the waltz would lead her thoughts toward the absent one, was cursing inwardly the blunder of Madame Martineau. He waited to hear Alice's refusal, and was agreeably surprised when she walked without any hesitation to the piano, which was at the further end of the salon.

"M. Vignory, can you read music ?"

The young man was surprised, for Alice knew him well enough to have no need to put the question, and he had to acknowledge that he did not know a note.

"Then my cousin will turn the pages for me."

M. Dorgères was delighted. His daughter had made an advance to the candidate who was under his protection. Vignory would gladly have followed and sat near Alice while he listened to her music, but he could not get away from his patron, who was just beginning a discussion of the recent rise of the rates of discount, and called him to give his opinion as to the cause and effects of this measure.

So Alice and Maxime found themselves tête-a-tête where nothing prevented them from speaking freely without failing in their obligation to society. The piano may have been invented with a view to favoring such confidences.

"Maxime," began Mlle. Dorgères, in a low tone, while she looked for the waltz, "I want to speak with you seriously."

"Good!" replied Maxime, in the same tone. "I begin to understand why you call in my services. Speak, I am serious as a governor of the Bank of France."

"You are on intimate terms with M. Vignory?"

"Of all that he has in the world, the most intimate."

"Then you can tell me if I may trust him?"

"What do you mean by such a question?"

"I want to know if M. Vignory is a man to defend an unfortunate friend."

"Assuredly. I answer for him as I would for myself in such a case."

"May I count on him to aid me to prove that M. de Carnoël is innocent?"

"Innocent! you believe that he is?"

"Do you doubt it?" she asked, quickly, in her agitation making a false note. Maxime, also agitated, forgot to turn the page. An illusion had just vanished from his mind. Her first words led him to suppose that Vignory was gaining a place in his cousin's favor. He now saw his mistake.

"You embarrass me a little," he said, after a moment's reflection, "and if you wish me to speak frankly, begin by being frank yourself. You love M. de Carnoël?"

"Yes, I love him," said Alice, without hesitation, "more than ever now that he is unjustly accused."

"Good! That is a plain confession. I thank you for your confidence, and am going to tell you what I think of the situation. But play a little louder, I am afraid we shall be overheard."

Alice struck a few vigorous chords which made Madame Martineau prick up her ears.

"First, I affirm," resumed Maxime, "that I have nothing to say against M. de Carnoël. I knew him but slightly, but have always regarded him as honest and brave. Moreover, Vignory, who knew him well, had a high opinion of him."

"He has just assured me that he was ready to maintain it against his accusers."

"Your father, for instance. This is generous on Vig-

nory's part, and is like himself. You have not yet learned
to appreciate him, but you will some day."

"I am already grateful to him for consenting to become my ally."

"Then you are undertaking a campaign to reinstate
M. de Carnoël. I cannot conceal from you that you will
find it no easy task."

"What if it be not easy ? The honor of M. de Carnoël is mine since we are betrothed."

"What ! You wish to marry him still ? "

"I wish and I expect to do so."

Maxime made a gesture of astonishment. He could not
but regard with admiration the courageous girl who had
not yet suffered herself to give way to despair. Nothing
in her appearance betrayed to an indifferent observer
the agitation of her mind. There was no lack of precision or harmony in the clear and brilliant notes her
slender fingers drew forth as they wandered over the
keys, and her charming head followed the movement of
the waltz, which lulled to sleep the groups at the farther
end of the salon.

"This marriage which you dream of is a pure chi-
mera," said Maxime. " M. de Carnoël is at this hour near-
ing America or the Antipodes, and will never return to
France."

" I am certain, on the contrary, that he is still here," replied Alice, firmly.

" May I ask on what you found this certainty ? "

"He could not have gone without an attempt to see me once more. I am certain that he is still in Paris."

" In that case it is unpardonable in him to remain in concealment without coming forward to vindicate himself."

" You forget he does not know that he is accused."

" In truth, you are right—how could he know? All that passed was between Vignory and this Russian. It is strange that the simplest ideas are sometimes the last to occur to us."

" And now that you do see it, I hope you see that the absence of M. de Carnoël is no proof of his guilt."

" I must say his situation is deplorable. To be reduced to silence for want of any knowledge of the charge when he need only appear to vindicate himself, seems indeed cruel. And I declare that if you authorize me, I will spare no pains to find him."

"Really? You also will become my ally ? "

"With all my heart, my dear Alice. I was so already without your knowledge. But no more talking is possible now. The waltz is ending. I have just turned the last leaf."

" I am going to begin again. No one will observe it."

" The fact is, your father is off on his favorite theories. M. Camaret is recounting to the ladies his travels in the Argentine Republic ; Vignory is watching us out of the corner of his eye, but he will not stir while my uncle has him. You can repeat the Wave while I give you the

affair of M. de Carnoël from my point of view. And
first you are aware that fifty thousand francs only were
taken when it might have been millions.. That is set
down against M. de Carnoël. An ordinary thief would
have carried off all."

"Neither do I believe the safe was opened by an ordinary thief. But is that a reason for condemning M.
de Carnoël ? "

"No ; but in order to acquit ·him the object of the
theft must be ascertained. Now with the money was
stolen a casket belonging to Col. Borisoff, and which
must have contained something else than titles either to
revenue or nobility."

"That is precisely what justifies M. de Carnoël. Ad-
mitting that he was capable of it, what interest had he
in appropriating the secrets of a foreigner whom he did
not know ? "

"Very well reasoned, cousin. Only Vignory said that
Borisoff remarked to my uncle that M. de Carnoël's
father had been for a long time an attaché to the embassy at St. Petersburg. He said that the son must
have kept up some intercourse with Russia, and added
that Robert might have acted in the interests of one of
these Russians, enemies of Borisoff."

"It is absurd. M. de Carnoël saw nothing of his
father's friends."

"Let me finish what I was saying and mind your playing. You skipped ten bars just now. You know, of

course, that Borisoff is engaged in a search after Robert, and means to make every effort to find him. My uncle gave him carte blanche, and he left Paris the same day."

" He has returned, then, for I saw him yesterday in the Bois de Boulogne."

" Oh ! oh ! can it be that he has given up the pursuit, or has he discovered that Robert is still here ? "

Mlle. Dorgères did not reply. Her father's old valet had just entered and approached the piano with a silver waiter in his hand.

He put the waiter on the piano and went out on tiptoe, after a significant glance at Mlle. Dorgères.

" What is the matter, my little cousin ? " he asked, seeing that she turned pale.

She made, for the moment, no reply. Her fingers ran feverishly over the keys, and the waltz continued to lull with its sweet melody the talkers round the fire.

The young man looked at the waiter, and concealed in the half open fan he saw a letter.

Evidently it was not there by chance, and the old servant who had taken care to hide it so adroitly must be the confidant of Alice's secrets. This discovery surprised Maxime.

" It is from him," she said faintly.

" I had no doubt of that. But this valet, then, is acquainted with the situation ? "

" Yes, he was here when I was born ; has always been

much attached to M. de Carnoël. He saw what I had
endured, and came to me yesterday to say that if I would
authorize him he would undertake to put in my hands a
letter from M. de Carnoël."

"My uncle has done holding forth on discount, and is
looking this way. I advise you to possess yourself of
the letter as soon as possible."

"No, I shall not touch it. You have just said you
were my ally. Then you will do what I am about to ask.
Listen, Maxime. This letter contains my destiny. When
I know its contents I shall know whether I have still a
conflict to maintain, or whether nothing is left me but to
die of grief. I beg you to read it first."

"Never! Your affairs of the heart are not for me to
regulate."

"You do not understand that I dare not open it for
fear I might find an avowal——"

Maxime started. He began to read the thoughts of
the unhappy Alice. Doubt had glided into this heart
that beat only for the absent one. She was asking herself
tremblingly whether this abominable accusation could be
true,—whether the man she loved had allowed himself to
be led into some dark dealings wherein he had made
shipwreck of his honor.

What were they? A conspiracy, perhaps. The vengeance of some woman against Colonel Borisoff.

"Here is what I expect of you," she said with surprising firmness. "The waltz is nearly ended. You will

hand me my fan when it is finished, and in doing so will take the letter. I will rejoin my father, and you will make some pretext for leaving the room ; you will say, for instance, that you wish to smoke, and withdraw to the library. There you will read the letter."

" The letter of your lover ? What do you take me for ? "

" Let me finish. If this letter justifies M. de Carnoël, you will return it before the end of the evening, and I will show it to my father. If, however, it condemns——"

" Well ? "

" Burn it and then return to the salon. My eyes will meet yours, and the first glance will tell me so, if there is nothing more to hope."

Maxime was about to protest, but she ended the last bars of the waltz as she spoke, and as she did so rose, saying : " Give me my fan. I am suffocating here."

The moment was critical.

M. Dorgères was approaching. One more step and he would see the letter ; so, much against his will, Maxime adroitly took it up, and at the same time handed her the fan.

" I give you a good mark, nephew. A half hour's work over a piece of music is meritorious, and I authorize you to go off and smoke a cigar by way of recreation. I know you are dying for the opportunity."

" No, no, uncle, I would rather play whist with you."

" Hypocrite, go. You would be served right if I

accepted. But we are four and I exempt you from
duty.   You will find on the table a box of Havana
cigars."

Everything seemed against Maxime. Alice had just
heard her father make himself the unconscious ally of
her project, and she threw a glance of entreaty to her
cousin.

He had not courage to refuse, and walked slowly in
the direction of the room to which he had been banished
in spite of himself.

"Bah!" he said to himself. "I will let her suppose
I am obeying her orders, while I will content myself with
trying my uncles panatellas. In a quarter of an hour I
will return, draw Alice to a corner and hand her the letter
without a word. She will consider it a good sign, will
not look to see if it has been opened, and find out only
when she retires to her room that I decline this office
of judge, and then—then—*ma foi!* she must do as
she will."

With this conclusion he entered the library, selected a
cigar, and buried himself in a leather arm-chair before
a beautiful fire of beech wood. His position was emi-
nently favorable for dreaming, and he sank into a profound reverie.

The adventures of the preceding night and the incidents of the last hour passed before his half-closed eyes,
and seemed to link themselves together in some mysterious way. Then his thoughts came back to the letter. In

thinking over it, it presented itself to his mind in a new light.

"If the young man has acknowledged his guilt, it would be rendering her a real service to spare her the pain of reading so sorrowful a confession. But it is hardly conceivable that M. de Carnoël has written to the girl he loves that he has stolen. It was very simple of Alice to fancy he was going to make her his confessor. The letter is crammed with professions of eternal devotion, but not a word of confession. And when I have waded through all this sentimental fiddle-faddle, I shall be compelled to replace in her hands a letter which will only turn her head more completely than before. Positively I shall return to my first idea, and leave the seal unbroken."

Having reached this conclusion, his thoughts wandered back to the unknown of Rue Jouffroy, and then to the circumstances his uncle had mentioned concerning Georget, and he made up his mind to ask some questions about the Countess Yalta who protected him. His friends had more than once offered to present him, and the little mystery surrounding her connection with Georget stimulated his desire to become one of the guests of this superlatively rich stranger.

"What an excellent opportunity for exhibiting the bracelet in this exotic world, where there are no doubt many rich adventuresses!" and by a natural association of ideas his mind reverted to the great project which had been somewhat overlooked during the last twenty-four hours—the search for the woman with one hand.

" If Alice knew of this, she would regard it as conclusive proof of her lover's innocence.   It would be useless to suggest that he had an accomplice, and that the next evening he acted alone."

He examined once more the probabilities, whether the letter did or did not contain a confession.   A third alternative presented itself to his mind.

" What if he should let it be seen that he is the victim of a plot ; if he should designate even indirectly the authors of the plot, the situation would be changed.   We shall all be interested in a discovery that would put me on the track of the real culprit ; yes, all, even Vignory, who has nothing to gain by continuing in uncertainty. *Ma foi!* great evils call for great remedies.   I am going to break open the letter."

Leaving no time for further reflection, he drew it from his pocket, tore it open and read :

" MADEMOISELLE :

I have loved—I love you still, and have believed I was beloved by you.   Your father reminded me that you were rich and I was poor, and that you depended on him.   I understood and am gone.   Resolving to expatriate myself, I yet could not leave France without kneeling once more on the tomb of my mother.   So I went to Carnoël and passed two days amidst the ruins of the house where I was born.   Why have I returned to

Paris? I returned, because I hoped still, I hoped that
M. Dorgères had deceived me, that you had not dared
to disobey him, but that you had not forgotten the
past.

"I have ventured to approach an old servant of your
father who will place this letter in your hands. He tells
me that no one speaks of me now, but he tells me more—
that you have wept, that you have suffered. And then
it came into my mind to beg you to see me once more.
I have no reproaches to make. I do not ask you to keep
the faith you pledged to me. I know that all is at an end
between us. But I do not want you to despise me, as
you would have a right to do did I not explain to you the
cause of my abrupt departure. You will see then that I
could not act otherwise than I did. To-morrow, at three
o'clock, I shall be in the Bois de Boulogne, at the corner
of the Route de l'Etoile and the Route des Bouleaux.
Have you the courage to meet me there with your governess? Madame Martineau may report the whole interview, which will be short, to your father. If you do not
I shall leave Paris to-morrow evening never to return.
Au revoir or adieu!"

"*Parbleu?*" exclaimed Maxime, "here is a singular
billet-doux. This gentleman claims an interview and ac-
knowledges his guilt in the same breath, for what else does
he mean by 'I could not act otherwise'? Poor Alice!
what a blow! Yes," he went on, talking to himself, "this
lover wants to plead extenuating circumstances. What

assurance! It is incredible! Now the question is, what am I to do about it? Alice told me to throw the letter into the fire if I saw in it evidence of M. de Carnoël's guilt. But I can see already the scene when I return into the salon. Her eyes will question mine and will read there the condemnation of her lover; then there will be a scene. I know her—my little cousin. She was very brave a while ago in the belief that this letter would clear the writer and rally me to the cause of the fugitive. If I burn it, who knows what may happen?"

The banker's nephew held in his hand the untoward letter which one little movement would deliver into the flames that were burning on the hearth. But he shrank from the thought of doing so, and resumed his promenade to and fro. The voices of the guests reached him through the open door. He heard the exclamations of the whist players, the prattling of the women, and now and then a clear musical laugh that he knew well,

"Poor child!" he murmured, "she laughs that it may not be discovered that she is on burning coals, and suffers all the agonies of suspense while she awaits her sentence. *Ma foi!* I have not the courage to pronounce it. Yes, but then I must return to this letter. *Diable!* a letter in which this gentleman appoints a rendezvous! That is a responsibility I do not care to take. I am brought to a pretty pass by consenting to mix myself up with my cousin's affairs."

And he relapsed into infinite perplexities. He read

again the letter from beginning to end with more careful attention, weighing every word.

"He is guilty ! I do not doubt it ; but has lost nothing of his pride ; and there may be a mystery beneath all this. Something about women, perhaps ; but no, he wouldn't tell that to my cousin. One thing is certain, that this theft of the casket complicates the affair singularly ; and that severed hand still more. What if Carnoël knows the owner of this bracelet ? What if he has been dragged into some political intrigue? That would not explain the theft of the fifty thousand francs, but things might change their face a little. Ah ! if I could only talk for ten minutes with my uncle's secretary."

Here he stopped short and exclaimed :

"*Parblue !* an idea strikes me. Why not wait for my man to-morrow in the Bois de Boulogne? I shall soon bring him to confession. If by chance he is innocent, I should propose to him to aid me in finding the guilty one—or ones. That is settled. I go to-morrow to the Bois de Bulogñe.

"Ah ! *diable !* and the letter ! Must I return it to my cousin ? In truth, why not? The proposed rendezvous is not compromising since the governess is to be present. And I could be there too, if I judged my presence necessary. That will depend on the result of my interview with M. de Carnoël. So, that is decided. I shall return the letter to poor Alice."

Maxime had just arrived at this point when Vignory entered the library, his face radiant.

"Your affairs are progressing well, I should judge," said his friend.

"Yes, I have just had a long talk with Mlle. Dorgères. She sent me to see if you have finished your cigar, and to beg you to come and take some tea."

"The time has seemed long," the cousin said between his teeth.

"One more whiff," he said aloud, "and I will follow you."

"Poor fellow!" thought Maxime, as Vignory left the room; "he little knows I have in my pocket a letter that is to have such influence on his destiny. I shall say nothing to Alice till I have seen the young man, and, to avoid explanations, as soon as I have rid myself of the letter, I shall vanish!"

He folded it in his hand and passed into the salon.

Alice was standing, a cup in her hand, but her paleness betrayed to Maxime her agitation in spite of the smile that wandered over her lips.

In pity for her suspense he reassured her by a glance.

"Well?" she said.

He slipped the letter into her trembling hand, saying as he did so:

"You see I have not burned it."

"Ah!" she murmured, "I knew he was innocent."

"You will read, you will see for yourself ; remember, whatever happens, that I am your friend."

After whispering these doubtful words, there was nothing more for Maxime but to disappear *à l'anglaise*, that is to say, silently and without adieux.

He threaded the stairway, and left the house with the laudable intention of finishing his evening at the club.

But he took a carriage that he might not expose to the enterprises of night loungers the famous bracelet which, this evening, he carried in his pocket, deeming it unnecessary to exhibit it for the benefit of the respectable dames who represented the fair sex at M. Dorgères Wednesdays.

CHAPTER VI.

PARISIANS are not early risers, and at nine in the morning the cafès are still well nigh empty. Clerks have not time to enter them before appearing at their places of business, whilst their employers rarely breakfast before noon ; so the proprietors of these public houses are in no haste to light their furnaces for the benefit of such passers-by as chance may bring them.

That is why on the morning after M. Dorgères' soirée, a young man who, toward nine o'clock, pushed open the door of a modest establishment of this sort on the Rue du Rocher, found the boy occupied in sweeping the room.

The solitude was not apparently displeasing to the new comer, for, braving the cloud of dust, he entered and took his seat in a corner where some late newspapers had been piled.

He had a good figure, and though plainly dressed and with a low hat on, there was that about him which caused the indefatigable sweeper to stop and ask politely what monsieur would have. Monsieur ordered a cup of chocolate, and taking up a newspaper which he selected from among a number of others, turned to the fourth page and ran his eye over the long columns of advertisements. Drawing a memorandum book from his pocket he began copying in lead pencil a notice which ran thus :

" North and South America.

" General Intelligence Agency.

" Information furnished gratuitously as to the best investment of funds in the two countries ; mines, agricultural and industrial enterprises. We can assure every person of intelligence and industry a remunerative position. Expense of passage defrayed by the Agency.

" Hours from 9 till 12.

" M. Briare, Representative of the Agency.

" 44 Rue de la Bienfaisance."

Evidently the young man who copied this advertisement was in quest of a transatlantic investment for either his energies or his capital. The last seemed the more probable, for he had not the air of a needy adventurer.

Whoever he was he did not seem disposed to exhibit himself breakfasting in a third-rate café, for he turned his back to the door, and instead of taking off his hat pulled it down carefully over his ears. But he had a face which once seen was not soon forgotten, and any-one who had frequented M. Dorgères' private office would have had no difficulty in recognizing the banker's ci-devant secretary.

But Robert de Carnoël had changed much. His com-

plexion was pale, his eyes hollow, and tokens of sadness
and unrest were visible in his features. He swallowed
absently the chocolate and rolls which the boy brought
at the end of twenty minutes, paid for them and went
out, after taking a look at his watch.

The Rue du Rocher is little frequented, and he met
few passers-by. He turned to the right into Rue de la
Bienfaisance. There was no indication of industrial or
commercial pursuits in the house toward which he directed his steps, and he had to inquire of the porter
whether that was the Agency of the two Americas.

"M. Briare?" asked a voice from the ground floor.
"He is on the second story, the first door to the
left."

The form of this reply suggested the idea that M.
Briare constituted the whole personnel of this inter-
national administration. It mattered little however to
M. de Carnoël; he was glad indeed to be relieved of the
necessity of passing offices occupied by clerks curious
and staring.

He mounted to the second floor, where he was received by a man, tall and large as a beadle, with enormous side-whiskers.

This imposing personage motioned him in silently as
soon as he pronounced the name of M. Briare, and
leading him through a passage-way to a door which he
opened without knocking, Robert found himself in presence of a gentleman with a very blonde complexion

and gold spectacles, seated before a table covered with papers.

The room had a low ceiling, and was badly lighted by a window at the back of the gentleman, whose face was thus not distinctly visible. On the walls were pigeon-holes filled with cards. A clock of black marble, ornamented with a statuette of Christopher Columbus, was on the mantel, and a good fire of coke was burning in the grate. Three straw chairs were placed for the benefit of visitors. The furniture was not luxurious and it was all new, whence it might be concluded that the agency had not been long in operation.

"What is the object of your visit?" asked the representative of the agency, politely indicating a seat to M. de Carnoël.

"I want some information concerning the States of the American Union, and I read in a newspaper—"

"That we were prepared to furnish it. Exactly so, sir. We have direct relations with California, Mexico, Louisiana—"

"It is of Colorado I wish to speak."

"That is most opportune. We have mining enterprises in that State which yield us superb revenues. You are not," he added incidentally, "seeking a situation of any sort?"

"That will depend on circumstances. If I found one that suited me I should be disposed to take an interest in the business and accept a position with a satisfactory remuneration."

"Consequently, to settle in America?"

"Certainly. I wish moreover to set off at the earliest possible moment."

"Very well, sir. May I ask to whom I have the honor to speak?"

"That is of no consequence. At present I wish only a little preliminary information."

"I beg your pardon, but we have invariable rules. The information furnished by our agency is of a confidential nature, and we must know to whom we are giving it."

"I shall scarcely furnish you with any valuable guarantee when I say that my name is Robert."

"Robert," repeated M. Briare, taking his pen to inscribe the name. "The first name, if you please; excuse me, sir, it is a mere formality, but the director lays great stress upon it."

"Henri Robert," replied M. de Carnoël with an impatient gesture.

"And you live?"

"209 Boulevard des Bategnolles. Should you like also my age and birthplace?"

"No, sir, the information you have been obliging enough to furnish is sufficient."

"Then I may hope that you will furnish me with information rather than questions?"

"I am entirely at your service, sir. Only let me give the person who admitted you orders to request a gentle-

man with whom I made an appointment for this morning
to wait until I am at leisure."

M. Briare pressed a bell, and the man with the whiskers presented himself so promptly that one might have
been tempted to fancy he was concealed behind the
door.

His chief made a sign to him, and spoke to him in a
language which M. de Carnoël did not comprehend, making use of a much greater number of words than could
be needed for the execution of so simple a commission.

"Your plan, then," continued M. Briare, "is to select
Colorado as the field in which you hope to utilize your
intelligence and capital. An excellent idea. Colorado is
a country where, with youth and intelligence, a man may
hope to realize a rapid fortune. We have on hand, as I
have just said, a large mining enterprise, whose principal
centre is a little town called Golden City, a town which
fulfils all the promise of such a name. I must not conceal from you that the business depends for success upon
a process for the treatment of auriferous and argentifer-
ous minerals, which it is of great importance not to di-
vulge ; consequently we cannot take too many precautions in procuring the surest agents—that is to say, the
agents must be pecuniarily interested in the success of
the enterprise. May I inquire what sum you have at
your disposal."

"About fifty thousand francs, but I wish to reserve ten
thousand for my personal needs."

"I will obŝerve that the administration will defray the expense of passage and allow you a liberal salary. You are, however, free to fix the sum to which you limit your share of capital. Are you in a condition to deposit it without delay?"

"I have the bank notes in my pocket, but you scarcely expect me to place them with you without further and fuller information."

"Oh, sir," said M. Briare, in an injured tone, "I beg you to believe that we do not desire to have persons engage with us except on the most perfect understanding. All the documents relating to our business, however, are in the hands of the director, and you must treat with him."

"When may I see him?"

"To-day, at three o'clock."

"Three o'clock? no, I shall not be able to call at that hour."

"Then you must wait till to-morrow; let me see—no, to-morrow the director presides over the administrative council; Saturday he attends a meeting of stockholders. You cannot see him before Monday."

"I cannot wait till then," said the young man rising.

"Now I think of it, why not go to him yourself this morning?"

"Where?"

"At his house, Rue de Vigny."

"Will he receive me?"

" He is much occupied ; but a note from me which you
will remit to his valet-de-chambre——— " .

Robert showed by his manner that this proposition was
not acceptable.

" But I can do better," resumed M. Briare.   " I have a
message from the director to come to him at ten o'clock.
Shall we go together ?   He will, in all probability, send me
his carriage."

M. de Carnoël reflected before replying.

" The horses of M. le Directeur travel like the wind.
M. le Directeur is very prompt, and in twenty minutes
you can obtain all the information you want."

" So be it," replied Robert, moved especially by this
last consideration.

" Then permit me to leave you for a moment.   I have
orders to give in case there should be callers during my
absence."

·M· Briare rose quickly and went out.   Robert awaited
his return standing, and had not long to wait.

In five minutes the agent reappeared, his overcoat on
and hat in his hand.

" M. le Directeur's coupé is at the door," he said.

M. de Carnoël followed him to the door, and was surprised to see, seated by the side of the coachman, the
colossus with the whiskers.

The coachman, covered with a fur robe, was not out of
keeping with the equipage, but the liveried usher at his
side cut a strange figure.

The agent had not boasted without cause of the horses of his director. They went truly like the wind, and never relaxed their speed during the length of the Boulevard Malesherbes.

The windows of the coupé were closed,· but did not prevent one of its inmates from seeing those who were walking in the direction of Rue de Juresnes.

What would he not have given to be free as formerly to pass the threshold of Alice's home !

And as if fate had determined to revive as vividly as possible the memory of the past he caught a glimpse of one of those fortunate ones who frequented in full light of day the neighborhood of the Madeleine.

This was Maxime Dorgères who sauntered along, his nose in the air, and his two hands in his overcoat pockets. Robert turned quickly, not wishing to be recognized by the banker's nephew, but their glances had met, and Maxime had good eyes.

M. Briare remarked this movement of his ccmpanion, and observed drily :

" Paris is a city where one always encounters those one would like to avoid. Happily our horses are travelling fast enough to distance all the tormentors in the world."

This observation displeased M. de Carnoël who deigned no reply. He thought this head of bureau was disposed to meddle with what did not concern him, and then began to wonder what might be the consequence of this

inopportune *rencontre*. Maxime was not a man to keep
a secret, and would, no doubt, inform his uncle or at least
Vignory. "If he should see his cousin this morning,
heaven knows what she would think if she heard that I
pass my time driving out in a luxurious coupé drawn by
ten-thousand-franc horses. No matter. If she comes to
the Bois de Boulogne, I can explain about the carriage."

"Here we are at Parc Monceaux," said M. Briare.
"See what lodgings he has ! There are not many such
bureaux in Paris. Oh ! he is a man who takes life as he
does business,—grandly, largely ! There is nothing nig-
gardly about him."

The coupé, on coming out of Parc Monceaux, turned
to the right, and brought up before a monumental gateway.
The man in usher's livery descended slowly and disappeared, while the coachman turned the horses preparatory
to entering.

The Rue de Vigny is not much frequented, and Robert saw only some boys playing on the sidewalk, a sight
which would have passed unnoticed had he not observed
among them the groom Georget.

The child looked at him with wide-open eyes, and his
face showed plainly enough his astonishment at this meeting with his patron's former secretary.

He knew, like every one in the house, that M. de Carnoël had lost his place, and he must have heard that he
had decided to leave France, for his abrupt departure

had furnished matter of gossip for all the employés of every grade.

"Really, I am the sport of misfortune," thought Robert. "In a passage that has not lasted ten minutes to be recognized twice,—it is too much!"

But he had not leisure to reflect long before the gateway opened and the coupé entered the court-yard. He might have remarked, however, that Georget examined the carriage, the horses, the fur robes, and especially the face of M. Briare, and was astonished that, unlike his habitual politeness, he failed to bow to him in passing. M Briare might have supposed he had never known or even seen the young man who wished to set off for Colorado.

The gateway was closed immediately by the porter, and the equipage drew up before a massive flight of stairs. Robert was struck by the imposing appearance of the habitation of M. le Directeur : the main building flanked by two wings and surmounted by a pediment in the style of the Renaissance, and a large space surrounding the court-yard.

M. Briare introduced his client into a vestibule filled with rare flowers, from the midst of which rose up a bear holding in his paws a waiter for visiting cards. The director of the agency must have brought this curiosity from foreign lands.

But the bear was sole watcher at the entrance of this princely mansion ; not a valet de pied was there to receive, not a valet de chambre to announce a visitor.

But the windings of the house were familiar to M. Briare, who led Robert through a long corridor with a splendid salon furnished in excellent taste and filled with specimens of art.

"You will wait here, if you please, sir," said the representative; "M. le Directeur is in his office. I will explain to him in two words the object of your visit."

Robert bowed and remained alone in this immense apartment, the high windows of which overlooked a large garden filled with venerable trees. One would scarcely have believed the owner of all this luxury to be a man engaged in recruiting workmen or capital for transatlantic enterprises.

A quarter of an hour passed by, when the colossal usher appeared and requested him to follow him. He had changed his costume, and now wore a sort of military coat reaching down to his feet. M. de Carnoël hesitated, so strange did this transformation appear, but it was no time to retreat, so he directed his steps toward the door his singular guide had just opened.

"Walk in, sir," he said, moving aside to allow M. de Carnoël to enter, and then, closing the door, remained standing with his back to it.

The room to which he had just been introduced had not the severe aspect of an office devoted to work, but of one appropriated to the use of a gentleman of leisure: furniture in old oak, ornamented wainscoting, richly-bound books, high chimney-piece, and mantel with armo-rial bearings.

But what surprised Robert more than all these ele-gances, was to see, intrenched behind an ebony table, M. Briare himself. He also was transfigured. There were no longer the gold spectacles and the obsequious air. His insipid face now wore a supercilious expression, which impressed M. de Carnoël most unpleasantly.

"I came to speak with your director, where is he?".

"Take a seat," said M. Briare, dryly.

"It is useless. I have no further business with you, and if the director is not visible I shall leave."

"But I have business with you, and you do not leave."

"Do you undertake to interfere with my doing so?"

"Precisely."

"And by what right, if you please?" asked M. de Carnoël, red with anger. "Does your agency obtain re-cruits for Colorado by force?"

"It is not Colorado which concerns us; it is the affair of Rue de Suresnes."

Robert started and remained mute with surprise.

"Your name is Henri Robert de Carnoël," resumed M. Briare. "You were, a week ago, the private secretary of M. Dorgères, banker. Do not deny it; I know you."

"Why should I deny it? I have no cause to be ashamed of the name I bear."

"You concealed it, however, when I asked you just now."

"It did not suit me to give my name to every one who might ask it. Will you be kind enough to inform me why you are playing this comedy in which I have no desire to figure?"

"Since you feign not to understand, I must tell you that I act in virtue of an order from the prefect of police."

"I comprehend still less now. What has the prefect of police to do with the agency you represent?"

"The agency of the two Americas? You are still on that? Know then that you have permitted yourself to be caught in a trap. It will, I fear, be painful to you to be informed that it does not exist, and the time has now come to question you."

"Question! I will see whether it suits me to reply."

"I warn you that silence is a poor mode of defence. You have too much sense to keep to that line of policy. You would do much better to acknowledge that you are guilty."

"Guilty of what?"

"Of the theft which has been committed at M. Dorgères."

"Miserable wretch!" exclaimed Robert, advancing upon him with clenched fists.

M. Briare's situation would have been critical, but the colossus who kept the door advanced to the assistance of his master, and placing himself in front of the table, interposed between them a living obstacle.

"I advise you to calm yourself," said the agent, who had not lost countenance. "Violence is also a bad system, and will not serve you. There are two men in the salon; I have only to ring and they will enter and lend their assistence to their comrade there, who alone would be sufficient to cope with you. I advise you, therefore, to compose yourself and resume the conversation where we left it."

Robert was suffocating with rage, but he made a great effort to command himself.

"I told you," M. Briare resumed, "that a theft had been committed at M. Dorgères. You do not pretend, I suppose, to be ignorant of what all Paris knows?"

The question was artfully put. If M. de Carnoël confessed his knowledge of the crime it would be equivalent to an avowal of guilt, since the secret had remained between the robbed and the robbers. But he replied with perfect naturalness:

"I was absent. I have not read the papers, and since I left M. Dorgères have seen no one."

"When did you leave it?"

"Eight days ago."

"Last Tuesday, was it not, between half past eleven and twelve? You returned at ten and went out with a parcel in your hand?"

"Yes."

"Why did you leave so precipitately?"

"I will tell you when you have told me why you ask."

"You cannot guess?" asked M. Briare, ironically. "It seems simple enough. At eleven your employer's safe was opened with a false key, and a half hour after, you were gone. The coincidence is singular, you must confess."

"What! it is the safe that has been robbed? Then M. Dorgères is nearly ruined. They deposited there that evening an enormous sum."

"How do you know?"

"M. Dorgères said so in my presence; it was more than three millions. And you pretend to say I am accused of having stolen it! It is absurd, you must see. A man who carries off millions loses no time in crossing the frontier."

This argument seemed to strike M. Briare, for he leaned his elbows on the table and was lost in thought.

"Sir," he said, after a moment's reflection, "you would be mistaken if you suppose I wish to find you guilty. I should be only too happy could you succeed in justifying yourself. You will do well then in your own interests to give me all the information I desire. You have just objected that you were in no haste to escape, and I recognize that the fact of your having remained pleads in your favor. You left Paris, however."

"Yes, I went into Brittany where I was born. I took the train when I left the house of M. Dorgères."

"We knew that and I take note of your frankness. But you remained a very short time for the agents we sent there the day after your departure were unable to find you."

" The agents ! " exclaimed Robert, bitterly. " Then they know in that county that I am accused of theft."

"You are mistaken. These researches are managed more quietly. The country people took our agents for your friends and replied that you had taken the train they did not know for where."

" I returned directly to Paris."

"Where you took a furnished lodging under the name of Robert. All that was natural enough. You had re-solved to expatriate yourself and wished to break with your old acquaintances. The object of your journey into Brittany was, no doubt, to borrow money on the property which remained to you."

" This property is a castle in ruins on which no one would lend."

"You have money at your command, however, as you proposed to put in business in Colorado thirty thousand francs. Was not that the sum you named ? "

" No, fifty thousand," replied M. de Carnoël, without hesitation.

" You are right. I rememember you said fifty thou-sand. Where did they come from ? "

" How does that concern you ? They have taken at least three millions from M. Dorgères. My little capital is far from amounting to that sum."

" If you should say that to an examining judge he

would reply that you had concealed the rest somewhere, —at your castle at Carnoël, for example."

"I should write him to make his search there," replied Robert, disdainfully.

"They would find nothing I am satisfied. I must also ask whether the sum is in gold or in notes.

"In notes, since I have it with me. But I must ask in return, why these useless questions?"

"Useless?"

"Yes, and impertinent."

"You shall see presently that they are very useful and also very pertinent. The sum that has been stolen is precisely a sum of fifty thousand francs, just what you have in your pocket."

"Fifty thousand francs! A thief would not have been contented with that when he might have taken a fortune."

"Oh, but this is no ordinary thief! He has never been mixed up with the police, and we have abstained from searching for him among the habitués of Mazas. We saw immediately that he was of a different stamp, and we thought immediately of you."

"Why?"

"I am going to tell you, and when I have done, you will see that we could not but think of you. Observe, in the first place, that the author of the theft must be familiar with the house and be able to enter at all hours, since nothing has been broken open. The door of the office had not been forced nor had the windows."

"You forget, I was not the only person who could go and come freely."

"You are right. There was the cashier, your intimate friend. Do you suspect him ?"

"Certainly not. Vignory is the most honest man I know. But there other employés."

"Who leave at five o'clock in the evening and return at nine in the morning."

"The servants—the errand boys."

"They are old and tried servants. They have been suspected, however, and secretly watched, and it is certain, were not mixed up with this business. Besides, the safe was opened with a false key. Well, to make a false key, one must have access to the real key. Now, you alone could be that person."

"I ?"

"Yes. M. Dorgères had his key; the cashier his. That of M. Dorgères had been entrusted to you more than once."

"I deny it."

"Your patron said that he sometimes left it on his table, at your disposition, therefore, since you worked in his office. But that is not all : To open the safe it is necessary to know the word—a word of five letters. This word you might have read, for you were at the office during the day while the letters were in place. Do you deny that also?"

"No," said Robert, after a moment's hesitation, "I

even remember that I remarked the word. Is that a reason for accusing me?"

"But I have not yet done. The safe was protected by an ingenious contrivance."

"Yes; a claw placed so as to seize the arm of whoever should attempt the lock. I am, moreover, surprised that the thief was not caught."

"It was because he knew not only the password, but the means of preventing the trap from acting. Now, M. Vignory had shown you the arrest crank and explained to you how to work it."

"It is possible, but I paid very little attention to it, and should have been much puzzled had I found it necessary to manœuvre the spring. Is that all?"

"No; there are moral proofs."

"What do you mean by moral proofs?" asked M. de Carnoël, contemptuously.

"It seems to me they are before your eyes. Your flight would be enough to cause a jury to find you guilty."

"I went away, but I did not fly, You forget I had been dismissed by M. Dorgères."

"Not exactly. He had relieved you of your duties as secretary, but desired you to remain until your departure for Egypt, where he offered you an advantageous situation. But you had reasons for preferring America," added M. Briare, sneeringly.

"Enough, sir!" exclaimed Robert; "you will scarcely

persuade any one that I have dishonored myself for the sake of appropriating the paltry sum of fifty thousand francs. Take me before a magistrate. This ridiculous parody of justice has lasted too long already. I will not lower myself by answering you further."

" Patience ! you will find yourself there perhaps sooner than you think. But I have yet something to say as to a singular circumstance. You are free to reply or not as you will. Know, then, that this thief, whoever he is, was not content with the theft of the fifty thousand francs ; he carried off also a casket."

" A casket ? "

" Yes."

" And which belonged to a Russian."

" Ah, you know that ? "

" Perfectly. I was present when the owner called upon M. Dorgères and proposed to withdraw it next morning."

" And the next morning, when the cashier arrived, he found the safe open and perceived that the casket had disappeared. What do you say to that ? "

" Nothing."

" Our opinion is that the object of the thief was to obtain possession of the casket, and that he took the money as a means of passage into a foreign country."

" It is very possible."

" When I say ' we ' I allude to Col. Borisoff, who had deposited this casket with your patron."

"Was it his device to bring me here instead of leading me before a magistrate?"

"No; on the contrary, it was by order of the justice that you were first brought here to be confronted with the complainant. You are at this moment in Col. Borisoff's house."

"The magistrate who gave you such an order has a singular mode of proceeding," said M. de Carnoël, dryly.

"I am not qualified to pass judgment upon his method," replied the agent. "You are not aware, perhaps, that a magistrate is at liberty to act as he pleases, and is responsible only to his conscience."

"So be it. But what hinders one from being led into Col. Borisoff's presence?"

"Nothing. I have ended my questions. Follow me, if you please."

So saying, M. Briare rose and indicated by a gesture a door at the other end of the room. Impatient to be confronted with his accuser, M. de Carnoël accepted the silent invitation unhesitatingly.

M. Briare held open the door while M. de Carnoël passed in first. Politeness of this description is merely tactics. A prisoner cannot well escape with some one at his heels, and there were two to prevent Robert from beating a retreat, for the colossus in military coat locked up the steps of his captain.

But Robert did not dream of flight. He entered the room with a firm, proud step, and was not a little surprised when the door closed behind him, and he entered an immense gallery or hall. The high ceilings and walls, ornamented with ancient tapestry, gave an imposing aspect to this place, which was only tolerably lighted by windows opening fifteen feet from the ground. A feudal lord of the middle ages might have held here the court in which he pronounced sentence upon his vassals. Before a hearth on which burned a bright fire, such as might have been seen formerly in a feudal manor-house, were two arm-chairs in carved wood, and on a table within reach of whoever might take a seat at this seignorial fireside, was an assortment of oriental pipes and a pile of cigar boxes.

But the lord was not there, and M. de Carnoël assumed that before making his appearance he wished to receive from his vassal a report of the interview which had just terminated.

Everything appeared to Robert more and more strange. Without being versed in the criminal code, he knew that a French magistrate was not at liberty to modify it to suit his fancy, and felt disposed to believe it all a hoax.

He was not left long in this uncertainty.. A door concealed by the woodwork opened noiselessly and M. Borisoff appeared.

Robert had never seen him except in fashionable dress —Parisian in manners as well as costume—and could scarcely recognize him clad after the fashion of a Russian lord in his own country—caftan of brocaded velvet, large pantaloons *a la tartare* and Turkish slippers. The military air was there still, and one could recognize the colonel under this Asiatic accoutrement.

He bowed slightly and invited the young man to be seated.

"Sir," said Robert, abruptly, "let me ask first why you have brought me here, using a ruse which I abstain from qualifying as it deserves?"

"You know well, sir," replied the colonel, quietly. "The agent who brought you here has just made you acquainted with the cause."

"This man pretends to act under virtue of a regular warrant, but I am not his dupe, and am satisfied that he acts only under your orders."

M. Borisoff reflected a moment, and then replied with a gentleness which surprised M. de Carnoël :

"It seems to me, sir, that you are taking a wrong course. Why discuss the validity of an agent's powers when it relates to facts that concern your honor ? Were I the only one who believed you guilty, a gentleman must have some regard for the opinion of another gentleman."

"You forget I am not free. Were we on neutral ground I should take the trouble to prove to you that I am not a thief, and then ask satisfaction. Here in your own house I refuse absolutely to reply."

"You are wrong, for it rests with me whether this affair shall have unfortunate results or whether it stops here."

"Do you pretend to control justice? We are not in Russia that I know of."

"No, but in all countries he who lodges a complaint has the right to withdraw it."

"That is to say that it is for you to dispose of me as you please. That I will not believe."

"Listen to me, sir, and you will appreciate more clearly our relations to each other. I had strong reasons for believing that my casket, which has disappeared from M. Dorgères' safe, was taken by some one who had an especial interest in appropriating the papers it contained ; therefore, I had no thought of you. I was only led to such a suspicion by the circumstances narrated to me by M. Dorgères—your precipitate departure, your facilities for obtaining access to the safe. But you know all this. The agent has enumerated those evidences, and it is useless to rehearse them. I wish to make you understand that the only point in question is the loss of my casket. The rest is of no importance."

"You call the theft of fifty thousand francs of no importance!" said Robert, sarcastically.

"Yes ; if that only had been taken the affair would have been dropped. It is only my papers that are in question, and I long hesitated to believe you had taken them. If you had not acknowledged to the agent that you were the possessor of fifty thousand francs I should still have hesitated to push this matter further."

"I have not deigned to explain to this man how I had

them. To you I will say that I received them three days ago."

"From whom?"

"From a person who owed them to my father?"

"The name of this person?"

"I do not know. The amount was brought to me with a letter, saying that I might without scruple accept the money, which was only a restitution."

"Have you preserved the letter?"

"Yes, sir, I have it with me."

"Will you show it to me?"

"No; I will show it only to the magistrate who shall examine me."

"I should not recommend you to do so. This would seem like a very insignificant justification. To return to my argument. The person who took the fifty thousand francs took also the casket. That person is yourself. Therefore you have my papers, or you know at least where they are. I ask you to return them to me, or if, as I fear, they have passed into other hands, to put me in the way of recovering them."

"You are still disposed to insult me," said M. de Carnoël, disdainfully.

"Mark well the proposition I make," said M. de Borisoff, without noticing this haughty reply. You are on the brink of a precipice, and if the authorities take hold of this affair you are lost. Everything is against you. The explanation you have just given is absolutely inadmissible. You have but one means of saving yourself and it is this : tell me what you have done with the casket, and I give you my word of honor that all pursuit will immediately cease. I will inform the magistrate that the papers have been returned to me, and will remit to M. Dorgères, by some unknown hand, the fifty thousand francs. I will not stop even there. I will see M. Dorgères, and endeavor to remove from his mind all suspicion of you ; and I swear to you that there shall not remain one trace of the accusation against you."

"Not even in the mind of that agent who was questioning me ? " asked Robert, bitterly.

The colonel reflected a moment, then, raising his head like a man who has just come to a decision, he said :

"I see that it is time to tell you the whole truth. You doubt my power to arrest an inquest already begun. You think that if I consent to be silent and succeed in persuading M. Dorgères to be so also, I shall not prevent the agent who has just questioned you from speaking. Have no fear. The man is Russian and is my steward."

"Then, sir, you lied to me when you said the authorities had taken hold of this affair, and all this is simply a comedy. The fellow who undertook to interrogate me is your steward. The other rascal in livery is doubtless your servant."

"He is an old subaltern of my regiment."

" I doubt it. He looks like a bandit."

" Sir," said the Russian with marvellous sang-froid, " you are irritated, I perceive, and wish to make me lose my patience. You will not succeed. You are my equal by birth, and I would consequently owe you satisfaction were you in a natural position toward me. But things changed their face a week ago and I am not obliged to follow the course to which your words would lead. It is not customary to cross swords with those who owe you money, still less with those who have taken your property."

" That is a system very convenient for cowards. In order to refuse-satisfaction to one whom you insult it is sufficient to say, 'I suspect you of an infamy.'"

" You persist in avoiding the question. You are wrong. Let me remind you once more of the facts. If I cannot succeed in drawing from you a confession which would set all this straight again, you admit that it is in my power to change the mode of proceeding, and place you in the hands of those who will examine you with less consideration than I have done."

" Do so," said Robert, undauntedly.

" You forget, sir, that in your country a person accused is, however innocent, a person lost in the public opinion. If you appeared before the Court of Assizes you might be acquitted. It is not probable, but anything is possible. But not one of your old friends would consent to take your hand, and your dishonor would be reflected upon the house where you have lived, upon M. Dorgères, upon his daughter."

"I forbid you to speak of Mlle. Dorgères," exclaimed Robert.

"You turn pale. I have touched the right chord. You see the danger I point out. This danger it rests with yourself to avert, and I ask you—I beg you, if you will—not to persist in following a path which will lead you to an abyss. Accept the facts as they stand. Explain yourself frankly to me. I have promised secrecy. I will keep my promise."

"And if I refuse, what then?"

"One of two things will happen : either I shall deliver you to the authorities, which I should regret—"

"That is what I wish."

"Or I should detain you here until you return to wiser counsels. And it is more probable that I should take the latter course."

"I have a third to propose : Take me to M. Dorgères ; to him I will explain all."

"M. Dorgères has abandoned the case to me. He has forgotten the loss of his money ; the theft of the casket was the main thing, and that is my affair."

"You have said yourself that the two affairs were one. If I prove that I have not taken the fifty thousand francs I shall prove that I have not taken the casket."

"You persist, then, in denying it?" said M. Borisoff.

"You persist, then, in accusing me?" replied M. de Carnoël, in irony.

"I see," said the colonel, "that we shall arrive at no understanding to-day at least, and I return to my plan of leaving you time to reflect."

"By imprisoning me in this house?"

"It is you who force me to it. How could I send you to M. Dorgères? What guarantee should I have that you would not escape on the route? I have no cellular carriage at my disposal."

"You have _sbires_ disguised as valets. That should suffice, it appears to me. You do not suppose I should cry out to call passers-by to my aid. Besides, what prevents you from accompanying me?"

"It would not be proper for me to be seen with you."

Robert started under this insult, and resumed, in a voice suffocating with rage in spite of his efforts to appear calm: "If I gave you my parole to return before the end of the day and place myself at your disposition, should I be permitted to go out."

"You would not engage, I suppose, to see no one during this interval, without making known to me your object. Therefore, you will not be surprised if I refuse to sanction a proposal which might disarrange all my plans."

"So be it. I supposed I was dealing with a gentleman. I was mistaken. You are simply a jailor."

"The jailor of a very agreeable prison," replied the colonel, with a smile that exasperated M. de Carnoël.

"You would be worse off at Mazas. My servants will be at your orders. You have only to ring and they will appear. My *cuisine* is excellent. There are well selected books here, and cigars of exceptional quality. And above all, you are free to tell me where to find my casket, as soon as you please."

CHAPTER VII.

MADAME PIRIAC.

WHILE Robert de Carnoël contended for his honor and his liberty with Colonel Borisoff, Maxime Dorgères was passing his time in quite another fashion.

Wonderful to relate, he had not retired very late and he rose quite early. On leaving his uncle's, he found nothing more entertaining at his club than a languishing game of baccarat, which he had not been at the pains to try to reanimate.

His conversation with Alice, and the expected interview in the Bois de Boulogne, occupied his mind entirely, and he was asking whether he might not have cause to repent of having put the letter into his cousin's hands. He was more than ever determined to meet the lover in the Bois and bring him to a full confession. It was a delicate measure and demanded a thorough preparation. He went home to reflect, and found many other causes for reflection besides ; the marvel of the Rink, the hand to be exhibited at the morgue, the history of Georget protected by this Countess Yalta, whose eccentricities furnished the theme of gossips. With so much to think about, it was long before he went to sleep, and he was troubled by strange dreams till aroused by the valet, who came to light his fire.

Maxime had been installed for a year in an elegantly furnished apartment on the Rue de Châteaudun, and he dispensed his money with a lavish hand.

Not that his establishment was ordered on a grand scale. He had no carriage, and contented himself with a single riding horse. Nevertheless, his uncle was not wrong when he reproached him with advancing at ·rapid strides on the road to ruin.

The young man practised every known method of getting rid of a fortune, except those which relate to the gratifying of one's vanity. If necessary, he would have invented them. In the way of investments, he was acquainted with only his pocket, which emptied itself with surprising rapidity.

But this miscreant had a heart, which was capable of a passion in the best sense of the word; this skeptic was an enthusiast; he had even preserved at heart a certain simplicity; he was neither mistrustful nor blasé.

To be passionately in love there wanted but the occasion ; but it was not in parading his bracelet at public balls and before eccentric foreigners, that it was likely to occur. Moreover, it was the last thing he desired, for his independence was dear to him, and the only woman he was impatient to find, was the one who had left a haud in the claws of M. Dorgères' safe.

The day after the soirée at M. Dorgères, Maxime had risen with the light, resolved not to lose the morning, since the afternoon was to be given to an excursion to the Bois. He found that at the end of a week, his enterprise was very nearly at the same point ; the mystery was, indeed, rather complicated than unravelled. But at present, there was nothing better to do than to follow up the affairs already entered upon. So he went out quite early, with the laudable intention of paying a visit to the grandmother of Georget, and rewarding the youngster with something more substantial than a recommendation.

He took a fancy to pursue the route he had followed on leaving the Rink, and go on foot by the Rue de Tivoli, Place de l'Europe, and Rue de Constantinople.

He seemed still to see the flashing eyes of the adorable skater ; to feel on his arm the gentle pressure of the delicately-gloved hand of this strange creature who had the air of a sultana, and who called herself Madame Sergent.

Rue Jouffroy was almost on his path, and the temptation to shorten the delay she had imposed on him became too strong to resist.

He took the Avenue de Villiers, and passing Rue Cardinet without entering, went as far as Rue Jouffroy, where resided the marvel. It was not yet nine o'clock and all was asleep in this quiet neighborhood. He recognized perfectly the house with its two stories and two doors, and planted himself in front of the building in the middle of the solitary street. The blinds were closed, and not a particle of smoke was seen rising from the elegantly constructed chimneys.

There was no appearance of the house being occupied, and Maxime concluded that the princess of the Rink had not deceived him when she announced her intention of leaving Paris the next day.

Then he reflected that there must be some one in charge of the house and that this was, perhaps, the best moment he could have selected to obtain some information concerning the lady of the establishment. Porters are not usually incorruptible, and the sight of a piece of gold might be expected to have a happy effect in untying their tongues.

Maxime took from his pocket a louis quite new, and advanced to the door, holding it between his thumb and forefinger. He rang boldly, but no one appeared.

After a second and third attempt, a man showed himself on the step, who had not the appearance of a valet, but a genuine military air, the type of a bourgeois subaltern.

" I beg pardon," said Maxime, avoiding the application of the epithet *monsieur* to this singular personage, " is not this house for sale ? "

" Neither for sale nor for rent," said the man with

the large moustache, who had not let go the door, and held himself, evidently, in readiness to close it.

"It is astonishing. I was told the owner was seeking a purchaser. However, is it here Mme. Sergent lives?"

"I do not know that name."

"Can it be possible? I have had the honor of accompanying the lady as far as this, and it was she who told me that—"

"Once more, I do not know who Madame Sergent is. Try the next house."

Maxime was about to insist, but the door was slammed in his face. This proceeding was not pleasing to M. Dorgères' nephew, and he rang violently, but the door did not reopen.

He rang still more violently, and even went so far as to attack the door with feet and fists; but the sole result of all this uproar was the appearance on the threshold of the door opposite of a man in cap and linen apron, a real porter this time, who leaned upon a broom, the badge of his office, and looked at Maxime with a wonder-struck air. This apparition succeeded in calming the young man and giving his thoughts another direction. He still held the coin in his hand, and it occurred to him that the money disdained by the bear with the moustache, might have a happier effect upon his neighbor. He was not mistaken. The man with the broom saw a piece of gold gleaming between the fingers of a well-dressed monsieur, and raised his cap, smiling with an engaging air. This settled Maxime, who now crossed the street in pursuit of his game.

"I have just encountered an ill-mannered boor," he said, toying with the piece of gold he held in his hand.

"Ah, yes, the Prussian," replied the man.

"Is that fellow a Prussian?"

"Prussian, Pole or Bavarian, it is hard to tell, as he speaks all the languages ; but we call him the Prussian, because he's gracious as a prison door."

"He is the porter of the house, I presume?"

"Oh, no. Porters are more polite. He only takes care of the house."

"It is occupied, is it not?"

"No, sir, at least I've never seen any but him."

"It is singular. I thought a lady resided there."

"A lady! It's the first I've heard of that. Nothing has been seen but that creature and the cart-loads of furniture that it took a week to unload and put in place ; and nothing can be got from the pretentious bear who guards it but oaths in all kinds of stupid jargon. He can speak as good French as you or I, though, when he pleases ; but that is not often. He never goes anywhere, and heaven knows what he lives on."

"But does this original never receive any visitors?"

"Never, unless it is at night."

"I don't understand it," Maxime said, gliding the louis

into the man's hand, "I thought the house was occupied by a Madame Sergent."

"Madame Sergent," repeated the obliging porter. "Let me see; I know a woman of that name who keeps a store. Her husband is a postman."

"She is not the one I am looking for."

"What is she like?"

"Very elegant, very young and pretty. A brunette with great dark eyes."

"Good, I see how it is. A *cocotte*, hey?"

"Perhaps."

"She has given a false address to monsieur. On Rue Jouffroy they rent only to married women."

"Yes. I begin to believe she was fooling me," said Maxime, between his teeth.

"All the same, sir. If ever I hear of a person of that name, monsieur has only to leave me his address; I will let him know all I have discovered."

"Thank you. It is not exactly she that I am in search of to-day, but a good woman who lives on Rue Cardinet."

"Hum! It is pretty long—Rue Cardinet."

"And I know neither the name nor the number. I only know that she keeps a lodge, and is grandmother of a boy about twelve years old named Georget, who runs errands at a bank."

"Georget! I know him—the little dog. He is bright as a hunchback, but is too fond of racing the streets; ha·

queer ways, and I shouldn't wonder if he came to no
good. His grandmother is Madame Piriac, No. 159, not
far from here. Would monsieur like to have me go with
him ? "

"No, it is not worth while—but I must go, for it is
late. I think I shall see you again."

"Monsieur will find me always at my post," replied the
loquacious porter, " and monsieur may count on my letting him know about Madame Sergent."

But Maxime was already out of hearing, being in haste
to give audience to the reflections that had been awakened
by the strange discovery he had just made.

" The brunette played me a singular trick. Was it my
heart she wanted, or was it my purse ? Evidently not, as
she cut short our acquaintance without turning it to any
account. She may have had grave reasons for not wanting to receive me till the end of a fortnight. A husband,
perhaps, who watches her and who is expecting to be
absent. I may have ruined my prospects in coming
before the appointed time, for who knows if she was not
hidden behind the blinds ; if she saw me she must have
thought me ridiculous indeed. Bah ! I am easily discouraged. I shall return, and in the meantime will
ask my friend Georget to keep a lookout in the neighborhood."

These reflections brought Maxime to the entrance of
Rue Cardinet, where he began observing the numbers on
the houses. He soon found the one he was in search of,

which proved to be an old building occupied by laboring people.

"If the Countess Yalta comes often to see her protégés here, she is indeed eccentric," thought Maxime. "The porter's lodge belonging to such a hole as this must be a dog-kennel."

He crossed the dirty entrance, and encountered bravely a dark passage-way whose walls were reeking with moisture. At a few steps from the entry he saw a glass door and knocked on one of the panes. No one responded to the appeal, but he heard confused noises within, which suddenly ceased, and a woman's head showed itself behind the window panes. Not caring to talk through a casement he pushed the door open.

"What do you want, sir?" asked the woman, placing herself so as to bar up the entrance.

"I wish to speak to Madame Piriac."

"I am Madame Piriac, sir. You came, no doubt, from M. Vervelle for the flowers which were to be delivered this morning?"

"No, madame, I do not know M. Vervelle."

"Then be kind enough to tell me to whom I have the honor to speak."

This well-chosen language surprised Maxime, and moved him to examine the speaker more closely.

She was a tall woman, a little bent with age, but whose features preserved an appearance of youth out of keeping with her hair, which was white as snow. Her eyes were

bright, her complexion fresh, and it might have been
divined she had been beautiful in her youth. She was
dressed simply and appropriately, and her appearance
betokened something different from her circumstances
and surroundings.

"I am the nephew of M. Dorgères, banker."

Madame Piriac made a movement of surprise and
seemed slightly embarrassed. She turned away, probably
to see if her lodging was in a condition to receive a dis-
tinguished visitor, and a minute passed before she spoke
again.

"Be so good as to enter, sir. You will excuse me for
receiving you in this poor lodging."

Maxime was greatly astonished to hear her express herself in the tone of good society, and not less so to find a
large, well-lighted room furnished with a certain sort of
elegance. There was a canopied bedstead, chairs covered
with Utrecht velvet, and a Louis XVI clock over the
mantel. Behind a curtain of ancient tapestry was a door
which must give access to another room. Nevertheless,
Madame Piriac worked with her hands, for on a table
were spread out all kinds of materials, such as are used
by workers in artificial flowers.

"Sit down, sir," said the widow, offering a chair.
"My grandson has often spoken of you, and I am
honored by your visit."

"It is of this child I came to speak with you," said
Maxime, as he took the seat offered. "Georget has no

doubt told you that the other evening he rendered me a great service ? "

" No, sir ; he has not told me of it."

" What ! he did not tell you that he aided me to escape a party of scoundrels who wanted to rob me ?

Madame Piriac was silent.

" I am under obligations to him, and wish to pay the debt I owe him. As he is too young to make a proper use of the little sum I design for him, I thought it would be best to place it in your hands, so I came—"

Whilst speaking Maxime felt for his pocket-book. The widow stopped him by a movement.

" Thank you, sir ; but I cannot accept anything. My grandson gains an honest livelihood. I am still able to work, and I beg you not to insist."

This was spoken in a tone that made the young man feel he had made a mistake.

" I ask your pardon, madame. I should have recognized that you have not always been in the position in which unmerited misfortune has placed you."

" You are mistaken, sir. I am the widow of a poor artisan ; that is no reason why I should accept a bounty. I do not know how much my grandson may have deserved it, but I am certain that he would refuse it."

" I may at least recommend him to my uncle, and that I have already done. I asked him yesterday to increase Georget's salary and give him something else to do than carrying letters."

" I am exceedingly obliged to you, but I wish Georget to be a soldier like his father, or to enter the navy. He is still too young to enlist in a regiment, but may become a cabin-boy. He will not remain long at M. Dorgères, where he entered against my will."

" Under the protection of the Countess Yalta."

" You know that ! " exclaimed the widow.

" My uncle told me so. Do you see Madame Yalta often ? "

" Never, sir," aswered Madame Piriac, quickly. " My son knew her when a prisoner in Russia. She was then a child, but has never forgotten him ; and when she came to Paris sought out Georget, announcing her intention to take charge of his future, which she began by finding him this place. I did not like to refuse a token of benevolence that was bestowed in honor of the memory of my son, but I intend shortly to write to Madame la Comtesse begging her to permit Georget to pursue another vocation."

" I hope, at least, that you will not forbid me to take an interest in Georget, and to serve him if ever he have need of me. He nearly saved my life by a certain house in Rue Jouffroy, which you probably know ; it is the subject of much talk in the neighborhood."

" I regret, sir, not to be in a position to give you any information," said Madame Piriac, rising from her seat. " I go out rarely and receive no one. And it only remains to thank you for your interest in my grandson.

We are not accustomed to the kind of protection you are pleased to offer, but I am happy to learn that he has deserved it."

This was a leave-taking bestowed in a fashion that struck Maxime dumb. So he stammered a few words of apology, made an awkward exit, and departed, feeling that he knew somewhat less than he did on his arrival.

"*Parbleu!*" he grumbled, as soon as he found himself on the sidewalk. "This is a portress such as one doesn't often see. It is only in Paris you can meet with a phenomenon like that. Certainly there is a mystery here. A great Russian lady who takes charge of the grandson without consulting the grandmother, and places him at a banker's to run errands, when she could so easily have kept him with herself. I believe if I want to find out the truth of all this, I must question the boy himself. I shall have occasion pretty soon to have a talk with Vignory at the office, and on coming out will find my Georget in the waiting-room, will get him some cakes from a pastry-cook at the corner, and a glass of madeira will soon untie his tongue."

The idea of the cakes reminded him that he had eaten nothing since the evening before, and his appetite, sharpened by the morning air and exercise, claimed a prompt satisfaction.

Maxime usually breakfasted at home, but to-day it seemed more practicable to betake himself for refreshment to Tortonis. It was some distance from the Boule-

vard des Italiens, but he felt disposed for the exercise,
and determined to take it on foot, saving a hack ride *en
route* if he felt so inclined. So he began his walk toward
the Madeleine, thinking, as he did so, of the Cerberus of
Rue Jouffroy and the surprising portress of Rue Cardinet.

He was in the habit of reflecting his nose in the air,
like the real Parisian that he was, but his meditations did
not hinder him from giving a glance at the female toilettes that passed, or even following them up when beneath
a lowered veil he thought he caught sight of a pretty face.

On reaching the height of Rue Lisbonne, he saw coming toward him an elegant coupé drawn by two superb
horses. Maxime paused for the purpose of watching the
splendid equipage pass. He was somewhat disenchanted
to observe on the box a man in office boy's livery, and
greatly astonished to recognize, seated inside, Robert de
Carnoël. There was but a second's time for recognition,
but it did not escape Maxime that Robert made a motion
of concealment.

"It is certainly he," said Maxime, following with his
eyes the coupé which disappeared like a meteor. "I
learned yesterday that he was still in Paris but I did not
know, and poor Alice does not know that he is rolling
about in carriages. Here is a discovery that upsets all
my ideas again. Where is this young man going? What
is he doing in that beautiful equipage? Hum ! this desperate lover has all the appearance of leading a pleasant
sort of life. I mean to have a nice little explanation with

him, and I defy him to justify his conduct. Alice shall
know that her gallant's ways are very suspicious. Come!
my friend Vignory's stock is going up."

With this comforting reflection, Maxime concluded to
take a hack for Tortonis. Hunger was urging him on,
and he had had enough of walking, so a quarter of an
hour later found him seated at the café, and ordering,
with visible satisfaction, a dozen *marennes*, and a slice of
pâté de foie gras, the breakfast of a man who possesses a
good digestion and a tranquil conscience. He took up
the newspaper, and saw an article with the heading in
large capital letters.

"MYSTERY UPON MYSTERY.

"Yesterday, at a late hour in the evening, the hand
that was exhibited at the morgue was stolen; how or by
whom, no one can tell. We learn that it was carried away
while the guardians of the morgue were at dinner. The
watchman, on making his round at ten o'clock, perceived
that it had disappeared.

"Our readers may count upon receiving prompt and
exact information as to the result of a new inquest that
is to be made, which will probably throw light upon this
mysterious affair."

"Yes," said Maxime, between his teeth, "count upon
this, kind readers, and you will have long to wait. I
alone can give you the information, and I shall keep my
knowledge for my own use. This is the work of the ac-

complice. He has entered the morgue as he did my uncle's office—without violence. His process is always the same. Ah! these are people with long arms," he concluded, as he swallowed a glass of chablis to reanimate his faculties.

He had need of the reinforcement, for the second blow had somewhat stunned him. ·

For the first time since he had undertaken to give chase to the thieves he recognized the alarming elements of his enterprise.

"What would they not give to regain possession of the bracelet?" he thought.

This reflection was as a flash of lightning illuminating certain incidents of his career. He thought of his adventure on Rue Jouffroy, and said to himself that those loungers had been posted there by the brunette of the Rink.

"This creature is not the thief; one does not skate immediately after submitting to an amputation from the wrist. But she was doubtless an emissary sent to draw me into a snare. *Diable!* I must keep my eyes open; I am walking over a ground covered with pitfalls. Henceforth I distrust all pretty women."

Deliberating thus, Maxime swallowed his last oyster, when he saw enter M. Villagos, whom he had not seen before since the evening of the Rink.

He came toward Maxime smiling, and offering his hand, and took a seat by him at the table.

" You do not come to the club now," said Dorgères. " I have been there many times without meeting you."

" It is true. I have passed several nights with an invalid lady, who has caused me considerable uneasiness. But she is on the mend now, and this evening I hope to resume our whist."

"Have you read the papers this morning ? " asked Maxime, his companion having given his order for mutton chops, broiled eggs, and a bottle of Pontet-Canet.

" No, *ma foi !* Indeed it must be confessed I hardly ever read them. Politics bore me, and as for Parisian news, I get all that from my patients, who are chiefly women, and women are always wonderfully well informed."

Then you know the strange story I have just been reading—this hand stolen from the morgue ? "

" Yes ; some one spoke to me of it. It is curious. To brave the penal code in order to carry off an anatomical preparation. But nothing is sacred to a thief."

" And what is your opinion of it ? "

" I never had the least skill in guessing riddles. Besides, judicial problems interest me very little indeed. But tell me something of the end of the romance of which I saw the beginning. That would be more lively."

" What romance ? "

" The romance of the Rink. May I inquire how it terminated ? "

" Very deplorably, my dear doctor. The lady led me

into a neighborhood with which I was very little acquainted; then before the door of her house she bade me good-evening, and withdrew."

"A strange skater. Her conduct is as inexplicable as the affair of the morgue."

"That is not all, doctor. On returning I was pursued by rascals, and should have had a sorry time of it if I had not, by the happiest chance, met with a youngster employed in my uncle's bank, who warned me of the danger and found me a hack."

"*Diable!* the marvel begins to look suspicious. It appears as if there might be some agreement between her and the knaves who gave you chase."

"I thought of that, but it was repugnant to me to believe it. She has the bearing of a princess."

"Appearances are very deceptive, above all in Paris. A pretty rag-woman might be picked up out of the streets, dressed by a fashionable modiste, installed in a beautiful apartment, and made to pass for a great lady. In less than a month she would play the duchess to perfection.'

"The like has been known; but I would swear that this brunette has never carried a rag-basket."

"What is her name?"

"Oh, she gave me a fancy name of the commonest sort, Madame Sergent. I declare, doctor, this woman is an enigma. For the matter of that, for the past few days everything I see or hear is extraordinary. Would you believe that this *gamin* who runs errands at my uncle's, was taken by recommendation of a superlatively rich foreigner, whom you must know at least by reputation, the Countess Yalta."

" The Countess Yalta ! She is one of my patients, and . I am going there after breakfast."

" Indeed ! My uncle told me she had gone to Nice or Monaco."

" She did go, but returned yesterday. It seems her trip was not a success as she sent for me."

" *Parbleu !* doctor, since you are her physician you can tell me something about her. I am entertained every day with fantastical episodes in which she figures. She seems to me like ·a princess in the *Thousand and One Nights.*"

" She does remind one of them."

" In what part of the world is her principality ? "

" You ask too much of me. All I know is that she is very rich, and is a person who cannot stay long in one place. The other day she left for Italy to spend the winter, and after a week's absence is back again in Paris. And to-morrow I should not be surprised to hear she had determined to explore the Nile as far as the third cataract."

" All Russians appear to me to be built after this model."

" But I do not think she is Russian. I am almost sure she is a subject of the Sultan, was born in one of the Asiatic provinces of the Ottoman Empire, and married a ·

Greek ; one of the families which claim descent from the Byzantine emperors."

" This illustrious husband is dead, I suppose ? "

" Yes, the countess has been three years a widow."

" Pretty, is she not ? I have only seen her at a distance."

" And I have seen her very closely, but should be much puzzled to say what I think of her face. I can only assert that she charms all who approach her. I have nearly been victimized myself."

" An eccentric charmer, from all accounts ? "

' "Your accounts are correct. She is given to all kinds of masculine amusements ; hunts, is expert with sword and pistol, and is addicted to every known sport. But these peculiarities do not prevent her from becoming, when she pleases, the most elegant and adorable of women. She knows everything, is a musician, painter, and if it pleased her to write plays or romances, they would meet with a prodigious success."

" A blue-stocking, then ? "

" By no means. She has more simplicity than any one I know. By the way, how does it happen you have never visited her? All your acquaintances of the club go there."

" To her balls. That is a kind of diversion little to my taste. I have a horror of a rout."

" But you might see the countess in her salon if you ·wished to do so."

" How is that ? she is not aware of my existence."

" Would you like to have me present you ? I know her very well, though not intimately ; but I can answer for your success. You have precisely the character and mind to please the countess ; and if you would consent to see her often, you would be doing a benevolent act, for she is dying of ennui."

" What ! a millionairess like her ! It seems to me that in the matter of diversions she must be puzzled which to choose. Has she any lover ? "

· The doctor shook his head, and answered in a tone almost confidential :

" Dear sir, you put your finger on the wound. The countess does not, and I believe never has loved any one. Between ourselves, I fear that when she was created the heart was left out."

" That is a very hazardous diagnosis. Every woman has a heart ; only there are hearts that do not speak till late."

" There are some that never speak. I have studied the countess ; she is as cold as the North Pole. She has a great deal of imagination, but not the least sensibility. · That accounts for her leading the life she does. And for my part, I have given up the hope of curing an ailment against which medicine is powerless, and content myself with treating her for a nervous rheumatism which she contracted last month, hunting in the marshes. I ought to warn you that should you be entrapped into making love to her, you will lose your time."

"Don't be uneasy, doctor; I shall not try. She is blonde, and I care only for brunettes. That reason would suffice if there were no other. It is a pathological case, and I give it up to you. I shall go to her house purely from curiosity, as one goes to Chamounix to contemplate Mont Blanc; and also, I confess, to speak to her about this little protégé of hers."

'That would be an excellent pretext for your visit. When would you like to have me introduce you to the Avenue de Friedland house?"

'When you wish; next week, for example."

"Next week the countess may have gone to America or Constantinople."

"You must have time though to announce my visit."

"Wherefore? My patient is much better pleased with unexpected meetings."

"Well, to-morrow, if you say so."

"Why not to-day? When we have smoked one or two cigars we can take a carriage for the house of the countess."

"What are you thinking about, doctor? I am in morning dress, and the countess must be still in bed."

'She! it is clear you know little of her habits. She rises with the day, and I venture to assert we shall find her in the garden breaking a horse or practising some gymnastics."

"That is the way she takes care of her rheumatism," said Maxime, laughing.

"She has her own method, and consults me only for form's sake."

"But you don't suppose she would receive me Amazon-fashion, or perched upon a trapezium?"

"*Ma foi*, yes! I forgot to tell you that coquetry is a feminine instinct unknown to her."

"Like love. Decidedly, your countess is a phenome-non. I shall not be sorry to see her in the midst of her sports."

"It is said, then. You come with me?"

"Yes, since you take on yourself the responsibility of any impropriety I may commit. But I must be at the Bois de Boulogne by half past two."

"The Bois de Boulogne! That suits precisely. The countess' house is two steps from the Place de l'Etoile. You may pay a long visit without missing your rendez-vous, for I suppose it is a rendezvous. This is hardly a season for strolling through the lakes."

Maxime did not care to entrust to the Hungarian the secret of his promenade in the Bois, so he replied in an indifferent tone :

"I am going to try a horse that will be brought to me at half past two in the Allèe des Longchamps."

"*Parbleu!* if you are fond of horsemanship you and Madame Yalta will soon come to an understanding. She leaps with a boldness that would cause all the fox hunters in England and Ireland to turn pale, and can control the most restless steeds."

"She will break her neck at that sport."

"It. is with some such idea that she attaches me to her. I am more surgeon than doctor."

"But I was not aware that you made part of her household."

"Not exactly. But she prefers me to my brethren of the faculty in Paris. And then we are in some measure compatriots."

"How is that? I was not aware that you were born in Turkey." .

"No ; but we Hungarians are something of Turks in the sense that we have no love for Russia. In the last war our country was very near taking sides with the Sultan. And I have contemplated serving under Osman Pacha.

"Did the countess command a batallion of Amazons in the army that defended Plevna ? "

"Not that I know of," replied the doctor, laughing ; "she would be quite capable of going to war if her caprice urged her that way, but hitherto she has thought only of pacific diversions."

"*Ma foi!* doctor, I must confess you have inspired me with a frantic desire to know her. I am ready to fol-. low you as soon as you have finished your cigar."

"I will finish it on the way. We will settle our account, get a carriage and set off."

Five minutes later the two were in a hack rolling over the Boulevard Haussman, which ends in the Avenue de Friedland.

The sky was cloudy. It had snowed the evening before and the snow still fell at intervals.

" There are chances that Madame Martineau would refuse to accompany her pupil in weather like this," thought Maxime, " and I hope Alice would not go alone. So much the better. I shall have the less difficulty in inducing him to decamp definitely ; it would be well to get the gentleman beyond the seas."

The hack stopped before a gate in the middle of a long wall, a gate designed evidently only for the servants or familiar friends of the countess, for it was not of a size to admit carriages. The front of the house and principal court-yard were evidently on the other side.

"You are favored in obtaining access to Madame Yalta," Maxime said, gaily ; "the guests who attend her fêtes do not take this route, I presume."

"The countess has authorized me to make use of it to avoid loss of time. If we had come in by the main entrance we should have had to defile under the eyes of a batallion of fellows in fine livery who transmit visitors from one to the other ; while, by passing through this private door, we avoid this solemn reception and go straight to the countess."

They entered a park ; not one of those gardens sparingly ornamented with trees transplanted at great cost, where all is artificial even to the turf over which one threads as on a drawing-room carpet. The venerable elms pread out their branches in full liberty, and the lawn extended as far as the eye could reach. Maxime saw in the distance an immense conservatory, and nearer, a large building in irregular style though charming.

"The cage is as strange as the bird," he said, half aloud ; "it must have been built especially for the countess."

"Oh !" said the doctor, "it has two faces, an English cottage in the rear and a palace in front. When you go out through the main entrance you will see that Madame Yalta inhabits a palace that would not look out of place at Versailles. But it is snowing in good earnest, so we will go in. It is hardly necessary to explore the park for the lady of the manor."

It was a new revelation to Maxime to find M. Villagos the accredited physician of a great lady who held his skill in high esteem. At the club he was said to be a philosopher expatriated for political causes ; an exile who had taken the precaution to see his money safely invested in a foreign country before putting himself in a position to be expelled by his government. The proscribed of this category, lead the pleasantest life imaginable in France. They are welcomed with open arms, feasted and honored. They enjoy all the delights which Paris can bestow upon the rich, and reap in addition a large benefit from the sympathy inspired by unmerited misfortune. Thus, they may be at once millionaires and martyrs. Maxime was surprised that the relations of this amiable practitioner with a lady of fashion were not more talked of in the Parisian world.

It is true he was modest, and rarely spoke of·himself. He conversed on the topics in vogue in the assemblies of his associates, and on these he rarely pronounced decidedly. No one could tell what his opinions were with any certainty, at least on any subject outside of his profession. And as nothing seemed to annoy him, he was one of those persons whom one meets with pleasure without desiring a closer acquaintance.

He led Maxime through sinuous pathways which wound through the massive evergreens to the house covered with ivy, up a flight of stairs into a vestibule filled with exotic flowers and shrubbery.

No one was there to receive visitors. The servants were doubtless at the grand entrance, as M. Villagos had said. This gentleman remarked to Maxime :

"I suspect the countess is at the billiard table."

"She plays billiards!" exclaimed Maxime.

"She plays all games, and excels in them too. She has a professor of chess attached to her establishment.'

"I begin to understand why she has not been in love. She has not had time. But where are you leading me, doctor? By these interminable galleries lined with pictures and statues I could believe myself in a museum."

"This is the cottage especially dedicated to the countess' sports. It contains a covered riding-room, an armory ; and as she worships art, painting and sculpture have also found their place there."

"And no one to keep guard over all these wonders?

This is the castle of the Sleeping Beauty of the Woods."

"You are mistaken. The countess is never asleep, and there is the proof—listen ! " said the doctor, stopping before a door of stained glass.

Maxime listened and heard characteristic sounds, the clicking of steel against steel.

"She is there practising with her fencing-master. Do you like fencing ?"

"Very much. I can make good use of a foil."

"Excellent ! The countess will be delighted to have a competent judge to witness her proficiency."

Maxime was about to protest. This mode, of introducing to a woman taking a fencing lesson a man whom she had never seen, seemed to him going too far.

But the doctor, without allowing him time to do so, opened the door and pushed him in, entering after him, and he thus found himself in presence of this singular creature who has so filled his imagination.

She was dressed in fencing costume, her face masked, a buckskin jacket, fencing gloves, sandals, black leather leggings, and velvet trousers clasped at the knee. Beneath the costume she wore, it was not easy to judge of her beauty.

All that could be determined was that she was tall and slender ; the mask revealed only a white neck of irreproachable outline.

"Good-morning, doctor," she said, without seeming to perceive Maxime, and continuing her combat. "I will be with you in a moment. One more touch with Kardiki, who contests the last stroke."

The Polish professor after a lively engagement received the button of the countess' foil, and acknowledged himself vanquished with a salutation of his weapon.

"Good-morning, countess," said the doctor, "I am delighted to see your rheumatism does not interfere with your exercises."

"You know that is my mode of treatment. I still suffer much, but fortunately it is the left arm."

While speaking the countess removed her mask, and Maxime was more surprised than charmed when he saw the face it had concealed. The complexion was a dead white, the lips full and red, the chin too prominent, the nose straight as that of a Greek statue, the brow encircled by rings of ash-colored blonde hair, forming an incongruous whole by no means pleasing at first sight. Her eyes were indescribable; sometimes they seemed the blue of a stormy sea, sometimes the gray of a winter sky, changing their color apparently with each shade of emotion.

The physiognomy was indescribable too ; mystical, and at the same time sensual, as may be observed in certain Byzantine images of the saints of that empire.

Maxime was lost in amazement, like an Englishman before the Colosseum.

There exist not on earth beings who are more the creatures of habit than the *viveurs* of Paris, and Maxime conceived of only two or three types of women to which he did homage, all of them approaching more or less nearly to those which figure in wax behind the show-cases of hairdressers. The brunette of the Rink repre-sented a variety admitted since Alfred de Musset had sung of Andalusian women, therefore Maxime was pre-pared to recognize her beauty. But this countess upset all his ideas. There was nothing ordinary about her ; and that sooner or later he should come to discover the charm boasted by M. Villagos, he had a confused percep-tion ; but this charm his character of *boulevardier* did not yet acknowledge.

"Countess," replied the doctor, "you have only to follow my prescriptions—exercise and distraction. Your practice of arms is well, and what is still better, I pre-sent to you the gayest, most agreeable and most humor-ous of my friends, M. Maxime Dorgères."

Maxime sought for a phrase which would not come, and ended by bowing awkwardly enough.

"You are welcome, sir," said the countess. "The friends of the doctor are mine," and she took off her fencing gloves to offer her hand to the young man.

"Are you a relative of M. Dorgères, banker?" she asked.

"His nephew, madame," replied Maxime.

"Then you are no stranger to me. I know him, and am indebted to him for taking a child into his service on my recommendation."

"Georget," replied Maxime, delighted to find a topic of conversation which placed him at his ease. "I am happy to tell you, madame, that the child has rendered me a service for which I am truly grateful."

"Really? How was that?"

"He saved my life by pointing out the means of escape when I was about to be robbed."

"His father saved the life of mine."

"My uncle told me that story, and it emboldened me to follow the doctor, who proposed to bring me here at this absurd hour. I hope you will excuse me for profiting by the occasion he offered me to speak to you of this Georget Piriac."

"Piriac; yes, that is the name of the man but for whom I had been left an orphan in my infancy."

"And whom you have never forgotten, since you watch over his son."

"My protection has hitherto been of very little use to him. I supposed I was doing well in placing him with M. Dorgères, but having observed that the child is remarkably intelligent, I am unwilling to have him pass his time carrying letters, and hope to find him better employment. But enough of Georget. Do you practise arms?"

"Sometimes."

"Then you will not refuse to give me a lesson."

Maxime was astounded. Certainly he had not come with any purpose of crossing swords with the countess, and was at a loss for a reply to so unlooked-for a proposition. . The doctor made a charitable effort to draw him from his embarrassment.

"Countess," he said to his patient, "I prescribed exercise, but it is not necessary to abuse it. An hour's fencing is more than enough for your rheumatism."

"I am not tired. See, doctor, my pulse is as calm as though I had just risen," and she extended to M. Villagos a hand in a white kid glove.

Her fencing jacket terminated at the wrist in long nine-button kid gloves. Here the fashionable lady reappeared in this eccentric creature.

"My dear countess," said the Hungarian, smiling, "how can I hope to cure you if you do not follow my directions? Besides, you see my friend Dorgères is not prepared for fencing."

"No matter. Your friend will oblige me by putting on a mask and fencing gloves. Nothing more is necessary. In one or two thrusts I shall know his play."

Maxime saw there was no retreat. The countess was looking at him earnestly out of her bright eyes, and her look moved him to the depths of his soul. He began to see the impossibility of resisting those eyes, and he no longer thought her ugly.

He unhooked from the wall a mask, foil and gloves, equipped himself slowly, and took his place opposite the countess, who was already prepared for him.

"Thanks, sir," she said gaily, "I see you know how to

yield gracefully to a woman's caprice," and she engaged him without further preamble.

Maxime had recovered his self-possession. He fenced well, and was not sorry to exhibit his skill to this Amazon, who believed herself invincible. He even expected to come off conqueror with no great difficulty, having a suspicion that the Polish professor yielded the advantage out of deference for his opulent pupil. He soon saw his mistake. Madame Yalta had a strange play that disconcerted him. It seemed at times as if he drew against a left-handed adversary. He recovered himself, however, and being an expert, succeeded in defending himself, though after a few skilful thrusts he was touched.

" I yield, madame," he said, lowering his foil.

" No, no," said the countess, " that doesn't count. You have not had time to accustom yourself to my attacks; but your play is more regular than mine, and in the long run you would get the advantage. Let us continue."

She put herself in an attitude of defence, and Maxime was compelled to do the same. He calculated carefully his feints and thrusts, in order to weary out his fragile adversary, who attacked with too much spirit to hold out long. But all his nice calculations were frustrated by one of those chances which cannot be foreseen by the most skilful fencer.

While the combat was liveliest, the countess' foil grazed Maxime's wrist. She drew it away quickly, but with some difficulty, for it had caught under the sleeve of his coat, and the bracelet, torn away in the effort, fell to the floor. Maxime, in his surprise, forgot to retaliate, and the countess threw aside her mask, saying :

"Have I wounded you, sir?"

"No ; it is not that," stammered the young man.

"Wounded at heart, perhaps," cried the doctor. "Countess, your foil has torn from M. Dorgères a bracelet which has very much the look of a love-token."

So saying, he picked up the bracelet and handed it to his noble patient. Maxime also was unmasked, and cut a stupid figure.

"If like the brunette of the Rink she should ask me to give it to her, *diable!* if I should know what to say !"

The countess had taken it in her hands and was examining it curiously.

"It is true, is it not, this souvenir is from a woman?"

"You would hardly believe I bought it of a jeweller," said Maxime, forcing a smile.

"And you have sworn to her to wear it?"

"No," he replied, stupidly.

"Then take my advice and preserve it carefully. Above all do not allow any one to take it from you. I have it now ; what would you do if I kept it?"

The poor young man blushed to his ears, and waited a second before he made the adroit reply :

"Madame, I should have the right to think that in confiscating it you made me a declaration. To show a man that you are jealous of his past is to confess that you love him."

The countess started, and a lightning flash passed through her eyes. She still held the bracelet and appeared unwilling to return it.

Maxime was on thorns, though he tried to keep his countenance.

The doctor was looking at Madame Yalta and appearing to take a lively interest in this little scene.

"You are right, sir," she replied, at length. "You might deceive yourself, and to prove to you that I love no one, here is your bracelet."

It needed no entreaties to induce Maxime to place it in his pocket, and M. Villagos said in a tone half serious, half jesting :

"Really, countess, you are too good. Many women would have had conditions to make before returning the jewel. In your place I should impose on M. Dorgères the obligation to come here every day for a month and give me a lesson in arms or horsemanship."

"A pleasant obligation, truly !" cried Maxime, who had recovered his fine spirits.

"I take you at your word," said the countess, quickly, "and hope you will be a real friend to me. You are so already, are you not ? "

Maxime assented earnestly.

"Then," said the countess, with a smile calculated to turn a head steadier than that of Maxime Dorgères, "you will go with me to the Bois. They say the lakes are already frozen, and I am impatient to skate."

This proposition, so suddenly made, recalled to Maxime that he had a duty to fulfil ; that it was incumbent on him to save his cousin from being led away by a fatal mistake.

"I beg pardon, madame," he said, with some embarrassment ; "under any other circumstances I should be most happy to accompany you, but to-day I have an engagement which it is absolutely necessary I should keep."

"With the lady of the bracelet ?"

"No, I assure you ; but—— "

"His rendezvous is in the Bois de Boulogne," said the doctor.

"Oh, then," resumed Madame Yalta, "you have no longer a pretext for refusing, and I shall never forgive you if you let me go alone. Besides, I shall not keep you long. I am going to order my sleigh, and you will get in with me. We will go the lakes, and you will leave me where you please. It is agreed, is it not? You belong to me for one hour. Doctor, M. Dorgères, if you please, into the library and entertain him while I dress. I shall not be long."

Maxime was still about to protest, but she disappeared, leaving him with M. Villagos.

"Well, what is your opinion of my patient ?"

"I begin to find her charming."

"Which means that at first you thought her ugly. The

countess never pleases at first sight, but intelligent men are always charmed before the end of a quarter of an hour. What is more uncommon is for her to be pleased by them, and I could read in her eyes the interest you have inspired. Come, see these objects of art while you are waiting."

Maxime followed the obliging doctor through long corridors, which ended in an opening masked by Gobelin tapestry. Behind this heavy enclosure was a zealous servant, who, on the first sound of their footsteps, hastened to raise it. This officer was a giant, six feet high, large in proportion, and bearded like the Farnese Hercules; nothing was wanting but the club. Bedizened too with gold lace and gimp, his appearance was well calculated to impose respect.

A simple *bourgeois* would have bowed low down to the ground. But it was he who saluted M. Villagos humbly, moving aside to make room for him to pass. The skeptical youth soon perceived that the doctor had not exaggerated when he made the assertion that the countess inhabited a palace, to which the cottage was but the antechamber.

This side was all sacrificed to fancy ; on the other began the grand establishment of a princess. Salon after salon, as at Versailles ; gilded salons, with ceilings painted by masters, representing mythological triumphs and apotheoses. At each door a *valet de pied* in grand livery of blue and gold ; valets in the uniform of the *cent-gardes*.

Maxime scarcely dared to breathe, and only recovered his speech when he found himself in a vast gallery lined with richly-bound volumes.

"*A la bonne heure!*" he exclaimed; "here I know myself. We are in Paris, in the house of a rich and intelligent woman. Whilst admiring the magnificence of the apartments we have just passed through, I was asking myself if I was about to be received by Louis XIV on his throne."

"You understand now how Madame Yalta is partial to the English house," replied the doctor. "This solemn luxury is imposed upon her by her great wealth, but she escapes from it whenever she can; it serves only for the formal receptions to which all Paris is invited. The aristocracy of two worlds are proud to dance here, and you may meet heiresses without number. I wish you the good luck to marry one of them."

"Thanks, doctor; but I expect to end my days in an obstinate celibacy, even should I end them without a sou, which is quite likely. But, upon my word, here is the sleigh marvellously equipped."

The windows of the library looked out upon the grand court of the house, and near the flight of stairs was drawn up a sleigh with three horses—one in shafts behind and the two in front driven abreast—held by a coachman who came, like all the rest, from the banks of the Neva,—a coachman encased in fur, and with an enormous fur bonnet reaching to the eyes. The horses pawed the ground, the bells tinkled, and these lively sounds had the effect of arousing Maxime, who had been considerably subdued by the splendor around him.

"*Parbleu!*" he said, "I should regret for the remainder of my life not having shown myself in the Bois in that unparalleled equipage, by the side of the most elegant woman in Paris. The question is, whether it is not a little premature. The snow has scarcely hardened yet."

"You are mistaken, my dear sir; it has been falling since yesterday evening, and the thermometer is twelve degrees below zero—real Moscow weather."

They were interrupted by the countess, who appeared transfigured.

She wore a cap of otter, which was marvellously becoming, and was enveloped in a pelisse of blue fox, which was worth certainly more than the hereditary manor of the Carnoëls.

This time Maxime thought her ravishing. The color had mounted into the pale cheeks of the indescribable creature, and her eyes shone with an extraordinary brightness. It might have been thought she had a fever.

"Take care, madame," said the doctor, struck with this sudden change; "the cold is piercing and your horses are difficult to manage. You are not yet entirely restored, and excess of fatigue might occasion a relapse. Indeed, I think you would do well to abandon this drive."

The advice was given in a more serious tone than Dr.

Villagos had yet used with his patient, but it was not followed.

"If I relapse, you will set me on my feet again, my dear doctor," said the countess, gaily ; "besides, a bath of cold air would do me good. The voyage to Monaco failed. I am going to try a tour in the Bois while it is frozen. Who loves me follows," she added, looking at Maxime.

And Maxime followed, though he did not yet love. It was an active heroism on his part, for the least inconvenient result of such an expedition for a man so unprepared would be a heavy cold.

But once launched out, this seeker after adventures knew no obstacles.

Having said adieu to M. Villagos, who pressed his hand warmly, he descended into the court-yard with the countess and took his place by her side. The coachman handed his mistress the reins and whip, and took the box attached to the sleigh in the rear.

"Let us have a little talk," said the lady of the changing eyes to her companion.

Talk ! Maxime desired nothing more. But of what ?

He had known the countess only one hour, and had already disposed of the only topic of conversation in common between them. "If she should refer again to the bracelet, I should be perplexed indeed what reply to make," he thought.

Madame Yalta, occupied in the management of her

Russian horses, allowed him a little respite to prepare for his part in the conversation. Maxime was astonished to see how suddenly everything had frozen. He felt in the morning that it was turning cold ; but in the interior of Paris the aspect of things was unchanged, while on the heights of l'Etoile, the appearance presented was that of Siberia.

"It is enough to keep the polar bear indoors," was the observation the chilling atmosphere suggested to the cousin of Alice.

"And to rejoice my horses, who were born in the frozen steppes of Russia. On starting, I found it troublesome to hold them, but now I have them in hand, and we may talk. Tell me something of your uncle."

To this unexpected remark, Maxime scarcely knew what reply to make. "He has a daughter," answered Madame Yalta, "who appeared to me charming. I saw her one day in the Champs-Elysées. How is it she is not married ?"

"But," stammered Maxime—"I do not know—besides, she is only nineteen."

"You must be in love with her."

"I ! not at all, I declare."

"Then I am going to ask whether what that child told me is true."

"Georget ? what has he told you ?"

"That she was in love with one of your uncle's clerks."

"What ! the chap has been——"

"Don't be angry with him. I have sometimes amused myself by asking him questions to hear his prattle. He is a great observer, and, thanks to him, I know your uncle's household pretty well. He gave me an enthusiastic account of Mlle. Dorgères; has described also the old governess, the cashier, and the secretary, a Breton lordling whom your uncle has recently dismissed. Why did he do so?"

"I—I do not know," said Maxime, more and more disconcerted. "I believe, rather, that M. de Carnoël resigned. My uncle wished to send him to Egypt and, unwilling to go so far, he withdrew."

"Carnoël!" repeated the countess. "Was there not an attaché of the French embassy at St. Petersburg of that name?"

"He was Robert de Carnoël's father."

"Then how is it that the son——"

"Has accepted the position of secretary to a banker? Because his father left no fortune."

"And the son is a brave youth who is not afraid to go to work to recover one? Really, I don't know why I make all these enquiries. You must think me very inquisitive?"

"Not at all," protested Maxime, who did not say what he thought.

"Would you know," she went on, ".why I fatigue you with questions about your cousin and your uncle's secretary? It is, because, after having heard Georget's stories,

I fancied that Mlle. Dorgères loved M. de Carnoël, and that he loved her."

Maxime colored to the roots of his hair in spite of the biting wind that was cutting his face.

"Good! I see I guessed right," cried the lady. "And do you know what I propose to do? It is to take your cousin's part against your uncle—to plead his cause with M. Dorgères. It is absurd, is it not?"

"No," replied Maxime quickly; "only you are ill informed. If I thought my cousin would be happy with M. de Carnoël, I would do myself what you propose. But—I am compelled to say that you are wrong to interest yourself in this young man."

"Why? has he done anything wrong?"

"I do not say that," replied Maxime, who already regretted having said so much.

"He is accused of it perhaps—of what is he accused?"

"Of nothing, but his conduct is, to say the least of it, singular. He went away without saying good-bye to any one, and is now in concealment. A man does not act thus whose conscience is clear."

The countess made a movement which was felt by the horses, for they started suddenly to one side, and to the surprise of Maxime she ceased to urge the delicate subject into which she had launched so abruptly.

They had reached the enclosure of the Bois, and the broad road which ends in the largest lake was filled with carriages and pedestrians.

The report had spread through Paris that there was skating, and the crowd hastened to avail itself of a rare spectacle.

It required Madame Yalta's marvellous address to pass without accident ; in the twinkling of an eye the Russian "trotters" had cleared the nearer end of the lake and arrived at its terminus opposite the cottage of the islets. Just as the countess stopped them, Maxime saw a woman approach the borders of the lake on foot, and could scarcely repress an exclamation of surprise. He had recognized the brunette of the Rink.

It was even she, the brunette with the golden skin, the marvel discovered by Dr. Villagos.

She wore the same costume as at the Rink, and made no attempt at concealment, not even having lowered her veil. In what a discovery had this fortunate expedition resulted ? Madame Sergent had deceived him concerning her fortnight's absence, and he felt a violent desire to ask for explanations of this falsehood as well as several others.

" Well," said the countess, who was standing surveying the scene, " everything is frozen and the ice is solid, since it carries so many. I doubt if a club of skaters is yet organized on the lake of Madrid, and if you like this sport we will try it there."

Maxime asked nothing better, though the presence of Madame Yalta might interfere with his movements ; so he was not in haste to reply.

She guessed the cause of his embarrassment. "For what hour is your rendezvous fixed?" she asked.

"For three o'clock."

"And in what part of the Bois?"

"On the route des Bouleaux."

"It is some distance from here, but is near Madrid. It is now half-past two. If you would take a single turn with me on the ice, I would drive you there. But no," she added, laughing, ".you prefer to go alone, for I do not at all believe you are going to try a horse. Well, then, you may leave me in twenty minutes. My coachman will take you to your meeting place and return for me."

Maxime neither accepted nor declined. He reflected. He thought Alice would not come to the Bois, and that the occasion was a rare one for following up Mme. Sergent and unravelling the mystery that enveloped her. The caprice which she had been able to awaken one fine evening in his unoccupied heart, was already much weakened ; but curiosity impelled him.

Nevertheless it cost him something to quiet Madame Yalto, who perplexed him at least as much as the adventuress of the Rink.

"I repeat you are entirely free," said the countess, "but decide. My horses are impatient."

Maxime was about to accept the skating when he saw approach his uncle's berlin drawn by two sturdy mares, and driven by a coachman who seemed unacquainted with his business.

"I verily believe," he murmured, "there is Joseph with the coachman's greatcoat over his livery, and Alice inside. Ah, the infatuated child! She has come in spite of everybody and the ice too."

"I am waiting," the countess said, impatiently.

"I beg pardon, madame," said Maxime, "I thought I recognized there—in that carriage—"

"Mlle. Dorgères," finished the countess. "Yes, it is she, and she has seen us."

The windows were raised and the blonde head of Alice showed itself for an instant and immediately disappeared. Joseph also had perceived his master's nephew, and whipped up his horses into a brisk trot.

"Well?" asked the countess.

Maxime was heroic.

"Madame," he said, without hesitation, "to my great regret, I am compelled to leave you."

"To follow that young girl, is it not?"

"No—but—"

"Why not speak the truth? It is plain that it is Mlle. Dorgères that you are to meet on the route des Bouleaux. If you go on foot she will arrive before you, and it will be unfortunate that you should be here in the carriage with me instead of at the rendezvous."

"I assure you that my cousin is not expecting me, and I go—"

"You will go to repair your delinquencies, and this is how. My horses travel faster than those of your uncle.

They will have made the tour of the other side of the lake before the berlin reaches the spot from the Porte Dauphine. I will put you out near the route des Bouleaux, at the place which you will indicate, and then leave you without looking behind me."

This arrangement was by no means agreeable to Maxime, but the countess left him no time to object. She had not relinquished the reins, made a sign to her coachman who resumed his place in a twinkling, and the impatient stallions set off at full speed.

" I see that this is another abduction," said Maxime, with a forced laugh.

" A very disinterested one," said the lady. " I lead you to the feet of the woman you love."

" I protest Mlle. Dorgères is my cousin and nothing more."

" I defy you to prove it. Why, then, should you be in such haste to meet her ? "

" It is not I who love her."

" Would you have me believe you came to this rendezvous on behalf of one of your friends ? "

" No ; on the contrary, I came to prevent a meeting which I apprehend."

" You must speak more plainly if you mean me to understand."

The trotters· flew like the wind, and the rapid motion intoxicated Maxime already confused by the countess' abrupt questions.

" The lady presses me because she is jealous," thought the young man with flattered vanity; " it is worth while to prove to her that my heart is not my cousin's."

"Well, madame," he said, not without a moment's hesitation, " know that Mlle. Dorgères has suffered her affections to be engrossed by a young man who is unworthy of her. That is a secret that does not belong to me, but I feel sure that you will not abuse my confidence."

" The young man is M. de Carnoël, is he not ? "

Maxime started ; but he had gone too far to retreat.

" Why do you regard M. de Carnoël as unworthy of Mlle. Dorgères ? " she asked quickly.

" He left my uncle's house under unfavorable circumstances."

" Ah, then, how is he still in Paris ? "

" I believe he remained for the purpose of seeing her again. He has written her that he would await her to-day in the Bois de Boulogne. And you see she has been weak enough to come. The interview will take place in presence of her governess who is with her in the carriage ; therefore the case is only one of heedless folly, whose consequences will not be very grave. But I have promised myself to see M. de Carnoël and to make use of language that will cut short this new attempt. And now, madame, you know all."

There was silence. The countess seemed agitated, and Maxime was asking himself whether he might not have cause to repent so delicate a confidence.

"Sir," she said at length, "you are the most loyal man I know, and it is in your power to become my most cherished friend. Here is the Allée de Longchamps. The route des Bouleaux is near. I give you your liberty, but I count upon your coming to see me to-morrow. And I shall not receive you in my armory," she added gaily. "From three o'clock the Countess Yalta will be at home for M. Maxime Dorgères, for him alone."

She held in her horses and Maxime descended from the sleigh, protesting that he would not fail the next day on the occasion so graciously offered him. She did not wait to listen to his words of gallantry, and Maxime followed with his eyes the sleigh which glanced down the Allée des Longchamps, then turned to the right and disappeared.

He remained standing, and it took him several moments to recover himself. He seemed to have had a fall from a balloon. The episodes which had succeeded the breakfast at Tortonis crowded upon his mind,—the presentation in the armory, the incident of the bracelet, the apparition of the brunette, and the meeting with his cousin Alice. But one object stood out clearly in this mixed horizon, and that not a dark one. The countess had just made him advances so marked that he could not doubt having pleased her; and his triumphs hitherto seemed very little worth compared with the success he had just obtained without seeking it. Recalled at last

from his fit of oblivion he remembered that he had come
to the Bois to watch over his cousin.

"Quarter to three," he said, taking out his watch.
"Carnoël must be already at his post. By hurrying I
shall have time to address a few wholesome words to this
gentleman before Alice arrives on the ground." And he
began to run at full speed to this rendezvous where no
one awaited him. It was the work of a few minutes to
reach the cross-roads indicated, but to his amazement he
did not find his uncle's secretary.

"This is certainly the place," he said, taking a look
at the inscriptions on the posts, "and not the least Carnoël. It is incredible! That Alice should have to stay
here waiting for this monsieur! *Ma foi!* I am not sorry.
She will be better disposed to listen to the sermon I am
about to deliver. As for this Carnoël, he is decidedly a
coxcomb, and the first time I meet him I shall— yes,
but then I shall never meet him. He has decamped. He
concluded that there was nothing to expect from this
scene of adieux, and that the air of this country was un-
wholesome for him. The coupé he was in carried him off,
no doubt, to the North Pole. And to travel in such an
equipage, Master Robert must have wealthy friends;
friends—that is to say, accomplices."

These reflections were interrupted by the striking of a
whip, which announced the approach of the berlin.

The place was solitary and the Bois silent. Snow covered the ground, and the trees were hung with icicles.

"A sorrowful spot and a sorrowful rendezvous," muttered Alice's cousin, striking the ground with his feet to try and get some warmth in them. "Poor Alice! what a taking in when she finds me here in place of her lover!"

The carriage approached the cross-roads slowly. Mlle. Dorgères put her head out of the window, and Maxime advanced deliberately.

Alice was very pale, and her governess had an utterly confounded air that, under any other circumstances would have made Maxime smile. Joseph, too, seemed ill at ease, and tried to hide his face in the furred collar of his overcoat.

"Do not be vexed, I beg you, and listen to me."

"You come from him?" said Alice, in a trembling voice. "You have seen him?"

"I come from no one," said Maxime, trying to look both grave and sympathetic. "Like yourself, I expected to find M. de Carnoël here, and it was to him especially I wished to speak. But he has not appeared—nor will he."

"Then some misfortune has befallen him," cried Alice.

"Not that I know of; but he has probably good reasons for not showing himself. You ask if I have seen him. I saw him this morning in a beautiful carriage drawn by superb horses. He also saw me."

"And he did not get out to speak to you?"

"On the contrary, he tried to conceal himself in the depths of his luxurious equipage."

"Where could he have been going?" murmured Mlle. Dorgères.

"To take the train perhaps. Who knows?"

"It is impossible. He has declared he would not go without seeing me."

"He may have changed his mind, or — would you know my real opinion? Yes? Well, I think he does not deserve that you should sacrifice yourself for him. I will not affirm that he has done what he is accused of, but his conduct authorizes the most unfavorable conjectures. What is to be thought of a man who dares not show himself, and who rolls about in carriages to favor his concealment? Whence does he derive his resources? You will say the coupé was not his. So be it. But he was never known formerly to have these relations with millionaires. Then certainly there is ground for suspicion in this sudden change of fortune. I see in Madame Martineau's eyes that she agrees with me."

The governess, thus drawn in, felt called upon to declare her sentiments.

"My dear Alice," she said, "your cousin is right. I consented to accompany you because it was not seemly that you should come alone, and because you agreed to tell all to your father. But I hope you are enlightened now on the moral worth of M. de Carnoël, and will not compromise yourself further for his sake."

Alice did not replied. She looked alternately at Maxime and the route des Bouleaux, where no one appeared.

"Swear to me that you believe him guilty," she said*
after a long silence.

"On my word of honor, I believe it," replied the
cousin, without hesitation.

Alice turned pale as death, but she conquered her emotion, and in a firm voice replied :

"You have pronounced my sentence. I will submit
courageously. Tell Joseph to take me home."

Maxime did not wait to be told twice. Without leaving her time to reconsider so sage a resolution, he pressed
her hand affectionately, saying :

"My dear cousin, if you wish to be happy, follow the
advice of your father ; " and he cried out to the driver of
contraband : "Rue de Suresnes ; the ladies wish to return."

Joseph did not understand, but he obeyed, and the
berlin resumed its route through the solitary road.

"I have just done a good deed," thought Maxime, as
he followed with his eyes the carriage which contained
the desolate Alice. "The blow has struck home, and
now that I have a tranquil conscience on that side, I may
look after my own affairs. The brunette is perhaps still
on the lake."

So he travelled on at gymnastic pace, but it was less the
brunette than the countess whom he hoped to find. But

his race and his search proved of no avail. Madame
Sergent was no longer there, and the sleigh had disappeared. Vexed and half frozen, he was forced to retire
discomfited from his chase after beautiful women, and
finding no hack at his disposal, was compelled to proceed
on foot to the Arc de Triomphe.   Virtue on this day did
not find its reward.

CHAPTER VIII.

WHILE Maxime Dorgères was awaiting his cousin in the Bois de Boulogne, Robert de Carnoël was pacing with rapid strides the gallery in which he was confined. Since M. Borisoff had disappeared by the secret door his solitude had not been disturbed, and he had full leisure to reflect upon his situation. It was a frightful one, and the more so as there was no remedy ; for it was in the colonel's power to keep him there indefinitely, or to deliver him up to the officers of justice. And whatever course this evil-disposed Russian should determine upon, he felt that he was lost, for he would rather die than live dishonored, and he knew that Mlle. Dorgères would come to believe him guilty if he did not appear and justify himself. What would he not give for one hour of liberty !

Each minute, as it passed, bore with it his chance of safety, and the monotonous tic-tac of the clock, which measured time in his luxurious prison, recalled him incessantly to the thought that the moment for seeing Alice once more was passing forever. He would willingly have risked his life ten times over not to miss the rendezvous in the Bois de Boulogne, but he had not even the resource of attempting a perilous escape.

Escapes have been made in days of yore from the Bastile. There have even been escapes from modern prison-houses, though the art of incarcerating has made notable progress within a century. But no such thing is possible in a house arranged like that of M. Borisoff, and with a jailor who has but one prisoner whom it concerns his personal interest to guard, and who has numerous and devoted subalterns. The doors of the library were carefully locked, and undoubtedly closely watched on the outside. The windows, fifteen feet above the floor, seemed inaccessible, and if they could be reached looked out on a garden enclosed with high walls. Robert felt that it would be impossible to overcome these obstacles, and when three o'clock struck he was in the utmost despair. It was over. Alice was lost to him. What could matter to him now ? He threw himself on a divan in the corner of the fire-place—a Turkish divan arranged for sleep—and fell into the physical torpor which nearly always succeeds great moral crises. How long he remained there he never knew. It was night when the sound of opening doors aroused him from his stupor.

Two servants entered from one of the doors in the woodwork marked by movable panels, bearing a table. Robert rose suddenly, with the intention of desiring them to leave him alone, but a moment's reflection stopped him. "These men," he thought, "are obeying orders; perhaps do not understand French, and if they do, have undoubtedly been instructed not to reply if spoken to." So he concluded not to waste words on them. He was also nearly famished, having tasted nothing since the cup of chocolate in the morning. Of what. use would it be to refuse the colonel's dinner, since he must yield sooner or later to the demands of hunger, which the most violent agitations of the soul are unable to suppress? So he resigned himself, from reason as well as necessity, to a repast which a ten hours' fast had rendered desirable, and made no effort to restrain the Muscovite valets who were arranging the table in front of the fire. Whilst they were acquitting themselves of this duty, two others installed in a corner a camp-bedstead, with excellent mattresses and heavy coverlets, much more comfortable than a Russian officer is accustomed to during a campaign. They brought him also a basin, a night lamp, and a variety of other accessories. The colonel had overlooked nothing that enters into the arrangements of an elegant gentleman.

"He imagines I am here for a long time," thought the prisoner, "but he is mistaken. I shall make my way out or die."

"M. le Marquis is served," said, with perfect gravity, the man who had performed the office of landlord.

Having never borne this title his surprise was great at having himself addressed thus, but it did not suit him to ask explanations of a lackey.

The table was served in Russian fashion. By the side of his plate was a bill of fare which he did not care to study, and a bata.lion of glasses of all sizes and shapes ; in the middle of the table a silver epergne and a number of exotic side dishes, among which the national caviare played the chief part. M. de Carnoël did very little honor to the colonel's excellent cuisine, and scarcely tasted his excellent wines.

He ate merely enough to recruit his strength, and that being done arose without a word to his attendants. In a moment the table was removed. The mutes of the seraglio could not have operated more silently, and Robert found himself alone once more in the large gallery which served him for a prison.

The fire sparkled, the wax candles glistened, the water sang in the red copper kettle, and the atmosphere of the room, softened and moderated by a well-regulated air stove, was embalmed by the penetrating perfume of the tea. Nothing was wanting to this princely interior, which seemed arranged that one might sleep there and dream of hope and happiness. And Robert dreamed with bitterness that for him hope and happiness were no more.

He measured the height of the precipice which yawned at his feet, over the brink of which it seemed as if some invisible hand were urging him.

Death were better a hundred times than to live dishonored, and he called death to his relief. By insulting the colonel he might force him, if not to fight, at least to

avenge himself by killing his prisoner. As this idea oc·
curred to him, M. Borisoff entered by the secret door reserved for his own use. He appeared as calm as M. de
Carnoël was agitated, and came forward to greet him, a
smile on his lips.

"Good-evening, sir," he said, in a tone of careless
ease. "I hope you have not had to complain of my servants, and will excuse me for having left you so long
alone. I have had important business to-day, but ·I
must not forget that you, as my guest, have a claim on
my society. I am going out this evening, but shall return to have a talk with you whilst smoking a cigar
watered by a cup of tea."

Robert was pale with rage. He was looking for an
insult strong enough to reply to this insolent politeness.
In the meantime M. Borisoff established himself comfortably in an arm-chair, and set to rolling up in a piece
of rice paper a pinch of oriental snuff.

He was in full evening toilette and covered with rib-
ands and crosses.

"Yes," he went on, "I am invited to a fête given by a
financial prince, but should have remained in the corner
of the fire with you, had I not expected to meet there
persons of your acquaintance, M. Dorgères and his
charming daughter."

"You will see M. Dorgères? Do you mean to tell him
that you have drawn me into a trap through means
which a brave man would blush to employ?"

The tone was aggressive enough, and Robert counted on an irritated reply. But the colonel did not frown.

"That will depend absolutely on the result of the conversation we are to have this evening. And first, believe me, sir, it is useless to try to draw me into a quarrel with you. This is a case in which interests so grave are at stake, that I wish to control myself, and I forewarn you that I can do what I wish. To return to M. Dorgères. Though he is convinced of your guilt, that is not what concerns him at present. It matters little to him that you should be the author of the theft; it concerns him much that you should not prolong your sojourn in this city."

"Is he afraid I should return to break open his safe?" asked Robert, ironically.

"No, he fears you would compromise his daughter."

"I have already told you that I forbid you to mix the name of Mlle. Dorgères with this affair."

"You forbid me!" replied the colonel, smiling disdainfully; "I shall not take the trouble to remind you that I alone have the right to give orders here. It is enough that you should hear me to the end. Hitherto, I had but a slight acquaintance with M. Dorgères. Our relations were simply those of banker and capitalist. And it has only been in the past few hours that I have learned this reason for relieving you of your duties as secretary."

"You inspire him with great confidence, it appears," said M. de Carnoël, turning pale at hearing the colonel boast of the private confidences he had received from the father of Alice.

"An absolute confidence," replied M. Borisoff; "he has thanked me for entering into his views in conducting prudently an affair that touched him more nearly than I thought. During the days that followed your departure, hearing nothing more of you, he assumed that you had crossed the frontier, and rejoiced that the pursuit I had undertaken ended in nothing. He felt that in the interests of his daughter nothing better could be desired than this dénouement, which cut short all difficulties without anything more serious than a trifling loss of money. I confess that my reasoning was not precisely the same, as I was greatly concerned for my casket. But to pass on. It was with the greatest consternation that he heard of your return to Paris, for he guessed that it was with the hope of seeing Mlle. Dorgères again. She is only too well disposed, it appears, to grant you an interview, for my frankness obliges me to make known to you that she has not forgotten you, and persists in maintaining your innocence."

"Her father told you that!" exclaimed Robert, with an emotion he could not disguise.

"He told me so, and I have had a proof of it this very day. He told me that she went out with her governess to drive in the Bois de Boulogne. Now, it is snowing at this moment as it snowed on the road to Moscow in 1812, and I asked myself what a young girl could go to the

Bois for at such a time, when I remembered that this morning you requested the liberty of going out for a few hours. It was not difficult to guess that the cause of your anxiety was that you might have an interview with Mlle. Dorgères. Was I wrong?"

"No."

"Very well. You wish to marry her, and you are right, for she is charming and will be very rich. And in order that you may do so, what is wanting? Simply to prove to her father that you are innocent of the act imputed to you; that you have been unjustly accused. The day on which he shall be convinced that you have been the victim of an odious calumny, he will hold himself bound to repair his wrongs toward you, and he has but one means of repairing them, that is to accord you the hand of his daughter."

"What are you driving at?" asked Robert.

"To let you know that it depends on me to turn this dream into reality."

"How, if you please?"

"Before answering, I must remind you that your reputation in the world is still unsullied. The theft is known only to three or four persons, who are all interested in its concealment. If, then, M. de Carnoël should resume his functions as secretary after a brief absence, no one would be astonished to learn that he was going to marry Mlle. Dorgères. It would not be the first case of an alliance between nobility and finance."

" You are mistaken. M. Dorgères has on this point
fixed ideas."

" Say rather prejudices which would yield to the necessity of making you an atonement. I answer for that,
and I conclude that if this evening I should say to him : ' I
have found the man who stole my casket and forced him
to return it, and this man is not your former secretary—' "

" You would do that ? "

" Why not ? Let me finish. If I added: ' For motives
personal to myself I do not want to denounce this man,
and beg to have the question set at rest ; but we have
suspected some one wrongfully whom it is incumbent on
us to indemnify for the injustice we have done him.' If I
held this language to the father of Mlle. Alice, what, think
you, would be his answer ? "

" I cannot tell, but I know I should have no right to
expect from you an act of justice which would be contrary to all your previous course toward me."

" I am, however, ready to act and speak thus. I will
even go so far as to return to M. Dorgères the fifty thousand francs that have been stolen. He will accept them,
for I will affirm that I have obtained from the thief a
complete restitution. Yes, I will do all that upon certain conditions."

" That is what I expected. What do you claim ? "

" That you should tell me where to find the casket of
which I have been robbed, if not by you, by those whom
you can point out."

"Still this infamous accusation!"

"Observe, sir, that I do not exact of you to return the casket. I do not believe it to be in your power. The persons interested in obtaining possession of it have put it in a place of safety,—have, perhaps, destroyed it. But these persons—I wish to know them. Give me their names, and so soon as I have ascertained that you have told me correctly, I shall seek M. Dorgères, and I promise you on my honor to repeat to him what I have just said to you."

"To be prepared to name them to you, it is necessary that I should have been their accomplice."

"Accomplice is a foul word. Listen. Shall I make known to you frankly my understanding of this affair in which you are implicated? A woman is the cause of all."

"A woman!"

"*Mon Dieu*, yes, as always! You have in France a mode of speech whose justice is striking: 'Look for the woman.' I do look for her and you can tell me where to find her. Having gone so far I see no reason for concealing that the papers that have been abstracted were State papers. I am connected, as you know, with Russian diplomacy, and am intrusted with a mission which consists in watching intrigues carried on in foreign countries by the enemies of my government. These enemies belong to a sect which disdains no means for the attainment of its end, and this end is to wipe out all social institutions. They shrink from neither theft nor murder, and it would not be surprising did they attempt my life, for I incommode them, and they are numerous in Paris. That is why I am prepared for anything ; why I take the precautions which you must have observed since you have been my guest. For the same reason I deposited at my banker's documents of which they knew the importance and were bent upon destroying. But they are admirably informed, and the precaution I took has turned against me.

"Amongst them are women, the best born, wealthiest and most charming. The sect has recruits from our middle classes, and even from among our nobility. But they are everywhere,—in Paris as well as elsewhere, and perhaps even more than elsewhere. And I can tell you what has happened. You have been the lover of one of these sirens. Oh! I do not suppose that you are so now. I know you to be sincerely in love with Mlle. Dorgères, but a former mistress always retains some sway over the man who has loved her. You have been carried away by beautiful phrases about tyranny and liberty, and have finally been led to favor the execution of a project whose success would promote the triumph of a holy cause and save the unfortunates inscribed upon the list of proscriptions contained in my casket. I do not blame you. Many others would have succumbed, and it was no crime in your eyes to give up the secret of the word with which the safe was locked, and the model of the key. For I admit you did not operate yourself. The fifty thousand francs were taken by this creature with an object that is plain enough. She knew you were going away that same evening, as she hoped, never to reappear, and she meant you should be accused to divert suspicion from her, and that it should not be believed politics had any part in the theft. She did more, as I am persuaded. It was she who, on learning that you were still in Paris, sent you the fifty thousand francs in the name of an anonymous friend. It was unpleasant to her to keep them—these ladies have queer scruples—and in compelling you to receive them, she compromised you still more. You see, sir, that you cannot be considered guilty; you have been weak, that is all; such is my conviction. If I thought you had stolen I should not treat you as I have done. And you must understand that your only honorable and profitable course is to confess all. Tell me the name of this woman, and in three months you will be the happy husband of Mlle. Dorgères."

"Sir," replied de Carnoël, looking steadily at the colonel, "you have much imagination, but the romance you have just invented will not have the anticipated effect. I do not know the woman who took your casket, if it be a woman, and I have nothing more to say."

"Then," murmured the colonel, as if to himself, "Mlle. Alice Dorgères will marry M. Jules Vignory."

"Vignory!" repeated de Carnoël. "What do you mean?"

"I mean that M. Dorgères has himself made known to me that for a long time it has been his plan to give his daughter to his cashier, and that he was much irritated at the discovery that you had made yourself pleasing to Mlle. Alice ; so it need not surprise you that he dismissed you abruptly."

"It is not that which astonishes me, but Jules Vignory was my friend. Had he loved her he would not have concealed it from me, and he is too loyal to try to supplant me."

"Sir," said the colonel, smiling, "you are at an age which cherishes such illusions. I thought, however, you knew men better."

"Do you assert that Vignory has betrayed me ?"

"No ; on the contrary, he defended you, and his merit in doing so was the greater, as suspicion might have rested on him. But because he has done so is no reason why he should not have been captivated, like yourself, by the charms of his patron's daughter. The sun shines for all. Mlle. Dorgères is ravishing, and the young man has eyes. He loves her, and has loved her long. Why should he have confided to you a secret which he scarcely acknowledged to himself, for he loved without hope ? Why should he have confided it to you—to you, who were beloved ?"

"And he told it to you, whom he scarcely knew ? No, no, it is impossible !"

"I did not say so. Here is what passed. M. Dorgères

is a man who goes right to the point, and he said to his cashier : 'You suit me ; will you marry my daughter?' After some hesitation, Vignory confessed that for two years he had secretly adored Mlle. Alice. You may guess that having obtained this avowal M. Dorgères had little difficulty in removing the scruples of his clerk. He announced that from that time he made him his partner, and left it to him to gain the good-will of his daughter. You may well suppose Vignory did not say no. There is the situation. What think you of it?"

"It seems to me," said Robert, in a husky voice, "that I have nothing to hope from the future, and that had I even committed the crime of which I am accused I should have no interest in accepting the odious bargain you propose."

"Pardon me ! You forget that did I prove your innocence to M. Dorgères the situation would change instantly. Only it must be done quickly. The feeling upon which you may count now will grow cold. Every day as it passes will diminish your chances, and when it is too late you will repent bitterly that you did not follow my counsel."

"No, for you counsel me to an infamy."

"Is it that which hinders you ? Do you fear to deliver up to the Russian government the woman who has stolen my papers? Even should she meet the punishment she deserves, your scruples would still be exaggerated, for it is this woman who has ruined you. But remember we are in France, where I can do nothing against her. My rôle is simply a defensive one. These people are formidable, and I ask you to aid me to defend myself. You can have no interest in sustaining them, since you are not their compatriot. Now, do I need to promise that they shall never know you have pointed them out to me? I swear to you that they shall not, whatever happens. I am prudent professionally."

"Enough, sir," cried Robert. "I have consented to hear you to the end, but if I knew the secret you wish to extort from me I would not betray it; but I do not know it, and should you put me to the torture you will hear nothing more."

"Is that your last word?"

"Yes."

"Then you have yourself only to blame, whatever happens."

"What worse can happen? I am your prisoner, but cannot remain so, for sooner or later you must deliver me to my judges. They will examine me, and to them I shall reply."

"Then," said M. Borisoff, with an ominous smile, "you fancy I shall restore you to liberty some day? You forget that in confining you to my house I have committed several infractions of the laws of your country, and that I have too much cause for circumspection to expose myself to the danger of having to render an account of my conduct to the commissary of police."

"Do you mean to kill me?" asked Robert, looking the colonel steadily in the face.

"For shame!" replied M. Borisoff, disdainfully; "such expedients are not employed by gentlemen, and I pride myself on a nobility as ancient as your own. Besides, I represent the Russian government, my house is Russian territory, and the penalty of death is abolished in Russia."

"You have replaced it by the knout," said Robert, in irony.

"Do not laugh. It is in my power to make use of this means to extort a confession."

"Try it!"

"To what purpose? I have one less repugnant and more certain. I shall keep you here until you have decided to speak."

"And if I persist in silence?"

"Then I shall send you to Siberia. I have all the means of doing so at my disposal. A post-chaise constructed expressly for the purpose, servants certain to watch over you during the passage, passports at sight of which no French or German authority would inspect your carriage. You would reach your destination, having seen no one nor been seen by any, and would never be heard of more. But before resorting to this extremity I wish to leave you time for reflection. I give you a month's respite."

"Neither in a month nor in ten years will you obtain anything from me."

"I shall not push the experiment so far," replied the colonel, quietly. "A month will suffice. You will then have no further interest to confess in order to buy my interest with M. Dorgères, for his daughter will be lost to you. I shall have used every means to open your eyes. If you insist upon throwing yourself over the brink of a precipice, at the border of which I have tried to stop you, I shall have nothing to reproach myself with."

"Nothing but an infamy."

"You have told me so already, and your insults have not reached me. I still hope that time will bring wiser ideas, and that you will decide before it is too late. I can follow, step by step, the progress which your rival and friend, Jules Vignory, is making in the regards of Mlle. Alice, and shall take care to bring you an exact report. In the present state of affairs I shall keep silence as to what I know, and let M. Dorgères think of you as he pleases. It is likely that, hearing nothing more of you, he will be reassured as to the danger to which your presence in Paris exposes his daughter. And he may well be, for Mlle. Dorgères must resent your non-appearance at the rendezvous. In order to pardon this offence she would need to know that you were not free at three o'clock, and it is not I who will tell her."

"Go on," said M. de Carnoël, bitterly. "Invent tortures more odious than the knout. You shall not weary out my courage."

"I have done," replied the colonel, unmoved. "There

remains only one point to be touched upon. The woman who has robbed me and whom you hope to save by your obstinate silence, will not escape me, you may rest assured. My agents are already on her track, and the sacrifice you are so infatuated as to make of your honor and your liberty will avail nothing. I leave you, for I fear to miss M. Dorgères and his charming daughter, whom it is important for me to meet, that I may bring you tidings of them to-morrow—and of M. Vignory who, I think, will accompany them to the ball."

After this cruelly ironical peroration M. Borisoff saluted his prisoner with an inclination of the head, and disappeared as he came.

Robert made no attempt to detain him. What could he say to this fair-spoken brute, who had been putting him cruelly to the torture for an hour. He had no hope of softening or convincing him, and did not care to prolong an interview so exquisitely painful. His strength was wellnigh exhausted. Anger, which had sustained him during this unequal contest, began to give place to profound discouragement. His pride was not conquered, but bitterly did he realize his helplessness, and he had not even the resource of yielding to that torpor of despair which brings to the unhappy the relief of oblivion. Every word of the colonel sunk into his heart and festered there like a poisoned arrow. And of all the wounds inflicted by this pitiless tormentor the most grievous was the one he received in learning that Jules Vignory was his rival.

Vignory, his best, his only friend, loved Alice and wished to marry her. And the odious Borisoff had not lied when he affirmed that M. Dorgères supported the pretensions of his cashier. Vignory fulfilled all the necessary conditions, for he was born for business and was not guilty of a title. He had, moreover, qualities to please a young girl. He was good-looking, young, intelligent, gentle, modest. And no one accused him—Vignory—no one attributed to him any base act; his honor was unscathed, and in taking on him the defence of M. de Carnoël he had given proof of an uncommon generosity.

"I owe him a debt of gratitude," murmured Robert, sorrowfully, "and it is by him I shall lose Alice, for why should she refuse to obey her father? My absence will release her from her pledge to me. She will cease to believe I have been calumniated—she believes it no longer now—she despises me."

He buried his face in his hands and wept. Around him the silence was profound, and nothing indicated that the colonel's servants would come to disturb his solitude on this night which was approaching—this night which Alice would pass at the ball. "I shall get out of here or die," he said, between his teeth. "If I find no other means of escape, I shall set fire to this cursed house."

The means were at his disposal, for a bright fire was burning in the vast chimney piece. But this violent measure would not save him. To all appearance his jailors were keeping watch; fire does not burn without noise or smoke, and they would not fail to discover it before it could open a passage way for their prisoner. So he quickly renounced this idea born of despair, and set to examining, more carefully than he had hitherto done, the gallery in which he was confined. A bright light was diffused through the room by means of wax candelabra; but the lofty ceilings were lost in shadow, and on raising his head he could see that the moonlight was streaming through the windows above an immense book-case. There were three, disposed like the windows of an artist's studio; each contained three large sashes which could only be raised by the aid of a peculiar mechanism. M. de Carnoël had no hope of accomplishing that, nor did he for the present think of breaking them; but could he succeed in reaching them, he might at least dis-cover whether they looked out on any practicable road. On arriving at M. Borisoff's, Robert had had no reason to study the approaches to this habitation, through which the obliging M. Briare had conducted him, not dreaming of being detained there by force. The most he could re-call was that he had entered a garden; what it concerned him now to know was, whether this garden extended under the library. Following this idea, he took up a light and began an inspection. At one end of the book-case he found a winding stairway. Mounting these steps he arrived at a cornice with a balustrade, ornamented with antique statuary. The cornice was on a level with the windows, and Robert set down the light, that he

might take a look outside. He recognized the garden
he had seen, planted with large trees and surrounded by
high walls. A sheet of snow extended as far as the eye
could reach. No footprints were visible, and no dark
figure was defined on the white ground. Robert concluded that the colonel's valets did not move about on
that side of the house, but they were probably mounting
guard immediately under the windows. He measured
with his eye the distance from the ground, thirty feet at
least, that is, much more than would be needed to break
one's neck. Then there was another object still more
impassible—the wall which separated the garden from another garden, or more probably a court, for above this
wall no trees were visible. But looking attentively, he
discovered on its top an object that was not motionless,
and he soon discerned the head and shoulders of a man.
What was he doing there? How did he get there? He
placed his lamp on the cornice, and his person masked
the light so he could watch unobserved for some explanation of this singular apparition. "It must be a spy of
the colonel's," was his first thought. But examining this
supposition further, he felt disposed to reject it. A sentinel would not be stationed on a prominent point, but
concealed in some obscure corner. Moreover, there was
no ladder on the inside of the wall, and the man leaning
on his elbow must have reached there from without. For
what purpose? Most probably, for theft. "No matter,
I am going to make him a signal. I shall risk nothing

in letting this prowler know that there is some one behind these high walls. No doubt, he will immediately
disappear, but if by any chance he has not come here to
steal, who knows what may happen?" Having come to
this conclusion, M. de Carnoël took the light which he
had placed behind him and raised it above his head. The
light of the wax candles was rendered still more visible,
from the fact that the moonlight, which streamed over
the wall, left the windows in darkness. He therefore
felt sure that the signal would be perceived, and waited
to see the man suddenly vanish. But the man remained,
and even raised himself a little on his elbows as if seeking a more convenient position to examine this light
which suddenly appeared before his eyes. Encouraged
by this first result of his manœuvre, Robert proceeded to
make a more decided demonstration. Holding his light
at arm's length, he moved it slowly up and down to indicate to the observer that this luminous telegraph was
meant for him. The design was understood, for the person raised himself on his wrists, placing himself astride
the summit of the wall and turning his face toward the
lighted window. M. de Carnoël had now a full view of
him, and he appeared surprisingly small, almost like a
child. He could not distinguish his features in the distance, but saw that he wore a blouse and flat cap.

The climber raised his two arms in the air and brought
them quickly back to his breast, which pantomime
seemed to say : "Is it to me you are making a signal?"

M. de Carnoël replied by waving his light twice and then bringing it to his head. The movement was evidently understood, for the child put one hand over his eyes as if shading them, and stretched his neck to get a better view. The heart of the prisoner beat fast. He had ceased already to look upon this urchin as the emissary of a band of thieves, and began almost to hope he came on the part of some friend. What friend? He had none now, if it were true that the only one who had remained faithful to him in misfortune, sought to supplant him in the heart of Alice. Besides, who could know that Robert de Carnoël was Col. Borisoff's prisoner? After looking at him attentively, the child raised himself, took off his cap and bowed.

"He must have recognized me," said Robert, in a low voice, "but where can he have seen me? One thing is certain, he has come here with no evil intentions, but what will he do now? Ah! he is going,—he puts his left leg over the wall, at the same time makes me an adieu, which is very expressive; it seems to say: 'Make yourself easy; I shall return.'"

M. de Carnoël was at this point, when he saw glimmer on the breast of the child three rows of brass buttons which, in consequence of the mysterious lad's change of position, were suddenly reflected in the moonlight.

"Georget!" he exclaimed, "why did I not think of it sooner?"

At the instant when he made this discovery, the daring

lad disappeared suddenly behind the wall ; it might have been supposed a trickster on the street had drawn him with a cord. The piece was played, and the only spectator whom it had drawn thought only of leaving his place. He first extinguished the candle which had burned there only too long already, and would infallibly have been perceived by the colonel's men if they had made the round of the garden. So he groped his way back to the winding staircase, descended with a light step and seated himself before the fireplace. The fire was still burning, the water was still singing in the kettle, the lamps of old Saxon porcelain still shed a soft light over the table filled with books and cigar boxes. No one had entered the library during his long excursion which had proved so successful.

He soon forgot the proximity of his jailors, and began to reflect seriously upon the singular apparition of Georget. He recalled that in the morning of his arrival, he had noticed the boy playing on the sidewalk of the Rue de Vigny, and his astonishment at the meeting with his patron's ex-secretary. M. de Carnoël had always been kind to the little foot-boy of the banking house. He liked his bright face and odd little ways, and Georget never lost an opportunity to show his partiality for the young secretary; it was, therefore, not extraordinary that he should interest himself in the fate of a protector whom he loved. But how could he have guesssed what had happened after the gate

closed on Robert and the so-called M. Briare ? It was
quite easy to conjecture that, urged by a feeling of
curiosity, he had been led to make the discovery that
this magnificent residence was the abode of the Russian colonel whom he had seen at M. Dorgères' bank ;
but by what prodigy of sagacity had he discovered
that M. de Carnoël had not returned, and conjectured
that he was retained by force ? And on whose part
had he come ? It could not be supposed he had himself conceived the project of rescuing the prisoner, or
that he proposed to execute it alone. He had made
a gesture which seemed to signify, "Count on me—
or on others."

Unable to solve these problems, and overwhelmed by
an uncertainty more difficult to bear than actual misfortune, Robert sank into an arm-chair, and was lost in despairing reflections. He took a bitter pleasure in torturing himself with the thought of Alice in the midst of
the fête, where, at this very moment, she was listening to
the perfidious compliments of Borisoff, or smiling upon
Jules Vignory.

"If she loved me still she would not have consented
to accompany her father to this ball," he thought, sadly.
But gradually these cruel images vanished, and oblivion
followed upon this unnatural excitement. After such
repeated mental shocks, his physical nature claimed her
rights ; he undressed and lay down upon the bed that
had been prepared for him, and fell into a profound.

sleep which gave him back his strength ; and when he opened his eyes the sun was lighting up the windows of the gallery. He had finished his toilette when the door at the farther end opened suddenly, and M. Briare appeared.

"What do you want?" asked M. de Carnoël, in a tone little encouraging.

"First to know whether you have slept well," replied the steward ; and, as the prisoner preserved a disdainful silence, M. Briare added : "And also to save you the trouble of searching for your pocket-book."

Robert made a movement toward the coat, in the pocket of which he had left all his papers and all his fortune.

"You will not find it. It is not there."

"You have stolen it while I slept."

"Not exactly. Col. Borisoff has no intention to appropriate its contents, as you know well. But he has commissioned me to take charge of them conditionally, as also of certain letters, amongst others, one in which an anonymous friend announces that he returns you fifty thousand francs which he owed to your father."

Robert turned pale. The blow had struck home, and he realized all its bearings. This letter was his justification. It established the fact that the money had been sent him by a debtor of his father, or at least that he had been made to believe so, and it was now in Col.

Borisoff's power to suppress the only evidence he could bring forward in his defence.

"So," he said, angrily, "you have taken advantage of my sleep to rob me. It is what might have been expected, and I shall not lower myself by complaining to you, who are but a valet, but shall lose no time in acquainting your master with my opinion of this new infamy."

"You will not see him to-day," the steward replied, unmoved. "He is a little indisposed, but has ordered me to hold myself at your disposition, and if you have need of me you have only to ring. Everything is at your command till it shall please you to leave the house. Tell my master what he wishes to know, and the doors will open to you immediately."

Robert dismissed him by a silent gesture. "Yes, I shall leave it," thought Robert, as the steward left the room, backwards, "but not on the shameful conditions this miserable Borisoff would impose."

CHAPTER IX.

THE VARIÉTÉS.

IN spite of the snow which had fallen so suddenly in Paris, the theatres opened their doors to such courageous spectators as the vigor of the cold did not retain by the corner of the fire. Maxime Dorgères was not among those who brave with a like indifference dog-days and freezing ; nevertheless, Maxime made his appearance at the Variétiés toward nine o'clock. After his expedition to the Bois de Boulogne, he had no call more urgent than to return home, and he reached there half frozen after a hack ride of fifty minutes. It took him a longer time to get warmed than it had done to ride from the Arc de Triomphe to Rue de Châteaudun, so that five o'clock struck before he had thought of dressing to go out again. The sound of the clock recalled to him that he had intended on leaving the countess to pay a visit to Jules Vignory, and recount to him some of the occurrences of this eventful day.

But when he reached Rue de Suresnes, the offices were closed and Vignory had gone to dinner.

He obtained this information from Joseph, whom he

found accidentally at the porter's lodge, and who mentioned that his master was going this evening to a ball with Mlle. Alice. Here was good news. Alice, then, was consoled, and all was going well.

He did not, however, relinquish the search after Vignory, but on arriving at his house in Rue d' Aguesseau, was informed by the porter that his lodger had returned to dress, saying that he should dine in town and go to a ball afterward. This information completed Maxime's satisfaction. If Vignory was to dine out, it was certainly with his patron ; if he was going to the ball, it was with Alice.

"Come," he said joyously ; "my little cousin is cured more quickly than I thought, and I have the satisfaction of having contributed toward this marvellous cure. I have done a good deed and earned the right to amuse myself this evening. But how ? At the club the dinner is good, but nine times out of ten the members bore you to death. I am going to the Café Anglais and imbibe inspiration in an old bottle of Château-Latour."

So he went, and the Bordeaux wine had the effect of making everything appear rose-colored, and when he went out, the boulevard, covered with snow, appeared to him charming. It did not, however, take him long to find out that the sidewalk, swept by the north wind, was not tenable ; and being at the door of the Variétiés, he entered, rather for the sake of getting under shelter than to see the play, which was not a new one. The house

was poorly filled, and he had no difficulty in obtaining a
seat in the front row of arm-chairs.

It was during the first *entr'acte* that he went in, but the
spectators were not taking advantage of the pause to cir-
culate through the passages or in the green-room, so he
was able to pass them in review at his leisure, and was
not surprised that he recognized no familiar faces. He
saw only women in country toilettes, and men devoid of
elegance. No one to speak to, not a pretty face toward
which to direct an opera glass. Maxime began to ask
himself whether he should have patience to wait for the
end, when his attention was attracted toward a box to the
right of the stage.

"That is a cackling that could only be made by that
turkey hen Delphine," he thought. And in looking he
ascertained the presence of this blonde with her friends
Cora ·and Bertha Verrier, who, on perceiving Maxime,
made an expressive pantomine, offering him the vacant
seat in their box.

The evening before he would not have disdained this
opportunity to enliven a dull evening, but within a few
hours past he had become converted and did not care to
attach himself to irregulars. These, especially, had not
the charm of novelty ; he knew by heart the jests and
current jokes with which they graced their conversation,
and contenting himself with a salutation of the hand,
turned his back on them without ceremony.

The box on the same side with himself, nearly touching him, was so placed with regard to him that it was difficult to ascertain whether it was vacant or occupied by persons who did not care to show themselves. Leaning forward to get a better view, he caught a glimpse of a woman's shoulders leaning against the partition of the box, and the vision of a profile which looked seductive. His state of mind was not such as to lead him to overlook the outlines of a pretty head, and he waited patiently till the lady should allow it to be revealed. Evidently she was not alone, for she suffered herself to be eclipsed now and then in order to speak to some one behind, a man to all appearance. This discovery calmed Maxime's ardor, as he did not care to be casting glances, too pronounced, in the direction of a tête-à-tête, conjugal or otherwise. So he resumed his position, leaving the pair to their isolation, and his eyes turned once more toward the box containing the demoiselles of the quarter world, when he observed the little Bertha making signs, but more complicated ones, in his direction. She beckoned to him with one hand, and with the other pointed to the box on the left. Evidently she meant to say .

"Come, I wish to show you something that will interest you, which you cannot see where you are."

"Can it be," he said to himself, beginning to scent an amusing adventure, "that I should recognize the couple that is niched here so near me ? Bertha Verrier is an insufferable prattler, but she doesn't want shrewdness, and knows the entire universe. *Ma foi !* I am going to see. I am bored to death here."

And as Maxime never hesitated when a folly was in question, he was soon traversing the circular passage way that ended in the box on the right.

"Here you are at last," said Bertha Verrier. "You are very lucky."

"Do you know that you are very disagreeable?" chimed in Delphine. "To turn your back on three women who were calling you, was the height—"

"The height of discretion, mesdemoiselles. I was afraid of incommoding you."

"Come, now," said the brunette Cora, "you know there are four seats here; the fourth is not in sight of the acting, it is true, but it is not the actors nor even the actresses we want to show you."

"What, then?"

"You do not deserve to be shown anything," said Bertha. "I take the trouble to beckon to you graciously, and you do not stir. I have a great mind to let you beg me to teach you to be less supercilious."

"Oh, I know, my dear friend! It is about the woman who is hiding there."

"Do you recognize her? Would you like my glasses?"

"What is the use? At this moment there is a total eclipse."

"Oh, she will reappear. Examine, meanwhile, the statellite who has just shown himself."

Maxime saw a man resting his elbows on the box who

wakened within him a vague recollection. He was a a huge fellow with broad shoulders and a forbidding appearance, and unbending as a lord whose native pride is supported on a respectable number of millions.

"Is it that I may admire this princely stranger that you graciously offer me a place at your side?" asked Maxime.

"No," replied Bertha. "He has outline enough, but is, I think, very ugly."

"Do you know him?" asked Maxime.

"I! not at all. It is the first time I have seen him."

"Then it is the woman you know?"

"Perhaps."

"And I, also, no doubt."

"Who is she?"

"Guess."

"How can I guess? I have not even seen the end of her nose."

"And the nose of the gentleman does not recall anything?"

"Nothing at all."

"Good! I suspected as much."

"Why?"

"Because I always thought she was not married. It is plain that that great mustached fellow is not her husband, for you would know if he were. You visit at her house, I presume?"

"My dear children," exclaimed Maxime, "if you continue to speak in enigmas I am going."

"I ought to let you go, but I am a good girl and cannot permit you to languish any longer," replied Bertha Verrier, laughing. "Have you your bracelet still, the one you wore on your arm the other evening?"

"Yes."

"Then you are still in love with her who gave it to you?"

"More than ever," replied Maxime, more concerned than he wished to appear. "Why the question, my dear friend?"

"Do you remember that I promised to name the princess who made you this pretty present?"

"Perfectly; and nothing prevents you now from following up the information you were about to give me when Dr. Villagos arrived."

"Are you very anxious for it?"

"Exceedingly."

"I warn you that I shall dispel some illusions."

"Proceed, nevertheless."

"Know, then, I have had the honor of supping with the lady of your thoughts—at Peters'—my good friend."

"You!"

"Yes, me. Your astonishment is not polite, but I pardon you. You are still believing you have made a conquest in the great world, and I—am not of that world. But neither is your adored one, I answer for it.

Would you like to have the particulars ? Then listen. The lady in question was, a month ago, the friend of a foreigner, who was the acquaintance of a foreigner who was my friend. The phrase is a little complicated, but it expresses perfectly the situation. Now, it happened one evening, at this same Variétés Theatre, these two foreigners, who came separately, each with his own, met in the green-room and arranged a square party, which took place after the play at Peters' restaurant. I vex you by telling you this, but you would hear it."

"And I still wish you to tell me all,—who she is—what she said—her name."

"You are superb ! You know better than I, for she did not think proper to tell me. It must be Carmen or Dolores, for she has a Spanish air though she speaks French perfectly. What she said ? Whatever might be expected at a supper. She is gay and not the least haughty or prudish, but she has no private confidences for the women she meets. Try as I might, I couldn't find out where she came from nor what sort of life she leads. I suspect she knows chiefly Russians, Turks, Wallachians, and other birds of passage like the two messieurs at our supper. Mine left two days after for Moldavia, and I have never heard of him since."

"But before he left he must have spoken to you of his friend's mistress ? "

"*Ma foi !* no, and never meeting with her I thought no more of her till you recalled her to mind with your bracelet. It was at this supper she showed it to me. A stone was wanting which she wished to replace, and she asked me the address of a jeweller. I gave her that of yours, Rue de la Paix, you know."

"And you have never seen her again?"

"Never till this evening. She is there in the box opposite."

"Impossible!"

"It is true, my dear. I have excellent eyes, and have seen her as plainly as I see you. Unfortunately, she saw me, and dived immediately. She doesn't wish to cultivate my acquaintance. I might lay a wager she was afraid I should pay her a visit in her box and inquire for the predecessor of the gentleman with the red mustache. She is mistaken. It is not I who would speak of an old lover before a new."

"Then that great devil who holds his head so high over there is not the same as—"

"The foreigner of the supper? No, my dear friend. The other having taken flight, the lady has not thought proper to advise you of the change. Now, do you owe me a grudge for having told you the truth?"

"On the contrary, I thank you. But you understand I want to get a sight of the lady. Now, she does not betray the slightest intention of showing herself. I must leave you, therefore, for the purpose of watching over the box in which she is concealed."

Maxime lost no time in making his adieux to Bertha

and her friends. and, passing through the passage way, regained his seat in all haste. The curtain was about to rise. He selected a seat in the front row not too far from the place of exit, and near enough to the box to be ready for any event. There was no change in the position of affairs in the box of the unknown. The screen which sheltered this mysterious person was still raised, the cavalier with the huge shoulders still turned his back toward him. But he had engaged in a conversation with the lady that must be very interesting, for he leaned over to speak to her more closely.

In the meantime, Maxime, keeping a sharp lookout, endeavored to arrange his ideas. That what he had just heard was true, there could be no doubt. Bertha had no interest in hoaxing him or inventing this story of this supper at Peters'. That the lady led this sort of life and changed frequently her protector, was no cause for surprise. But what astounded him was that she should be at the theatre fifteen days after undergoing a mutilation that would keep any honest woman in bed for two months.

"She must have the devil in her," he thought, "and her companion must be very stupid if he does not observe that his belle has lost a hand. But he was there when she lost it; this is the accomplice. I hold them now, and shall not let them slip if I have to climb up behind their carriage. I shall not be long in disposing of these people. I have had enough of police business, and shall spend my time better now with the countess."

While monologuing thus, Maxime, for an instant, lost sight of the box. One closes the eyes a little while reflecting seriously. When he opened them again all was changed. The man had disappeared, the screen was lowered, but the woman was no longer there.

"*Diable!* they are gone, or they are going! Oh, oh! they will not get off like that; I will catch up with them."

And he made precipitately, like some one frantic, for the exit, to the annoyance of the peaceable spectators, by whom he hustled without asking permission.

He reached the passage way just as the monsieur was donning a superb furred coat which the officer in charge had just handed him. He paid no attention to Maxime, but the idea occurred to him more strongly than before that it was not the first time he had seen this bony figure, yellow as parchment, this huge red mustache, these hollow eyes and bushy eyebrows.

"Where, *diable!* have I met him? But it doesn't matter; the lady remains, and now that she is not watched, will certainly show herself. Why should she hide? She doesn't know that I have her bracelet."

He regained his stall, not without occasioning grumbling on the part of the spectators whom he disarranged anew, when recollection occurred to him suddenly.

"That man resembles, feature for feature, the Cerberus who shut the door in my face this morning in Rue Jouffroy! If it is he, it will be strange indeed, and stranger still if the woman is—but we shall see."

What he first saw on taking his seat was Bertha Verrier, who pointed to the box and seemed to say :

"What do you wait for now that the place is free ?" .

He turned quickly, and could not repress an exclamation which drew forth some prolonged eh-eh-ehs.

Without a screen, in front of the box, in full light, he saw the marvel of the Rink. He could not believe his eyes ; yet verily it was she ! This brunette with the golden complexion was unrivalled, and was not of the number of those whom one can mistake or confound with other women.

"Impossible !" said the stupefied Maxime, "Bertha is crazy, the thief is one-handed and this one has two hands, at least if one be not artificial, surgery has made such progress—but no, I dream—she makes use of the left with ease ; presently I shall examine more closely these hands that were pressed within mine the other night. I shall watch, and if she stirs I will be in the corridor before her. Whether the bracelet is hers or not I must speak to her, for I have much to say." The lady appeared unconscious that her knight of the Rink was there and watching her.

She wore a princess dress of black satin trimmed with black tulle and jet ; two large pearls in her ears, and one enormous diamond which sparkled on her dress, were her only ornaments ; and beside them the turquoise bracelet would have made a mean figure. It was a ruinous simplicity which revealed at once the good taste of the wearer and the wealth that was lavished upon her. With a distrait air she passed in review the spectators, and when she directed her glass toward the opposite box, Bertha Verrier rose up the better to observe the bow she would receive. But it did not come.

"*Parbleu!*" thought Maxime, "she ignores her, she doesn't consider her good company, and when she comes to me she will have quite a different reason. My face will recall recollections she will not care to renew. That moment I will hold myself in readiness to dart."

The brunette continued to inspect the hall deliberately, but on a word dropped by one of the actors, which created laughter, she lowered her glass to look at the laughers with her eyes—eyes which met those of Maxime. It was a critical moment, but it did not pass as he expected. Madame Sergent bowed with a gracious smile.

"Good," he said to himself as he returned the smile. "I understand, she expects to make me give her the bracelet. She wishes to renew the first attempt and the opportunity seems a good one, as her monsieur is not here. She does not suspect that I know the jewel belongs either to herself or to one of her friends. But a man well warned is worth two, and if a battle is to come it is not I will have to pay the costs."

After the smile came a movement of the head, the most engaging, which there was no mistaking. She invited Maxime to join her in her box, and it may be believed he did not wait for a second invitation.

"Ah, Madame or Mademoiselle Sergent, you wish to lay immediate siege to my weak heart. You will see that I know how to defend myself, and the attack will cost you dear."

In an instant he was on his feet making for the door; but this new sortie was not effected without difficulty. The chairs had filled, little by little, with spectators, who this time were not content with murmuring against Maxime's repeated comings and goings. There was a general concert of complaint in which the parquet joined, though it was not interested, since Maxime only walked over the gentlemen seated in the front row of the orchestra. The play was interrupted; on all sides the cry was: "Put him out," and the police were near intervening. But the turbulent nephew of the sage M. Dorgères received without stumbling this shower of interpellations, and went on his way despising the abuse of the brawlers at the end of the hall, and saying in a low voice to those he was compelled to walk over: "If my apologies are not sufficient, I will send you my card."

The recalcitrants ended by yielding and allowing him a passage. The door of the box was opened to him immediately; he glided silently in and found the beautiful skater plunged in a semi-obscurity. She had raised the screen to protect her from the footlights and the public gaze.

"At last I have found you again," she said, extending her hand to Maxime, who felt very conscious as he pressed it that this was not a hand of wood.

"You were seeking me, then?" he said. "I fancied it was I who was seeking you."

"Then we were in quest of each other. And now that chance has brought us together let us have a talk. We have, as I think, much to say to each other."

"Much with which to reproach each other. You were fooling me when you announced your intention to leave Paris for a fortnight."

"Were you rash enough, in spite of my prohibition, to knock this morning at the door of the house in Rue Jouffroy?"

"Did you know that?"

"Did I know it? Have I not been subjected to frightful scenes in consequence? I have been nearly ill."

"Really? I thought I saw you toward three in the Bois de Boulogne."

"That is my mode of treatment. But since you saw me why did you not speak to me?"

"Because I was not alone."

"That is to say, you were with a lady."

"You were a few moments ago with a man."

"Alas, yes!"

"Why alas? Does he bore you, this monsieur?"

"To death."

"Then why do you suffer it?"

"Because I cannot help it."

"He is your husband?"

"Oh, no, indeed! I would not marry him if he gave me by a marriage contract all his millions."

"Well—but—if he is not your husband, by what right does he impose himself upon you?"

The lady suppressed a strong inclination to laugh, and hiding her face behind her fan, said:

"Do you ask me that seriously?"

"Very seriously."

"Then, on the evening when you escorted me home, you took me for a *femme du monde?*"

"You have the air, the manners and language of one. Besides you told me so. I had no difficulty in believing you."

"You are very flattering, but confess you know very well what to think on that point."

"I confess that just now a certain demoiselle was boasting of having supped with you at a night restaurant, but I thought it was mere boasting."

"Not at all. It is true."

"Is it true also that you were accompanied by a stranger, as this evening, only, as Bertha Verrier says, not the same?"

"Bertha Verrier is right. The other went away the next day."

"*Parbleu!*" exclaimed Maxime, "that is what I call frankness. Bertha does not pride herself on fidelity either. You understand each other perfectly, and may I ask why you affected not to recognize her?"

"Ah, pardon me, dear monsieur—monsieur—you told me your name, but I confess I have forgotten it."

"Maxime Dorgères."

"Well, M. Maxime, know that it has pleased me to separate myself from the associations in which I was reared; it has not pleased me to frequent the society of those who first saw daylight in a porter's lodge."

"Then you are not of the same race as these seekers after adventure?"

"No, and I do not resemble them, for it is the adventures that seek me. At the Rink, for instance, I came simply to skate, and I found there an idler who took the notion to make a conquest of me."

"The attempt was a failure," said Maxime, laughing. "You made an end of him there, and if the happy thought of coming here this evening had not crossed his mind he would never have seen you again."

"He would have seen me a fortnight afterward if he had taken the trouble to return."

"Why this fortnight?"

"Because in that time my lord and master expected to be absent."

"If you had said that, I should not have been guilty of the folly of calling too soon."

"And this morning he received you himself."

"Yes. I had some difficulty in recognizing him just now. I had taken him for your porter."

"Really! That is amusing. But I am not surprised; he is hideous."

"And jealous, apparently?".

"Horribly."

"But he must have recognized me in the orchestra, and still he has gone?"

"He did not see you; he sees no one but me, and if he has gone it is because he has a passion stronger than jealousy—the passion of play. To-night he is to be of a party of that sort, and I am delivered from his presence."

"Till to-morrow?"

"Probably, but I cannot tell. Sometimes he happens to win largely and leaves. He is avaricious."

"I see you are not far from detesting him."

"Cordially. I endure him because he frequently absents himself, but it will not be for long. I wish to be independent, and that can only be by being rich. And one of these days I shall separate from this savage."

"He is Russian, is he not?"

"I know nothing about his nationality. He must have been born in a cavern of the Carpathian Mountains, for he has the manners of a bear."

"On Rue Jouffroy they say that he receives no one, and lives on provisions stored away in his cellar."

"Ah! you 'have been questioning the neighbors? But will you be kind enough to tell me why you interest yourself in the life I lead?"

"You have a suspicion, probably?"

"You are going to say that you are in love with me—

you are going to speak falsely. I know perfectly that
you do not love me, you scarcely know me ; besides, I
have strong reasons for believing that you love another."

The occasion seemed propitious for speaking of the
bracelet, but Maxime wished to choose his own time, and
he did not think it had yet come. He was pondering a
plan he had in view, and meantime followed with his
eyes the evolutions the lady made with her hands, and
the freedom with which she used them left no room for
the suspicion that one had been manufactured at Char-
rière's.

"My protestations would be unavailing," he said,
"since you are determined not to believe them, but before long I shall prove to you that my heart is free."

"Do you mean to return to ring at Rue Jouffroy ? It
would be to have me devoured by my ogre."

"Never fear; I shall observe the interdict, and wait
till Blue Beard has taken the express train. But what
hinders you from supping with me this evening?"

"Decidedly, you do not take me for a *femme du
monde* ? "

"The *femmes du monde* sup like other people ; but you
know me well enough to accept an invitation which will
have no consequences except such as you please to
give it."

"My dear monsieur, it is much too soon for supper. I
must absolutely return by twelve—like Cinderella."

"You shall return at twelve ; you shall not lose your shoe, and one is always hungry for oysters."

"That promise decides me. We will go when you will."

Maxime had expected a little more resistance, though his opinion of the skater had been considerably modified within an hour.

"You do not care to wait for the end of the play ?" he asked.

"Oh, not in the least. I did not come here for amusement. It was my tyrant who brought me," replied the brunette, shrugging her shoulders.

"Then let me go first and make sure of a carriage ; it is not worth while to have Blue Beard's coachman know."

"Blue Beard is avaricious, as I told you. He hires a coupé by the month, and keeps it for his own use all night. But it is useless to go for a hack. I love the snow. I like to press my feet on this white carpet, and fancy my friends will recognize the tracks I make."

"*Ma foi!* if your foot is as tiny as your hand I should find no difficulty in tracing you. But the boulevards even are impracticable this evening. Let me take the precaution of looking up a conveyance."

"It is useless. We need not go far to get supper."

"Where, then ?"

"To Brebant's, for instance. It is but two steps, and the Carpathian bear will not come to look for me there. There are delightful rooms on the second floor."

"She seems to be familiar with all the night restau-rants," thought Maxime, and he replied :

"For Brebant's, then. We shall only have to cross the street, and since you love snow, nothing could suit you better."

They began to hasten, for the act was concluding and they wished to avoid the crowd. The boulevard was de-serted ; not a hack visible.

"Do you know," said Maxime, "that there is a chance of your remaining blocked up at Brebant's till to-morrow morning ; the horses can hardly stand, and when the time comes for you to return to Rue Jouffroy, if you must re-turn—"

"If I must ! At twelve o'clock, if you please."

"I must remind you that is now half past ten."

"Well, an hour for talking and a half hour to walk home."

Maxime did not insist, but he promised himself to take good care not to repeat the nocturnal expedition which had come so near costing him dear. A vague suspicion crossed his mind that the lady listened to his proposals because of some hidden purpose.

They made the transit without accident. The steps of the restaurant were solitary, and they were offered the choice of several rooms. Madame Sergent cast her eyes on a little salon, the only window of which opened on the boulevard several feet above the sidewalk, and ordered two dozen oysters, cold partridge, lobster and champagne.

It was, plainly, not her first supper. Maxime watched her with a lively interest, and when she took off her gloves took the two hands in his and kissed them one after the other.

The lady permitted it with a very good grace, and the last doubts of Maxime were dispelled. The hands were plump and flexible, the fingers slender, the nails rosy. Nature alone produced such *chef d'œuvres*, and that rarely. Satisfied from henceforth that it was not Madame Sergent's hand that had been left in M. Dorgères' safe, Maxime arranged his batteries accordingly. This discovery, besides, facilitated his task. He thought it would be easier to lead a woman to confess that she knew a thief, even that she had been the accomplice of one, than that she had herself stolen.

The oysters were served, and the lady attacked her dozen with a good-will which Maxime was pleased to see. He thought a good appetite inconsistent with remorse, or the meditating of any evil design. She permitted him to take a seat on a divan near her, and to pour out champagne, which she drank without ceremony. It was charming, and under other circumstances Maxime would have thought only of passing a joyous hour with a gay companion, but he did not forget that he had come to obtain explanations of Madame Sergent, and that all his politeness must be directed toward that object. But he thought it was not well to press at first this scandalous topic. By precipitating the attack he would be apt to frighten off the lady, who would no doubt be less guarded after a few glasses of champagne, and it was not unlikely would herself bring up the subject of the bracelet.

"Surely," he exclaimed, "life is a pleasant thing. I spent the day fatiguing and freezing myself for persons who are not at all obliged to me for it, and now that the happiest of chances has led to this meeting with the prettiest woman in Paris, and this supper in a warm little nest—"

"Not another word, or I open the window," said the brunette, laughing. "First, I am not the prettiest woman in Paris, and I did not come here for you to make love to me."

"For what, then ?"

"To eat lobster."

"Nothing else ?"

"*Ma foi!* yes; I haven't tasted any for a month. My tyrant detests it, and never consults me as to dinner."

"Happily his reign is coming to an end."

"Well, no ; he wishes to take me travelling."

"And you will let him do so ?"

"I don't know ; it depends on the fancy of the moment. I will go if I suffer from ennui."

"Tell me, then, quickly what must be done to amuse you."

"Not very much ; it is necessary to love me."

"That is easy,"

" No ; it is very difficult to love me as I wish to be loved. For you it would be impossible."

" Tell me how you would be loved."

" Madly. I am radical in love, and your heart belongs to the left centre. The man who loves me must be capable of committing a crime if I exact it of him.

" *Diable!* " thought Maxime, a little disconcerted by this unexpected sally. " A crime—that is radical, to be sure."

" How do you pass your time ? " she asked.

" Like other young men who have leisure and money."

" That is to say, in the pursuit of pleasure. Do you find it often ? "

" Well, yes. I would not give this evening for all the money in my uncle's safe."

" Bah ! you would amuse yourself better with Bertha Verrier. She is not exacting."

" You have a wrong opinion of me. I am much more sentimental than you suppose.

" Ah, yes ! " exclaimed the lady, with a burst of laughter ; " I had forgotten the bracelet."

" What bracelet ? " asked Maxime. It was a more prompt attack than he had anticipated, and he wanted time to prepare his reply.

" The one you had on your arm the evening you were kind enough to escort me home. You told me it was a family relic, but I did not believe a word of this polite explanation."

"Well, and you were right. The jewel did not come to me from my ancestors ; first, because I have no ancestors. But neither was it given me by a woman."

"You are not going to pretend you found it ?"

"Exactly so ; I found-it."

"And you wore it instead of sending it to the Lost Office ? You will never make me believe that."

"It is true, nevertheless."

"Then there is some history connected with it ?"

"You are right ; the strangest of histories."

"Oh, do tell it ! We are now at partridge ; this is the very time."

"Know, then, that this bracelet belonged to a person that—by the way, have you never seen it ?"

"No ; I have felt it, but you did not show it to me"

"Do you want to see it ?"

"Very much."

"There it is," said Maxime, putting it on the cloth. It was his great stroke, and he observed the lady narrowly.

She exclaimed, with a frown :

"*Ma foi!* it is not pretty. Bertha Verrier wouldn't have it."

"Bertha Verrier has seen it and is of your opinion. She thinks it is very ugly."

"Wait awhile !" cried Mme. Sergent. " I have seen it too. It belonged to me once ; it belonged to me a month ago, and this girl, I knew, remarked that I wore it the evening I supped with her."

Maxime cut a silly figure. He was in the situation of a huntsman who, having laid a trap for a fox, sees him set it aside with his foot instead of falling into it.

"What!" he exclaimed, feigning astonishment, "this bracelet was yours?"

"*Ma foi!* yes," said the brunette. "I ought not to acknowledge it, for no elegant woman wears such hardware. It was the first present of my Moldavian, and to please him I wore it several times. I remember even that, having lost one of the ugly stones, I went to a jeweller, Rue de la Paix, to have it replaced. But after the departure of the hospodar—in Moldavia they are called hospodars—I hastened to rid myself of this pretty present."

All this was said so naturally that Maxime never conceived a doubt of the truth of so plausible an explanation.

"May I ask into whose hands it passed?" he inquired immediately.

"That I do not know myself. I took it to an auctioneer and asked him to include it in a sale that was to take place in Rue Dronot. It found a purchaser, and I received, after expenses were paid, twenty-three louis. There is my history. Now let me have yours."

"Mine!" stammered Maxime.

"Certainly. Tell me where you found it, and why you attach such value to it."

"You wish to know?" asked the young man, after a moment's reflection.

"Do I wish it! I scent a tragedy, and tragedy, you must know, is my element."

"Well, this bracelet was lost by a woman who committed a theft."

"Nothing but a theft? that is very vulgar. I hoped it was at least a murder, jealousy, vengeance; that would be something like—but a theft!"

"This was a very extraordinary one."

"It must have been for you to be so much interested. Have you undertaken to discover the thief?"

"Yes, and I expect to do so."

"A queer fancy. Then you take up for your own amusement the business of police agent?"

"Every one has his peculiarities. You love to patter in the snow. I love to guess riddles."

"Now I think of it," said the lady, with a burst of laughter. "You must have thought I was the thief?"

"I swear—"

"Do not swear. I guess all. Bertha had seen the bracelet and told you it was mine. Armed with this precious information you set off for the war, and when you put the bracelet on the table just now expected to see me faint. Really it is too droll. In your place I should send for a policeman."

Maxime protested, and Mme. Sergent went on as if trying to repress an excess of merriment.

"No? You do not wish to? You do me the honor to believe I have not stolen? Well, then, ring for them to bring the lobster, and open the window. I have laughed until I am stifling."

Maxime was quite out of countenance, and to gain time and recover himself, hastened to obey. He rang, he opened the window, notwithstanding the fifteen degrees of cold outdoors, and returned to take his seat beside the charming creature whom he was repenting of having suspected.

He found her engaged in examining the bracelet. She held it in her slender fingers, turned it round and looked at it curiously.

"It is the very same," she murmured. "See, this is the stone I had replaced. It may be easily recognized, being more brilliant than the others. To think that this ugly jewelry might have brought me before the Court of Assizes," said the lady, laughing. "A judicial error, like the Lesurques affair."

Maxime was searching for some word that would enable him to reënter the lists, when he heard the sound of a rough voice calling:

"I tell you I will enter."

"Ah," murmured Mme. Sergent, "it is he! I am lost!"

Maxime rushed toward the door with the intention of defending her, and as he reached it met, face to face, the Carpathian bear himself, his eyes shining, his hair bristling.

Maxime was not terrified, and placed himself so as to bar his progress, saying in a firm tone :

"What do you want?"

The bear retreated two steps, and growled the beastly response:

"I want the woman who is in this room. She is mine."

"There is no woman here, and if that doesn't satisfy you here is my card."

The enraged bear took the card Maxime had offered.

"Very well," he said, "to-morrow you will receive my seconds, if I do not receive yours. You know where I live, since you came there this morning as a spy. But your card is not enough; I want the woman."

"You do not enter, and if you persist I shall—"

Maxime did not finish. A cloak brushed his shoulder. Mme. Sergent, all cloaked and hooded, passed near him, and quickly gained the stairway.

The bear precipitated himself after her, and the stupefied young man remained face to face with the frightened boy who was bringing in the lobster.

"*Ma foi!*" said Maxime, trying to console himself, "it was the best she could do. A discussion with that animal would have resulted in a fist fight, and I much prefer to give him a sword in his sides."

At this moment his memory returned to him.

"The bracelet!" he exclaimed. "She has carried off the bracelet!"

It was too true. The bracelet was no longer on the table, and as Madame Sergent held it in her beautiful fingers at the moment Blue Beard announced his arrival, it was probable that in her fright she had carried it off. He was forced to confess that he had made a wretched campaign of it. All his wise combinations had procured him only a duel with a disagreeable personage, and the loss of the object on which he had counted to unravel everything. Not that he was disconcerted at the prospect of a duel, for he was an expert swordsman, and calculated upon giving a useful lesson to this boor who sequestrated a charming woman. He even hoped this sword-thrust would gain him credit with the incomparable brunette.

"She will know how to find me when I have been fighting for her," he thought, "and to recompense my chivalry will herself bring me the bracelet."

There was no time to be lost in looking for his seconds, for he expected to be awakened at daybreak by those of his savage adversary, and at such an hour the only hope was to look for them at his club.

He found a courageous coachman, and as he proceeded on his slow journey had leisure to reflect on the events of the evening, and to ask himself how this jealous lover made the discovery that his belle had supped at Brebant's.

"*Parbleu!* I have it. This ugly animal recognized me in the orchestra, and hoping to catch Mme. Sergent and me together, has had recourse to a classic method— that employed by the jealous in all ages. He announced to the lady that he would pass the night at play, and stationed himself as sentinel at some café near the theatre, or he may have paid some one to follow and watch us. We were seen entering a restaurant,—he has followed and hung around the door—bears are never cold—and when I opened the window he discovered where I was and entered, furious. What a brute! He must be very rich indeed for that woman to endure him, and she must be fond indeed of money to submit to such tyranny. Bah! she is no better than the rest. It is a pity, for she is very pretty. But I was a fool to think she had anything to do with the theft. When such creatures descend so far as to risk the Court of Assizes, it is not a casket of papers they take. This one would not have left a thousand-dollar note in my uncle's safe. And the history of the auction sale must be true. How shall I now find out the owner of the bracelet? I did not even think of getting the address of the auctioneer; it was gross stupidity. Through this man I might have found out into whose hands the bracelet fell, and still it is very doubtful. A person who buys at auction is not obliged to give his name—it is enough to give his money. *Ma foi!* I begin to think I shall never discover anything."

Maxime had just arrived at this conclusion when the hack stopped before the door of his club. It was the hour when ordinarily the salons were filled, the hour when the habitués assemble around the fireside to exchange the news and scandals of the day. Maxime thought that in mixing himself up with this council of babblers, he might perchance gather some information concerning the brunette of the Rink.

But to his disappointment he found at the club only about a dozen faithful members, and amongst these not a man whose services he could ask on the ground.

The Hungarian doctor arrived to relieve his embarrassment.

"My dear sir," said Dorgères, without preamble, "I am to fight to-morrow. Will you be my second?"

"With whom do you fight?"

"With a foreigner whom I do not know, and in the cause of a woman whom you know—the marvel of the Rink."

"You have seen her again, then?"

"Yes; this evening at the Variétés. I invited her to supper, and whilst there this monsieur who protects her tried to force himself into the room."

"Good! I can see the scene. You offered him your card; he took it and led away the beauty. I would bet any amount you never hear of him again. They belong to a class who come to Paris to amuse themselves, not to cross swords."

"If I do not hear of him he shall hear of me. I am strongly inclined to give him a lesson in manners."

"Bah! If there has been no violence, I would let it alone. You are not, I suppose, in love with the marvel?"

"Oh, not at all!" said Maxime, quickly.

"If you were that would change matters, but since she is indifferent to you I would wait till her lover claims satisfaction."

"Perhaps I shall, but in any event I may count on you?"

"Pardon me, but for a few days I shall not be at my own disposal. I shall be needed by the countess."

"How is that?"

"On returning from the Bois, Mme. Yalta was taken with a serious indisposition. The sleigh ride in such weather may cost her dear. She realizes herself that she is ill, for she has consented to go to bed, and I came to the club this evening in the hope of meeting you here. She wished me to say to you that she would be unable to see you to-morrow. And between ourselves, I cannot prophesy when she will be again on her feet."

"Doctor, you distress me," exclaimed Maxime, really agitated, "and when I think that I may have been the involuntary cause of this mishap."

"Oh, you have nothing to reproach yourself with. She would have gone alone if you had not been there. She takes counsel only of her own caprices."

"But, doctor, do you answer for her safety?"

"Yes, if she will undertake no new folly. I have prescribed for her the most absolute rest, and it is for this reason that her friends—you are one I am sure—must refrain from seeing her till she shall be completely reëstablished."

"I may at least go every day to inquire for her?"

"Assuredly, and I myself will keep you informed, for I am going to establish myself in the Avenue de Friedland house. Now let me say good-bye. I must return to my invalid. And take my advice; avoid fighting for this dark-eyed girl whom I unfortunately pointed out to you at the Rink. She does not deserve to have a brave man risk his life for her."

M. Villagos departed, leaving Maxime sorrowful and much perplexed; so sorrowful that he thought no more of his seconds; so perplexed that he left the club and went home to reflect at leisure upon the new situation which the events of this decisive day had brought about.

CHAPTER X.

A MONTH has passed. The thaw has come and the New Year too ; but Maxime has not seen again the Countess Yalta. Neither has he seen again the inexplicable creature who carried off the accusing bracelet. The day after the abruptly-ended supper, he waited all the morning for Blue Beard's seconds, but none appeared. In the afternoon, forgetting the doctor's wise counsels, he recruited two brave youths and despatched them to Rue Jouffroy. They found the doors closed against them ; reiterated appeals to the bell having proved unavailing, they were compelled to return without fulfilling their mission.

The day following, Maxime went in person to the house of the ogre, but his success was no greater. The obliging porter opposite recognized him, and came out for the express purpose of informing him that the bear had decamped ; that he had not been seen for thirty-six hours ; that the neighbors who detested him had signified to the commissary of police that some crime must have been committed in that mysterious house ; and that the

268

commissary had searched it from garret to cellar. They
had not discovered the least skeleton nor anything which
indicated that it had been a scene of violence. It did.
not appear that it had been used even, or that any one
had slept in its sumptuous beds. The conclusion of the
inquest was that the unknown had gone as he came, no
one knew why; but as the furniture he had left sufficed
to pay the rent, there was no cause for his occupying
any further attention.

Maxime not acknowledging himself beaten went to see
the owner, who told him that having signed a lease of
nine years and paid three in advance, he had no reason
to be concerned at the departure of his tenant. The
name of this tenant was composed of so many consonants
and so few vowels, it was impossible for a French tongue
to pronounce it, and M. Maxime Dorgères now found
himself at his wits' end. The best informed *viveurs*,
those who had all Paris on their fingers' end, had been
unable to give him any information concerning this shoot-
ing star, who had blazed one or two evenings and disappeared without leaving a track.

So Maxime, discouraged, ended by believing that
Madame Sergent had never made part of the *demi-monde* ;
that in conjunction with the Carpathian bear she had
played a comedy of which he had been the victim, and
that she had supped with her too confident admirer for
the sole purpose of getting possession of the bracelet.
She had succeeded and he should never hear of her

more. The trail was lost—the birds were flown. They had gone to rejoin the thief who could now sleep tranquilly. She had regained possession of her hand stolen from the morgue, and of the jewel which had adorned that guilty hand.

Though not indifferent to his defeat, Maxime consoled himself with no great difficulty. His business of police agent was brought to an end, but he had not had time to acquire a taste for this pursuit of· criminals, upon which he had entered so passionately. And then his mind was elsewhere. Since he had known this strange countess he had thought only of her, had thought of her all the more because he had not seen her again. He had gone every day to the Avenue de Friedland mansion to receive a bulletin of the health of the countess.

The Hungarian seemed now to be encouraged. Madame Yalta had entered upon convalescence, and it was no insignificant flattery to the young man's vanity to learn that she spoke of him and expressed a desire to see him.

Changes have taken place—many changes in the household of M. Dorgères. Vignory has been elevated to the dignity of partner, and better still, his patron has given him official authority to pay his addresses to Mlle. Alice, who does not repel his advances.

She also is much changed. After a few days of seclusion following her drive to the Bois, she told all to her father. Joseph, the too complaisant valet de chambre had nearly been turned away, but she succeeded in winning his pardon. Cousin Maxime, on the contrary, has risen considerably in his uncle's esteem, who is under infinite obligations for his well-advised intervention.

To her confession Alice added a declaration which delighted M. Dorgères. She said, henceforth Robert de Carnoël did not exist for her, and that she was ready to follow in all respects the paternal counsels. The banker profited by the occasion to urge the claims of his cashier, and she offered no objection to this pretender. She asked only for time to know him, but exacted also of her father that no steps should be taken against M. de Carnoël, and that his name should not be mentioned in her presence. These conditions were readily accepted. Vignory now dines every evening with M. Dorgères. Mlle. Alice has even begun to appreciate his good qualities and to accord him a welcome. No one can doubt that this state of affairs will speedily end in a marriage ; and this dénouement is more probable, as a month has passed and Robert de Carnoël has given no sign of life. Col. Borisoff had had several conversations with the banker, and it is agreed between them that the affair of the theft shall be abandoned. The colonel has accepted the loss of his casket, and is interested in the future happiness of Mlle. Dorgères. The father is grateful for his good conduct and his friendly sentiments. He would even have invited him to his Wednesday soirées but for Alice's opposition. The colonel recalls sad memories, and she positively refused to see him.

There is yet another change in the household of the banker.

Georget's place has been filled by a little peasant boy whom M. Dorgères brought from his native town to run errands in his offices. One December day, Georget did not appear, nor the day following.

On the third day the banker received a letter from the Widow Piriac saying that her grandson was dying.

M. Dorgères, who had a kind heart, repaired immediately to Rue Cardinet, where he learned that the child had been picked up the night before on the Boulevard Courcelles, his arm broken and skull mashed ; that he was delirious and his life in danger. The shock he had received had been so great that he had lost his memory, and was not in a condition to recount what had happened to him.

Such was the condition of affairs when Maxime Dorgères went out one morning, according to his daily habit, to inquire for Madame Yalta.

He had received encouraging news ; her strength was returning, the fever had disappeared, and with the aid of rest it might be hoped the convalescent would soon be in a condition to receive her friends.

Maxime was beside himself for joy, and as joy predisposes the heart to sympathize with the happiness of others, the idea occurred to him to pass by Rue de Suresnes and have a talk with Jules Vignory.

The sky was serene once more and the air soft. He

directed his steps toward the residence of his uncle, thinking as he did so of the strange course which events sometimes take in this world of ours.

Six weeks before, an attempted robbery had thrown him on a path which he had followed up with ardor, and which through a succession of unforeseen incidents had led him to make the acquaintance of an adorable woman, by the side of whom Mme. Sergent was simply an ordinary beauty. And now he had completely forgotten the severed hand, Robert de Carnoël, the brunette of the Rink, to think only of this countess whom he had but slightly known during one snowy day, but of whom he still kept a burning memory. He could scarcely even recall distinctly her features, and sometimes she seemed to have appeared to him in a dream, But the shadowy image haunted him, and he was impatient to have it assume once more form and substance.

The rest mattered little to him now. Vignory was happy, and Alice was cured of a senseless passion. They were approaching with full sails the tranquil port of marriage, which everything indicated they would soon enter.

The door was kept partially open during the hours when the public was admitted to the grating, and Maxime entered without meeting any one. It was necessary to pass through a vaulted passage way in order to come out on the court, and then turn to the right to reach the offices. It was there that the friends had come in collision with two individuals of doubtful appearance, who had quickly passed into the street five minutes before the discovery of the theft. Evidently the authors of the attempt had passed by them then, and one of these audacious robbers must have been a woman disguised as a man, the woman for whom he had so vainly sought.

The incident now came back to him, and for the first time since he had undertaken the pursuit of the rogues it passed before his mind that the tall one might have been the man of Rue Jouffroy—the same height, same figure. But the woman dressed as a man could not be Madame Sergent, for Madame Sergent had both her hands.

"All these bore but a subordinate part in the perform-ance," thought Maxime : "they acted on behalf of some one who has not yet been detected. The bear belonged to the first expedition, when the woman left her hand on the field of battle ; he was also of the second, and the woman was not, her wound confining her to her hospital. Afterward the bear despatched the brunette to obtain the bracelet from me by soft devices. But how could they know I was going that day to see the skating on rollers ? Mystery ! * * * like all the rest. But it is certain he knew it. The rascals who followed me were acting under his orders in the event of Madame Sergent failing. At the Variétés this pretty couple began again and I fell into the trap ; but I can laugh them all to scorn. *Au diable !* the bracelet, Blue Beard, the false Andalusian, the one-handed, the scamp of high degree who suborns all these subaltern scamps—and *Vive la Comtesse Yalta !*"

On arriving at the lodge he found the glass door partly open, and in the midst of a cloud of tobacco-smoke saw three men seated before a fire, their backs turned toward him. He recognized the concierge, the valet de chambre, Joseph, and Malicome, the watch. His first impulse was to call to account these fellows, who were converting the lodge into a smoking-room, but he was restrained by a sentence that met his ear.

" I tell you again," said Joseph, " that the secretary is as innocent as you or I."

"Then what did he run away for?" asked father Doulevant.

" Because the old one didn't want him to marry mademoiselle ; but I'll lay my life on it he didn't touch the safe."

Maxime was astounded. The theft, then, was known to the servants in spite of all the precautions taken to conceal it.

" But if the pretty secretary is innocent, why don't anybody hear from him ?"

" There are some as have heard," replied Joseph, with an important air. " But it is true nothin's been heard for a month, and about that I has my notions—it's because he's been sent to his grave."

" What ! you believe they've killed him ?"

" I am as certain of it as that that is a well-blackened pipe."

" Who is there would have killed him ?"

"Those he stood in the way of."

"Come, now, he has most likely taken ship for America, but I don't believe he's stolen. And do you wan't to know who has? It's the little groom."

"Georget? It ain't possible. I ain't over-fond of the little crab, for he's several times played me tricks passing by my lodge; but I'd never have believed he'd touch the safe. First, he didn't stop in the offices after six in the evening."

"No, but he was a cat. I caught him one morning asleep on a table. He said I'd shut him up the evening before without seeing him. He might have hid in the closet the evening of the robbery."

"If he did, he did it on account of other people. And if he's been three-fourths murdered in the street it's because there's people as want to put him out of the way, as they did Carnoël, who must have known something too."

"And Vignory didn't lose any time taking his place and courting Mlle. Alice. It's true he's permitted by the patron. But the poor little thing don't look much like getting married. She cries all the evening; the femme de chambre told me so."

"Bah! she'll be consoled," said Malicome. "And a nice thing it'll be for the cashier. He came here without a sou, and will die in the skin of a millionaire."

"It's not that 'll make him generous. Since I've known him I haven't found out the color of his money."

Maxime felt inclined to enter the lodge Tartar fashion and use his cane on these gossips, but he concluded it would not be well to commit himself, and so passed on unobserved.

Nothing is more instructive than the conversation of servants when their masters are in a position to be benefited by it, without their knowledge. One may learn many things of which he would otherwise remain ignorant, when the reverse side of servile platitudes is revealed. Maxime was acquainted with the class, and was not surprised at the liberty of speech in which they indulged, in such little gatherings as this ; but certain words that he had heard still rang in his ears. The settled conviction of the majority of the lodge was that the secretary had been unjustly accused, and that Georget was concerned in the theft.

"If it should be true ! " thought Maxime. " In that case I have been guilty of two blunders : first, in assuring my cousin that her lover was unworthy of her ; and secondly, in interesting myself in this little scamp who has been the cause of all the trouble. Yes, but it is not true. This rascal Joseph regrets the *pourboires* with which M. de Carnoël rewarded him for transmitting clandestine messages to Alice, and that was enough to induce him to hand over to him letters-patent of innocence. No matter, when I see the countess I shall ask her if she is certain of her protégé."

Pushing open the door of the waiting-room, he entered

the office, where he found Vignory writing a letter. He was radiant and almost ready to throw himself into the arms of Maxime, stage fashion, but the presence of the clerks moderated these transports, and he led the nephew of his patron into a little room adjoining the office—a temporary receptacle for old papers, which, since his change of fortune, Vignory had fitted up for the purpose of isolating himself at times from his subordinates. Taking care to close the door, he seized Maxime's two hands and pressed them warmly."

"It is true, then," said the nephew, sufficiently enlightened by this demonstration, "you are to be my cousin?"

"What! you know, then—"

"I know nothing, but I guess all. Your face is triumphant."

"I am the happiest of men."

"Dispense with these appropriate phrases and tell me simply what has occurred."

"That will not take very long. I dined at your uncle's—a family dinner. We were four, M. Dorgères, Mlle. Alice—"

"Mme. Martineau and you. *Parbleu!* if you enter so into particulars you will never get through."

"Well, after dinner your uncle was absorbed in reading the statutes of a new financial company, Madame Martineau had gone to sleep in the corner of the fire, so we found ourselves tête-à-tête, Mlle. Alice and I."

"And you seized the occasion to make an ardent declaration?"

"I was going to try, but Mlle. Alice did not give me time to speak. She said to me: 'M. Vignory, I know you love me and I appreciate your good qualities. On a recent occasion you showed that you had a heart, for you undertook the defence of an unfortunate friend. I esteem you, and know that my father wishes me to marry you. I authorize you to ask of him my hand.'"

"Hum! here is a consent very lacking in enthusiasm. What was your reply to this frank and moderate discourse?"

"I cannot tell—I was so agitated."

"Good! some disconnected phrases, protestations of gratitude—eternal devotion—I think I understand. But finally you accepted?"

"Do you doubt it?"

"No; you are rational enough to make a rational marriage."

"Of reason and inclination too. I have worshipped her for two years without daring to say so."

"You are not the only one."

At these words Vignory colored slightly, and Maxime, who never disguised his thoughts, resumed:

"Do not suppose I wish to discourage you. My little cousin is sincere when she says she esteems you; I am even inclined to believe that she will end by loving you, and that you will one day be the most cherished of husbands.

But do not forget that she has loved passionately a man whom she would have married but for untoward circumstances. Your position is a delicate one."

"I know it, but it does not frighten me."

"So much the better. In your place I should be a little jealous of the past. And there are moments when I feel disposed to ask if M. de Carnöel has not been unjustly accused."

This time the cashier turned pale.

"If he were innocent he would have appeared," he murmured.

"At least, if he be not dead."

"Dead! why should you suppose—"

"In passing by the lodge just now I caught a few very singular remarks. Joseph and Malicome believe that Robert has been murdered."

"It is absurd. He has left France beyond a doubt."

"Are you sure? I saw him in Paris eight days after the theft; and then he suddenly disappeared. It is not natural."

"On the contrary, it is all very clear. He went first to Brittany, and after remaining there two or three days, returned here. Col. Borisoff can prove it. But what are you driving at?"

"To say to you, my dear Jules, that all this affair of the theft does not yet seem clear to me, and I begin to think the real culprits have not yet been suspected. For instance, it never entered our minds that it could be Georget; but the servants maintain that it was."

"Georget ! your protégé whom you recommended so warmly to M. Dorgères ? "

"Oh, I don't answer for the assertions of these messieurs, but it is plain that the rogues had some communication with the house. Georget went and came incessantly here. Might he not have hidden somewhere, and opened the door to the rogues at a moment when no one was about ? "

"Why bring up all this sad story ? " asked Vignory, in an agitated voice ; " I made a fête day of the announcement of my marriage to you, and hoped you would sympathize with my joy : instead of doing so, you talk only of a young man who was my friend, whom I defended as long as I could, but for whose return it is impossible for me to wish."

"Pardon me," cried Maxime, touched by this appeal to his feelings, " I am a fool. *Du diable!* if I know why I interest myself in these people. All's well that ends well, and I am delighted that you are to marry Alice. When will the ceremony take place ? "

" M. Dorgères proposes the first of February."

" Then I have no time to lose in selecting my bridal present, and I give you my word of honor to talk no more of M. de Carnoël."

With that mobility of mind which was one of the young man's minor defects, he had almost come to believe for an instant in the chance assertions of a valet and an office boy, but was already regretting having considered them seriously, and that he should have distressed his best friend by reviving disagreeable associations instead of congratulating him on a marriage of which he heartily approved.

His usual hour for repairing to the Avenue de Friedland had gone by, and he found that having dedicated so much time to the affairs of others it was high time he should be engaged a little with his own.

He left his uncle's to make his daily visit to Dr. Villagos.

The liveried servants of Madame Yalta's mansion had become familiar with this assiduous visitor, and gave him every day the same welcome. A colossal porter received him at the entrance, announced him by a stroke of the bell, and passed him on to the *valet de pied*, who introduced him into one of the salons on the ground-floor.

He had scarcely entered when M. Villagos appeared. He had an anxious expression, and Maxime feared he brought bad news of his patient.

"Well!" he asked impatiently, "have you come to tell me of a relapse?"

"No; thank God she is doing well; her strength is returning, and I may pronounce that the countess is safe; that is, she is cured of her ailment, but I am not entirely reassured."

"You mean that you fear some imprudence? I hope, my dear doctor, you will use your authority to prevent it."

"My authority cannot be stretched so far as to give her repose of mind. She is filled with a thousand fancies, such as you would never guess and will hardly believe when I have indicated them to you, not knowing Madame Yalta as I do. She is a woman who throws herself passionately into everything, and interests herself in misfortunes which in no way concern her. Thus, you made known to her, it seems, that your uncle's secretary loved Mademoiselle Dorgères, that she loved him, and that he had been sent away."

"I beg pardon; it was the countess who spoke of it to me. I even sought to undeceive her."

"You did not succeed. She is persuaded this young man's misfortunes are unmerited. M. de Carnoël's father was formerly known to the father of the countess. That was enough to make her espouse the cause of the son. She is ignorant of what has passed at M. Dorgères', she merely pictures to herself two lovers who are unhappy, and has made a vow to undertake their cause. She has all the folly of a Don Quixote. She would redress the wrongs of humanity."

"And, like Don Quixote, she beats against wind-mills. My cousin is to marry in a month my uncle's partner. I am really distressed that Madame Yalta should have attached any importance to a child's gossip."

"Now, dear sir, I must beg you when with the countess to say nothing that may in any way excite her. She will try to lead the conversation to a subject that occupies her continually. Promise to do all in your power to give it another turn."

"It is understood. But you speak as if I might soon have the happiness of being received by Mme. Yalto."

"Assuredly. She is bent on seeing you."

"When?"

"This morning. She begged me to say to you that she wished to thank you for the interest you have shown during her illness. I will not conceal from you that I should have preferred not to have her receive you this morning. I am always apprehensive of any mental excitement ; but I content myself with reminding you of your promise to avoid a certain subject."

"I renew the promise ; besides, you will assist me in doing so?"

"No. I have patients who require my attention. Moreover, the countess will prefer seeing you alone."

This arrangement was very agreeable to Maxime, though he was compelled to assert the contrary to M. Villagos. The doctor contented himself with a smile, and taking his arm led him to the grand stairway which led to the private apartments of the countess. There he found a *valet de pied* who, on a sign from the doctor, preceded him to show the way.

The last words of the doctor, as he left Maxime were :

"Do not forget my instructions."

Maxime was firmly resolved to be true to his promise, and he had moreover no inclination to waste conversation on others during the time the countess should accord him. On the first story he was received by a femme de chambre, who requested him to follow her. She conducted him through various apartments which resembled the halls of a museum ; there were many objects of art and but little furniture ; nothing was conventional ; there was neither ante-chamber, nor boudoir, nor salon. Braving the prejudices which impose upon the rich the obligation to inhabit a mansion arranged after unvarying rules,. she. had sacrificed every thing to fancy. " This is .something uncommon," Maxime murmured, as he followed his conductress.

" The habitation is made after the image of the adorable'persons whom fools call eccentric."

To tell the truth, however, he expected to find her in some recess furnished after the fashion of the day.

The femme de chambre opened a door softly, and instead of announcing him, motioned him to enter. He did so, and found himself in a semi-obscurity in which he failed at first to distinguish objects clearly, so that he remained on the threshold without venturing to advance.

The room into which he .was introduced was oval, and was lighted from above. The walls were of polished faience, in oriental style, and all around the room extended a large divan ; in the centre were enormous baskets of flowers and bushes of camellias, which seemed to have their roots in the ground. There was no sign of a chimney place, nevertheless a soft warmth was diffused through the room and a penetrating perfume. It resembled much more nearly a harem than the apartment of an invalid. The astonished Maxime saw the door close behind him, and supposed the waiting-woman had left him alone to give notice to her mistress.

He advanced, however, and when he had passed the massive shrubbery, suddenly found himself face to face with Mme. Yalta. She was half reclining on a sort of stage formed of piled-up cushions—a Turkish couch—and covered up to the shoulders with a white bear skin.

Paler than of yore, but more beautiful, perhaps, with the beauty which revealed itself only to men 'capable of appreciating the brightness of her glance, and the strange irresistible charm of this speaking face.

"I was looking for you," she said, and her voice moved him profoundly; "you are welcome." And she extended a charming hand which Maxime did not dare to kiss but pressed warmly.

"If you could know how happy I am to see you once more!" he exclaimed.

"I know it," replied the countess, "and I beg you to believe that if I did not receive you sooner it was because the doctor absolutely forbade it. But I gave him notice this morning that I meant from to-day to resume my habits, and by way of beginning I wished to see a friend again. Would you believe that he opposed it? Had I listened to him you would not be here. But you are here. Sit down and let us have a talk."

In the way of seats Maxime saw only a heap of piled-up cushions, but though unused to oriental habits, he succeeded in establishing himself comfortably enough. It was less easy to find an opening for conversation, and the most skilful of talkers would probably have experienced the same embarrassment. What was he to say to a woman whom he had seen only once, and who, however, placed him on the footing of intimate friendship? The trivialities which make up conversation in the world seemed out of place, and M. Villagos had interdicted the only topic which it would have been easy to approach. The countess, doubtless, appreciated his embarrassment and spared him the trouble of commencing.

"I have formed many projects during my enforced seclusion," she said gayly, "projects of reform; the existence I lead wearies me and I have resolved to change it."

"You intend to quit Paris?" exclaimed Maxime.

"No, not at present at least. But I dream of being happy after the fashion of the quiet *bourgeois* who is content with the joys of fireside and home."

This beginning surprised Maxime greatly. Though he was no coxcomb, he could not help wondering if the countess was about to propose a quiet life in some retired corner with him.

His astonishment was so visible, that Madame Yalta laughed and went on: "I see you do not understand the meaning of the conversion I have announced. The insane countess whom you have known is no more. I have taken a vow to live simply, and to aid the accomplishment of this vow, wish to connect myself with a patriarchal family. I can think of no word that expresses my thought better."

" Such families are rare enough in Paris," said Maxime gayly, " and at least it would be necessary to search for them in a world—"

" Which is not mine, I know it. But it exists, for I know one—yours."

" Mine ? but I have none. I was early left an orphan. I have only an uncle."

" And a cousin. It is of these I am thinking. It was on my mind when the doctor brought you here and I have come to believe our meeting was predestined. I must tell you that I am superstitious to excess. It seems to me now that this chance is a premonition, and that my destiny is to know those who are dear to you, your uncle and his daughter whom I have but just seen. I am drawn toward her by a feeling which I cannot define, and have determined to beg M. Dorgères to present me to her."

" He would be delighted to be agreeable to you," stammered Maxime, who little expected an overture of this sort, " only—Alice is still so young."

· " And I—am so no longer," interrupted the countess ; " I am twenty-nine—ten years older than Mlle. Dorgères. And I have lived—I have suffered, while she is still at the age which cherishes illusions. Ah ! well, it is precisely this contrast which makes me wish to become her friend. I have gained at some expense an experience of life which I should love to make use of in contributing to the happiness of a pure girl whom I had learned to love as a sister.

"My cousin would be proud to hear you speak so, and let me assure you, madame, that she is worthy of the interest you feel. But let me remind you that she enters the world by the common door through which pass all our rich *bourgeoisie*, all the heiresses. She is about to be married.",

"What! her father has consented to accept M. de Carnoël?"

Maxime bit his lips. He had spoken hastily, and saw too late that he had already broken his promise to M. Villagos.

"No, madame," he replied with visible embarrassment. "My cousin marries her father's partner, a charming young man who is my intimate friend—Jules Vignory.

"And she loves him?"

"Undoubtedly; Alice would not be forced into marriage, and has made a perfectly free choice."

"Are you certain? You told me yourself she loved M. de Carnoël."

"She believed so. At nineteen a young girl may easily deceive herself as to her real sentiments," said Maxime, with a forced smile.

The countess was looking at him out of her large

bright eyes, and seemed to try to penetrate to the depths of his soul. There was silence which ended by placing Maxime at his ease. He was desperate at having been led to this subject in spite of himself, and was sending M. de Carnoël to all the devils.

"I am going to speak with you frankly," resumed Madame Yalta, slowly. "You have not forgotten, I suppose, our conversation—one very cold day?"

"How should I forget? That was a marked day in my life, for it was the day I had the happiness of speaking to you for the first time," said Maxime, glad to revert to these personal recollections.

"Then you remember that I had become acquainted with certain facts through my protégé Georget?"

"Madame," he said, "Georget has talked at random like the child that he is. He was fond of my uncle's secretary; he imagined the young man was to marry my cousin, and was grieved at his leaving the house."

"He left because M. Dorgères banished him. You gave me to understand that he was guilty of some unworthy act. Georget has told me more. He told me that a theft had been committed at M. Dorgères, and that M. de Carnoël was suspected."

Maxime started.

"You see I am well informed," the countess continued. "I know all that has transpired. I know that the safe was opened with a false key, and a casket taken belonging to a Russian named, I believe, Borisoff. I know, too, how the theft was discovered. Georget was there, and heard all. The cashier called M. Dorgères, who, on learning that his secretary had left precipitately the night before, did not hesitate to pronounce the young man guilty. You see I know all."

"Except the affair of the severed hand," thought Maxime. "If she knew that she would certainly tell me."

"And," resumed Mme. Yalta, "I am certain that M. de Carnoël is innocent."

"I hope so," murmured the friend of Jules Vignory.

"And I beg of you to tell me what passed between Mlle. Alice and himself in the Bois de Boulogne."

Maxime thought that, having gone so far, it would be puerile to have recourse to a subterfuge.

"M. de Carnoël did not come to the rendezvous he had appointed," he said.

The countess turned pale.

"Is that true?" she asked in an agitated voice.

"I swear it on my honor."

"And you have heard nothing of him since?"

"No ; he has had the good taste not to write to my cousin."

"And hearing nothing more of him, Mlle. Alice has accepted this silence as a confession of guilt? She has condemned without hearing him?"

"He has condemned himself."

"If he has not appeared it is because he is not free."

"I do not know whether he is free, but I know that he he is in Paris, or at least he was the day I waited for him on the route des Bouleaux. He may have concluded to cross the frontier."

"I do not believe it. I believe he has been put out of the way to prevent him from vindicating himself."

"What! you think he has been killed?"

"I hope not, but he may have fallen into the hands of those who were interested in his disappearance."

"The real rogues? You suppose they have seques-trated—confined him?"

"Perhaps; but if he is alive I shall find him. Do you see now why I wish to know Mlle. Dorgères?"

"Not very well, I confess," said Maxime, timidly.

"You do not see that I have pledged myself to break off a marriage which will be the misfortune of her life, for sooner or later the innocence of M. de Carnoël will be recognized, and I count on your aid to establish it."

"Mine!" cried Maxime. "You wish me to second you in this impossible enterprise—I, who am fully con-vinced that M. de Carnoël is guilty!"

"Your conviction will change; I am certain of it," re-plied the countess, unmoved by this protestation.

"I hope so, with all my heart, for I beg you to believe that I have no feeling of personal hostility toward M. de Carnoël. At the same time I must confess that it is not my wish to break off the marriage of my cousin. I can-not forget that her betrothed is my best friend."

"But would you not better prove your friendship by averting a marriage which would prepare for him ever-lasting regrets? Would not his situation be frightful if, after this marriage, M. de Carnoël should return completely justified—M. de Carnoël, whom your cousin has loved with all the ardor of a first love? Do not deny it. If she has renounced this love it is because she believes him dishonored, but she has not forgotten him. The image of her former lover is still present to her thought, and it is to drive it away, to save herself from reverting to this past, that she hastens to bind herself irrevocably. I am a woman, and know the heart of woman. Rest assured that Mlle. Dorgères, weary of the struggle against an inclination which dismays her, takes refuge in marriage, because she hopes to find there tranquility and peace. If she should recognize too late that she has been deceived, she will curse for the rest of her days the tie she is now impatient to contract."

The countess spoke so earnestly, her beautiful eyes so full of eloquence, that Maxime felt her emotion gaining upon him. He was not convinced, far from it; but he was perplexed like a judge who has just heard a skilful lawyer plead for a great criminal. At the same time, he had the mortification to ascertain that he—an earth worm in love with a star—held a very insignificant place in Madame Yalta's thoughts.

If she had set her heart upon seeing him it was that she might speak of de Carnoël, and the discovery astonished as much as it distressed him, for he could not conceive why she espoused so warmly the cause of this young man, whom she had never seen. The statement of Dr. Villagos that her father had known the father of Robert seemed a very insufficient reason why she should, in the face of everybody, espouse the cause of the son who was accused of theft.

An idea suddenly occurred to him. It was Georget who had recounted all this to the countess—Georget, whom the servants of M. Dorgères accused. Might it not be that the odd little *gamin* had made confession to his protectress, which involved a proof of the young secretary's innocence? This hypothesis admitted, the conduct of Madame Yalta appeared quite natural. She would not denounce Georget, but she owed it to herself to assist M. de Carnoël in the misfortune into which a fatality had thrown him, to repair the evil caused by the little scamp whom she had patronized. If it were so the cause of Robert was just, and Madame Yalta was right to seek to save Alice from a fatal error ; she was right to say the day would come when she would curse her union with Jules Vignory.

Notwithstanding his oddities, Maxime was above and before all an honest man, and he also would have had a life-long regret if he had suffered a wrong which it rested with him to resist. Friendship has its limits, and in order to serve his friend, Maxime could not go so far as to refuse to face the truth. At any rate he must reply to this countess, wnose captivating tongue had wellnigh converted him.

"May I count on you ?" she repeated, after allowing him a moment's reflection.

"Absolutely !" he exclaimed, carried away by an irrepressible enthusiasm. "Tell me what I am to do and your orders shall be obeyed."

"First, I beg you to assist me to find M. de Carnoël.

"There is nothing I should desire more, but how can I go about such a search ?"

"I will tell you. You spoke of the child whom I placed at your uncle's. Georget is very bright, and was devoted to M. de Carnoël. I feel sure he would have been able to tell us what had become of him if he had not been the victim of some mysterious accident. He is on his feet now, but his memory is not yet restored, and in order that it may be, I thought of you."

Maxime opened his eyes wide in astonishment.

"I know you are not a doctor," she resumed, laughing, "and I am not expecting to have him treated according to the rules of the faculty. M. Villagos has already done in that way all that could be done, but his task is now ended and yours begins. Georget is attached to you, is he not ?"

"I believe so. He proved it recently. He saved me when I was pursued by villains."

"Well, you could not show your gratitude better than by going to see him."

"I have been three times, but his grandmother would not permit me to see him."

"She is a woman born in a position superior to that in which her marriage has placed her, and has preserved of that origin a pride that is almost fierce. She distrusts all the world but myself, but she never refuses a request from me in memory of my father's kindness to her son. You will show her this ring, which she has seen me wear, and say that I beg her to leave you alone with Georget—to confide in you as she would in myself."

"Well, but what shall I say to the child?"

"Whatever seems calculated to awaken his memory. You will speak to him of this sad story which he appears to have forgotten, of Mlle. Dorgères and M. de Carnoël, and I am sure you will succeed in obtaining some useful hint. If I charge you with this delicate mission it is because I believe you would execute it better than I should do. Georget is devoted to me, but I intimidate him. With you he will be more at ease. I have, besides, another reason. Villagos is the strictest of doctors, and forbids me everything that he considers a dangerous excitement."

"I know it, for before permitting me to see you he made me promise not to speak of M. de Carnoël or Georget, and Heaven is my witness that it is not my fault if I have broken my word."

"He shall know nothing of it, for I count on your discretion. The secret of our plans shall rest between us two. And now that our treaty is concluded, now that you are my ally, my friend, pardon me if I beg you not to lose a moment in seeing Georget."

Maxime rose. He understood that the countess dismissed him politely, but he still waited for a word, a look. It seemed to him he deserved something more than this friendly farewell.

" Do you think I should hold this language if you were indifferent to me?" she resumed, penetrating his thought.

Maxime fell on his knees, but at this moment the femme de chambre entered just in time to arrest a premature demonstration.

" Au revoir, monsieur," added the countess, with a smile full of promise; "I hope you will not make me wait for your visit, and perhaps I may have the pleasure of seeing you soon at your uncle's, for the first day I am able to leave the house shall be the occasion of a visit to M. Dorgères and his charming daughter.

CHAPTER XI.

ALTHOUGH Maxime succeeded until he had passed through the gateway of Mme. Yalta's mansion in preserving the appearance of decorum, no sooner did he find himself on the public sidewalk out of sight of the majestic porter of the countess, than he began to gesticulate and talk to himself like a lunatic or a poet, the two classes of men whom lovers most resemble.

This time he was captured by the heart as well as the head, and if Madame Yalta in saying farewell had commanded him to throw himself into the Seine, he would have hastened to obey. Happily she had contented herself with sending him to Madame Piriac's, but there was some merit to be attached to Maxime's acquitting himself of this mission. It was to act precisely contrary to the sage resolutions just formed with a thorough understanding of the subject. Maxime was rejoicing in the morning in the prospective marriage of his friend, Jules Vignory, and in the afternoon going to work to put a stop to it. His conduct was much the same as that of a lawyer who, in the midst of a speech, should desert his client to go over to the opposite party.

298

It was actual treason. And still he felt no remorse. What were now to him the ties of friendship? All such sentiments had dissolved like sealing-wax before the first fires of rising passion.

After all, the affair was full of obscurity, and one might easily be mistaken. He concluded also that a supplementary inquest would not be out of place in the interests of Alice, who did not deserve to be allowed to make a marriage like this, out of pique, if her first lover were not unworthy of her. M. Dorgères could not deem it a cause of reproach that his nephew had sought to repair a cruel injustice. There remained Vignory who would assuredly owe him no ill-will for bringing to light a rival whom the poor cashier could never have sought to supplant while he was still Alice's lover. And Vignory was of a quiet, conciliating temper; his love for Mlle. Dorgères was a tranquil love which time would appease. Moreover, he possessed a nice little bit of consolation seeing his patron had just made him his partner. Whatever happened, this advancement which he owed to the project of marriage between Mlle. Dorgères and himself was secured to him. Maxime having by this reasoning calmed whatever scruples he may have entertained, did not hesitate to jump into a carriage for Rue Cardinet. Persons under the influence of passion have always at hand an assortment of sophisms which they make use of to justify the least logical of their acts. From the Avenue de Friedland to the Batignolles is not a short transit, but it did not prove wearisome to Maxime, for he contemplated without ceasing the ring the countess had just placed in his hands. Assuredly it was written that Maxime should pass his life wearing jewels that were not his. After the bracelet, the ring ; after the turquoises, the amethyst. But what a difference ! The bracelet called up only disagreeable recollections ; the ring was nearly a promise ! Madame Yalta had not requested him to return it, and he was ready to accept as a pledge of reciprocated love this talisman which was to reduce the restive Madame Piriac to obedience. Maxime's imagination frequently played him such tricks as this.

He easily found the old house and entered with deliberate step. The alley was dark as ever, and through the glass door of the little lodge he saw the grandmother of Georget at her needle in the corner of the fire. He concluded to open the door and enter without knocking. She rose up quickly, as if with the intention of barring the passage.

"Madame," he said, unmoved by this discouraging reception, "I beg you to excuse the liberty I have taken. I have been several times to see Georget, and you have not done me the honor to receive me. To-day I venture to intrude on you for reasons that I will explain if you will listen to me."

Maxime was careful to express himself in the most respectful tone, that he might show the ancestress of the groom that he was not simple enough to mistake her for a real portress.

She guessed his intention, for she framed her reply as if she were simply the salaried guardian of a house occupied by laboring people.

" But, my good sir," she said humbly, " everybody may enter my lodge, and if you have not seen my boy it is because the doctor has forbidden him to see any one. He is not yet in a condition to talk."

" Not even with the Countess Yalta ? "

The widow Piriac started slightly, which did not escape the watchful eyes of Maxime, but she replied without much embarrassment :

" The lady will not certainly come here, however great the interest she may feel in my poor child ; but if she did I should beg to be excused from allowing her to see him."

" She will not come, but she has sent me."

" I was not aware that you knew her."

" I left her an hour ago, and she begged me to see Georget, to have a talk with him, and even to take him to walk."

" My dear sir, madame the countess is probably ignorant that the child does not know what he is saying— the shock he received has affected his brain—and the doctor has advised me not to let him go out."

" The countess, madame, foresaw the objections you would make, and to prove to you that she has charged me with combating them, placed this ring in my hands."

The ancestress of the groom turned pale and looked at M. Dorgères in blank stupor. "What does she expect of me?" she asked.

"Madame Yalta is bent on learning the fate of a young man who disappeared a month ago, M. Robert de Carnoël, and she wishes me to make use of Georget in trying to find him."

"She forgets he has lost his memory."

"No, but she hopes that it will return to him; that some circumstance—some chance which I shall try to bring about if you will permit him to accompany me—will awaken recollections. For instance, if I carried him to my uncle's offices, who knows if he might not recall something."

Madame Piriac reflected deeply, and Maxime thought he saw a hesitation between the necessity for obedience to a command it was impossible to disregard and the fear of injuring her grandson.

"Is M. Dorgères aware of Mme. Yalta's project?" she inquired at last.

"No," replied Maxime quickly, "and I shall not speak of it to him."

"Pardon me, sir, if I ask you one last question. Will you swear to me that whatever may be the result of your researches no harm shall come to Georget?"

"Madame," replied Maxime, in an accent that left no

doubt of his sincerity, " I give you my word that Georget
shall not be compromised in any way. I will add that I
am not curious as to the circumstances that have led to
your connexion with the countess. If it be a secret I
shalt not try to penetrate it. I have but one purpose, to
serve a woman who inspires me with the liveliest and
most respectful sympathy. It matters nothing to me
why she wishes to find M. de Carnoël. She wishes it,
that is enough to make me desire to aid her with all my
power."

" Sir," said the ancestress, " pardon me for having
hesitated before trusting you with what is dearest to me
in the world. I no longer hesitate and will call
Georget."

She had hardly pronounced the name when the child
darted into the lodge, through a door concealed behind
a tapestry curtain."

Maxime was inclined to suspect the cunning little
urchin had heard the entire conversation and entered
just at the right moment, but he was soon undeceived.
Georget opened his eyes wide and his face expressed
such unfeigned astonishment it was impossible to suspect
him of acting.

" M. Maxime ! " he exclaimed joyously.

" Yes, little one, it is I," replied the young man,
patting his cheek. " You didn't expect to see me
to-day ? "

" *Ma foi !* no, but I guess, all the same, why you

came. The patron sent for me to pull my ears. I didn't go to the office yesterday."

Georget said this with the most comical air imaginable, —the air of a schoolboy who has been caught in mischief and is much more inclined to laugh than to apologize. His complexion was paler than formerly, his face and person thinner, but his eyes were as bright as ever, his mouth as laughing, and but for his arm, which he carried in a sling, it would not have been supposed he had had so narrow an escape from a dangerous accident.

"Don't be afraid for your ears, my boy. My uncle didn't send me here to scold you. He knows very well it is not your fault that you have been absent for a month."

"What! has it been a month?—true, I have been on my back since—since the great snow. But if it has been a month New Year has passed."

"Don't be afraid; you shall have your New Year's gifts,—everything you want, if Madame Piriac will let you."

"Good mamma, I declare the doctor has not forbidden me to have bon-bons."

"He has forbidden you to talk too much," said the ancestress so quickly that it struck Maxime she wished to prevent the child from mentioning this doctor who must be M. Villagos. "Yes," continued Georget, "but he will let me go to walk. He said yesterday that I didn't take exercise enough, and must begin to use my arm."

" The out-door exercise would be of service to him,"
said Maxime, addressing Madame Piriac, "and since you
agree to it, I am going out with my young friend."

" Not for long, I hope, sir."

" Oh, we will return before dark, and if Georget seems
fatigued, we will take a carriage."

The ancestress acquiesced, thanks to the all powerful
talisman.

They had hardly touched the street when the boy
raised his head and sniffed the air like a young horse
who has long been confined to the stable.

"It is good to be out-doors," he cried, " and not going
to the office, for we are not going there, are we?"

"Never while we live," replied Maxime, gayly. "Did
you think I came to make you do penance?"

"Good!" If you knew how the time drags when I
am shut up in four walls! Hold, M. Maxime, you wont
tell this to good mamma, but sometimes when I get very
tired, I spin away as far as the Madeleine to play marbles.
—ten minutes in all, no more—but if M. Vignory had
known it—"

"Bah! he would have said nothing ; he is a good fellow."

"May be so, but he don't laugh much ; with you, now,
it's like M. Robert—I'm not afraid. You wouldn't have
told the patron on me."

"Is it long since you saw M. Robert?" asked Maxime,
quickly.

"Well, no—that is—wait now. The last time I sa
him was—*ma foi!* I can't think. All I remember is I
passed by me to go to the office. I took óff my cap, an
he said good morning."

"That was a month ago—probably .the day he wer
away, or the day before."

"He has gone away, then? That is queer. Wher
did he go?"

Maxime did not reply. He was thinking.

"Hold!" said Georget, suddenly, "here we are at the
Boulevard Malesherbes, and the booths are up. It must
be near New Year's."

"It has passed, my boy," said Maxime, shaking his
head sadly. "You forget I came to buy your New
Year's presents."

"Did you, really?"

"I told you so awhile ago. It seems your head is not
quite steady yet."

"Oh, dear no; it's in a queer way—my head. I
would like to tell you how it feels if I could."

"You can try."

"Well, you see, M. Maxime, at times it is all right in
my brain; you might ask my name and I couldn't tell
you, and then all of a sudden my ideas begin to dance
the polka. It seems as if about thirty-six came knocking at the door and trying to come in at once. Then it
is like being at the theatre when the curtain is raised. I
see a crowd of things I didn't see before. This lasts

time awhile, then all is mixed up and then it all disappears. Try as I may, I can recall nothing. It seems as if I had been dreaming, but I couldn't tell what."

Maxime was moved as he listened to this recital. The boy's mind had been only partially eclipsed, and even his memory which had chiefly suffered would return at times to vanish almost instantly. He must profit by one of these momentary returns to question him, but how was it to be called forth? He could only trust to chance.

They were a few steps from Rue Jouffroy, and he would pass that way to see if the boy would recognize it.

"Have you been to the Rink on Rue Blanche since the evening I met you there?"

"The Rink! no, I never go there."

"Really I thought you spent many evenings there. You told me so yourself."

"If I did I was yarning; only it does seem to me I was there once. It is where they skate on rollers, isn't it?"

"Yes. Do you remember that I came out with a lady, and that you followed me to the corner of the Avenue de Villiers and Rue Jouffroy? You know Rue Jouffroy well, do you not?"

"As my pocket. It is the first to the left."

"We are just at the place where you got me a hack and the rascals who ran after me were outwitted."

"Yes, they were three," murmured Georget. "I knew

they meant to stop you when you had passed the street."

"How did you know it ?"

"That I couldn't tell you. But I remember I made up my mind they shouldn't do you any harm."

"And the lady who was on my arm, do you remember her ? A brunette with large dark eyes. She told me her name was Madame Sergent."

"Madame Sergent ? don't know. Droll sort of name, though. Why not Madame Corporal ?"

They were now at the corner of Rue Jouffroy, and Maxime was preparing for a stroke on the effect of which he calculated. He thought that if Georget had been even indirectly involved in the theft, he must have some knowledge of the woman of the Rink and her acolyte, the Carpathian bear. If he had known them he must have had access to the mysterious house which they occupied or pretended to occupy, and the sight of the house might awaken his sleeping memory.

"Do you pass this way often in going to the office?" he asked.

"That depends," replied Georget; "it is shorter by the Boulevard Malesherbes, but some days I take the longest route ; then I go by the Avenue de Villiers, the Boulevard de Courcelles, the Parc Monceaux ; I turn into the Avenue de Messine, where I sometimes find a party of boys to play with ; then I file along Rue de Miromesnil or the Boulevard Haussman, and bring up at Rue de Suresnes."

"Then it was on some of these streets that your accident happened?"

"Perhaps."

"Should you recognize the place if I took you there?"

"I don't believe I should. Grandmamma says I was picked up on the Boulevard de Courcelles, lying across the rails of the tramway; I didn't put myself there you may be sure; it follows somebody else did."

"To have you crushed to death, my poor Georget. You have savage enemies, then?"

Just at this moment they arrived before the house that had sheltered the problematical Mme. Sergent.

"*Parbleu!*" said Maxime, as he stopped before it, "this is a pretty house; it would be a better lodging than my second floor Rue de Châteaudun. It appears to be for rent. The shutters are closed. Do you know whose house it is?"

Georget did not reply He examined the house attentively, passing his hand over his forehead—the usual gesture when one tries to recover a fleeting idea.

"Ah—at last—I know it!" cried the boy. "No, no, it is not for rent—it is all shut up, but that doesn't signify. Some one is there."

"Who?"

"Ladislas, *parbleu!* the red horseman—the man that trains horses."

"What horses?"

"The lady's horses."

"What is the lady's name?"

"I do not know any more."

Disappointed, Maxime resumed his questioning from another point.

"You knew this Ladislas, did you?"

"Oh, not much. I have seen him two or three times, and that was enough."

"Have you been in his house?"

"No, he shut the door in my face.'

"But you had some business with him, as you came to see him?"

The boy reflected a moment.

"It is no use to ask me. My head is gone. It is night—you know."

Maxime saw it was useless to insist. Georget evidently was honest with him. He had lucid moments but his mind was quickly obscured. His brain resembled one of those capricious watches that suddenly stop and start off again when vigorously shaken.

"And the Countess Yalta, did you know her?" he asked suddenly, as he led Georget toward the Avenue de Villiers.

"That I do. She is a friend of grandmamma's."

"Then you go to her house?"

"Oh, very often. It is so pretty, and there are more pictures than at the museum, and she isn't a bit prouder for it all, the countess isn't. Whenever I go there she has served up for me—a queer kind of dish it is—fish roe on bread and butter."

This way of designating the Russian dish caviare, made
Maxime smile without diverting him from his investigation.

"What does she talk to you about?" he asked.

"All sorts of things. Wait! the last time I saw her
was—all I know is she was ill and received me on a great
bed like the one in the Louis XIV chamber at Versailles.
She asked me about M. de Carnoël."

"And could you tell her?"

"I don't know; it seems to me I hadn't seen him for
three or four days."

"Would you like to see him again?"

"Oh, yes."

"Then let us go to my uncle's. Vignory, may be, can
tell us where he is. For my part I don't know."

"I will go wherever you wish, M. Maxime, but if I
once set foot in the office they won't let me off again, and
I like better to walk."

"Never fear. They will not keep you. You are free
until you can make use of your arm again."

"My arm! I had forgotten that, but it is so; I am
one-handed for awhile yet, but I could run errands all
the same."

"I answer for it Vignory will not keep you, and that
he will receive you kindly too. They are fond of you
there—my uncle, and my cousin Alice."

"She is so good; is it true she is to marry M. de Carnoël?"

"I believe not. He has left the house."

"But he will soon come back?"

"No one can tell. I am trying to find him."

After this reply the conversation suddenly ceased, to Maxime's great regret. Georget, who had chattered incessantly since he left his grandmother's lodge, now fell into a profound meditation. Maxime looked at him out of the corner of his eye, and from the serious expression on his infantine countenance, he saw that the child was making prodigious efforts to collect his thoughts. Evidently the name of Carnoël had awakened confused recollections. The silence was prolonged, and while they passed down the Boulevard Malesherbes, George did not once open his lips. He suffered himself to be led by the Rue de Suresnes, and it was not until he had passed the door of the banker's house that he recovered his speech.

"Hold!" he cried, "that lad has on my vest buttons and cap. It doesn't keep him from looking like a simpleton though."

Maxime did not see fit to inform the boy that the groom in question was his substitute. He excused himself also from making any explanations to the porter who came out of his hole and looked at Georget, come back to life, with a thunder-struck visage.

He found Vignory busied in arranging the papers in the safe, and on seeing Maxime he exclaimed : "What! you again."

"Again is not very amiable, but I forgive you, for

you appear to be over head and ears in work. I will not disturb you long. I only wish to present a lad of your acquaintance. What has become of him ?" he added, turning round.

Georget had managed to glide behind him to avoid confronting the cashier, and was crouching down by the side of the safe. To bring him before Vignory, Maxime had to take the child by the collar.

"So here you are !" exclaimed the cashier, much surprised that Maxime had brought him a boy whom he had accused that very morning of being the author or accomplice of the theft. "You are cured, then ? But no, you have only one arm. How is the other ?"

"The other is hanging to my neck. I only beat with one wing, but it's all the same, M. Vignory, if you want me.'

"Then you don't know that the patron has filled your place ?"

"With this great canary bird that I met just now ? I suspected as much. Hold !".he cried suddenly, "you have changed the word. It was Mlle. Alice, and now—"

"How do you know that ?" asked Vignory, stupefied.

"Because I saw it. And before that there was another."

The nephew and the cashier exchanged significant glances.

"And the trap," continued Georget, "the iron arms which catch the thieves ? Ah ! here they are."

Maxime, as much agitated as his friend, took the

child by the arm and led him toward the closet which the new partner of M. Dorgères had arranged for his private use.

Vignory understood and followed. They pushed Georget in and shut themselves up with him.

"You have fixed this little hole up nicely. It was so full of old papers there wasn't room for the patron's Newfoundland."

"But you could get in, could you?" asked Maxime, quickly.

"*Dame!* I'm not as large as the dog."

"Then you did get in sometimes?

"I believe so—but I'm not very sure."

"Try to remember."

"I do try, but I can't."

Maxime made a sign to Vignory, who went apart with him to one end of the long, narrow closet.

'Well, what do you say to that?" he asked   "Do you think I was right in suspecting this boy of being concerned in the theft?' ·

"The chap must at least have furnished some indications to the thieves. But that does not prove M. de Carnoël to be innocent," he added, timidly.

"You suppose that he could have had an understanding with Georget—in fact, it is not impossible. Georget was devoted to him."

"And does he know where he is?" asked the cashier in a husky voice.

" He has known, most likely, but has forgotten—like all the rest."

" Do you believe this loss of memory is not acting ? "

" If it were, he would not have been so imprudent. He was not obliged to commit himself as he has done. At any rate, it would be well to question him thoroughly. The sight of the safe has brought him to the desired point. If I lose this opportunity, I might never re-cover it."

" Hey ! Georget, what are you thinking about ? "

" Nothing," replied the child, " I was just waiting for M. Vignory to send me on an errand."

" M. Vignory has nothing for you to-day."

" So much the worse. I would rather be on the streets than in the waiting-room, though sometimes you can have fun there too. Such droll people come in ! "

" We might lay a wager that you play tricks on them."

" Never, M. Maxime Malicome must have told you that.'

" Why Malicome ? "

" Because he don't like me. He is wrong. I could have had him sent off and I didn't."

" You ! "

" Yes ; I had only to tell that he was never at his post, and that in the evening anybody can walk in the office as if it were a mill. I've done it myself."

" Come ! you always decamp when six o'clock strikes."

"That's true. I have friends who wait for me before the Madeleine at quarter past six. Still, I'm sure I have stayed here,—at least once,—when nobody was about. I remember how afraid I was."

"Afraid of what?"

"Of everything. At night the office is only lighted by the gas jet at the corner, the great safe looks like a huge giant, and mice are running under your feet,—it makes your flesh creep."

"They shut you up while you were asleep?"

"Perhaps."

"And you didn't call to them to let you out?"

"I don't know."

"Then you saw no one?"

"No,—no one."

"How did you get out?"

"I don't know."

Maxime stamped his foot with impatience. The exasperating, "I do not know," came back like a refrain to cut short all progress. There was nothing left but to begin again.

Vignory knit his brows and shrugged his shoulders.

"Do you know Col. Borisoff?"

"Col. Borisoff! That I do. I have seen him at least three times. I was here when he came to get a box he had left with the patron. I don't like him, this Borisoff."

"Why?"

"Oh, first, because I don't like Russians.   Neither does grandmamma."

"What have they done to her?"

"Many things in former times,—things that I have forgotten; and I don't like the way he talks.   One might suppose he was a hand-organ grinding out the Grâce de Dieu.   What fun I had taking him off that morning! He saw me and began to growl at me, and I might have faired badly if M. Vignory hadn't opened just then."

"M. Borisoff would have done well to give you a les-son," said Vignory.   'The patron didn't pay you to make fun of his clients and listen at doors."

Maxime hastened to resume the conversation, fearing that Vignory's ill-humor would spoil everything."

"Bah!" he said, "everybody has a right to laugh a little.   And I don't think much of Col. Borisoff either. Did he get his casket?"

"No, for it was not there."

"Some one had taken it away?" he asked eagerly.

"For certain."

"Who?"

"Wait; let me think.   It was—now the fog is rising in my head.   I had the name and it has flown."

"Ladislas?" said Maxime, at a venture.

"Yes, that is it," cried Georget, clapping his hands.

"And the lady?"

"The lady—what lady?"

" The one that owned the horses that Ladislas trained ; you spoke of her to me."

Georget began to reflect, and replied slowly :

" I did not see the lady.   Ladislas was alone."

" Think well.   It was, perhaps, the same who left the Rink with me.   You know I met there a woman ; that I came away with her, and that you followed us."

" Don't tell me that, M. Maxime ; that mixes me all up."

" Then let us go back to Ladislas.   He didn't like Borisoff, as he stole his box ? "

"Borisoff is a brigand."

" Good !   But what did he do to Ladislas ? "

Georget put his hands over his forehead, but made no answer.

" I cannot," he murmured, with a despairing expression.   It is over.   I know nothing more."

Maxime was desperate.   He saw that his friend thought the scene ridiculous, and still doubted the good faith of the boy   Vignory in this affair could not be impartial.

He thought of his vanished rival who was still formidable, and cursed the fever of investigation that had taken possession of Maxime Dorgéres.

" What good is to be done by bringing up all this ? " he thought; " and what use can be made of the testimony of an idiot ? "

And drawing Maxime aside, he said in his ear :

" What are you hoping to arrive at ? That this frightful *gamin* knew and aided the thieves is evident, but
what of it ? For my part, I have seen enough of
Georget. Take him where he came from, and let us
talk of this nò more."

" So be it," replied Maxime, a little piqued. " Come.
Georget," he added, pushing the child toward the door.
Vignory made no effort to detain him. . The friends
shook hands and separated without another word. Vignory resumed his verification of accounts. Maxime
passed through the office and went out with Georget.

He was by no means of the same opinion as his uncle's
partner—this headstrong Maxime. The boy's silence on
certain points served only to stimulate him in the chase
after discoveries ; urged him forward in pursuit without
regard to where it would lead, and without respect of
persons. He had an unexpected meeting in the gateway with Mlle. Dorgéres, guarded by the inevitable Mme.
Martineau. She had grown paler, but was still lovely,
and her sweet face brightened as she perceived Maxime
and Georget.

The child uttered a cry of joy. She came toward
them, and extending her hand to her cousin, inquired
for the health of the poor boy.

" He is very well," replied Maxime. " I went to his
grandmother's for him, and am taking him to walk by
way of diversion. See what a good boy I am become.
May I ask where you are going ? "

"It is a secret," replied Alice, "but I will take you into my confidence. I am going to sit for my portrait. It is to be a surprise for my father."

"Where does your artist live?"

"Corner of Rue de Lisbonne and Rue de Courcelles. If you take Georget back to his grandmother, it is almost your route; will you come with us?"

"And you can tell us on the way about a lady who is dying to know my pupil—the Countess Yalta."

"The Countess Yalta!" repeated Maxime, who little expected to hear Madame Martineau pronounce this name.

"Yes, sir, this noble lady came to your uncle's an hour ago, and has expressed a desire to see your cousin. M. Dorgères did his best to decline the honor she wished to confer on his daughter. He is of the opinion that a foreigner who drives four horses is not the most suitable associate for a young lady. But the countess insisted so, that he was compelled to put her off with some evasive reply. So she left, saying she would return. We have been at a loss to account for this passion for Alice, and hoped you might have the answer to the riddle. Between ourselves, your uncle thinks she is crazy.'

Maxime was not quite of this opinion, but he was amazed that the countess whom he had left extended on a couch had so soon after driven out in spite of the orders of Dr. Villagos.

"See here, my dear Alice," he said, after a pause, "you

know that Jules Vignory is my friend and cannot surely suspect me of a desire to injure him Well, honesty obliges me to tell you that the countess undertakes to establish the innocence of M. de Carnoël."

Alice turned pale and made no reply, but Madame Martineau exclaimed: "What concern is it of this stranger's? And you, sir, cannot you see that you distress your cousin by recalling a past that she voluntarily ignores? And you must acknowledge that it sounds strangely to hear you undertake the cause of a man whom you were the first to accuse."

"I do not defend him; it is the countess who does. I seek only for the truth. She is convinced that M. de Carnoël is innocent, and that if he has not shown himself for a month past, it is because he has fallen into the hands of those who were interested in preventing him from doing so.'

"It is absurd," cried the governess.

"It doesn't appear very likely, I confess. You asked me the countess' intentions. You know them now, and can decide what course to pursue. I do not engage you either to see the lady or to decline to enter into any relations with her."

"The question is decided. M. Dorgères has refused your countess, and is determined to close his house to her."

"My uncle has the right to act as he sees fit."

"But you, Maxime," murmured the girl, "are you—"

"Oh! I know well enough what I am going to do. I shall finish what I have begun. The truth must come out. We are all interested in discovering it."

"Sir," said Madame Martineau, "if your uncle were aware of your projects, he would not thank you for these ill-advised proceedings."

"Dear madame, I should be grieved to displease him, but my part is taken. Alice will not see the countess. I shall continue to see her. Perhaps we are both right. It is late. I promised Madame Piriac to bring Georget back before night. Let me take leave of you and quicken my steps." And having bowed to the governess and pressed his cousin's hand, he walked on to rejoin Georget, whom he had sent on in advance.

"Well, little one," he asked, "are you pleased with your walk?"

"Oh, yes, it is good to breathe the fresh air."

"To-morrow I shall come for you again and we will take a different walk. Perhaps I shall take you to see the countess."

"What countess?".

"The one who has the beautiful house in the Avenue de Friedland."

"Ah! yes, Nadèje."

"Nadèje! You mean the Countess Yalta?

"Grandmother always calls her Nadèje. Ask her.

Here was another cause of astonishment. Maxime did not know the first name of the countess, and he little expected to hear it spoken by a *gamin* of Rue Cardinet.

"Ah !" said the boy, "here we are at the street where I have made such nice parties. See the sidewalk before this grand house ; it might have been made to play marbles on. I played there two hours the day I broke my paw."

"Ah ! really, you recognize the place ?"

"Oh, perfectly, it seems as if it was only yesterday. I didn't go to the office in the morning, and I said to myself : 'Just as well not to go at all to-day ; they will think I have been ailing.'"

"But you didn't stay there all day ?"

"No, I was sauntering round the fortifications ; but it seems to me I returned here, I can't tell why."

"It is, *parbleu !* a splendid mansion. Monumental entrance, superb court. There must be a garden in the rear extending toward Parc Monceaux. If you would like, we can walk around it. Do you know to whom it belongs ?"

"No ; yet I fancy I have been in there."

"I shall find out," thought Maxime, whose curiosity began to awaken

"Why did you go there ?" he resumed aloud. "To take a letter from the office, perhaps ?"

"No, I am sure it was not that ; I didn't set foot in Rue de Seresnes that day."

"Here is the Boulevard de Courcelles where you were

picked up," he said, pointing to a street which bordered a long wall.

As soon as they passed the corner which bore the municipal placard, the child's eyes brightened, and he exclaimed :

"It was here. I recognize the place. Come, I will show it to you."

After having run about twenty yards Georget stopped.

"Do you see this wall ? Well, I fell from there."

"Are you sure of that ?'

"Very sure. See, there is some plaster work that has been detached. I struck my head on this large stone at my foot."

"It was not here, however, that you were found. You were lying on the road across the rails of the tramway."

"Some one must have taken me there   I don't remember anything after I made the somerset."

"But why did you climb on the wall?"

"To see what was on the other side."

"And what did you see ?"

"Nothing ; it is night now."

Maxime made a movement of impatience, but he controlled himself.

"How, *diable !* did you get up there?"

"I believe it was with a cord. Yes, that was it—a cord with knots, and a hook at the end."

"And where did you get the cord ?"

"I have forgotten; but I answer for it that I made use of a knotted cord. It must have broken when I was getting down."

"Let us see, my little Georget. Try to remember once more. You had some idea when you tried to scale the wall?"

"No doubt, but I have forgotten what."

"Think. Take time, and don't be frightened if I press you a little. I am not Vignory, and have no orders to give you. I am your friend—as M. de Carnoël was."

Aladdin, in the "Thousand and One Nights," must have been amazed at the appearance of the genie his rubbing had evoked. Maxime Dorgères was not less so when Georget exclaimed :

"M. de Carnoël! It was he! I was looking for him when I climbed up there."

"You knew, then, that he was in that house?" asked Maxime, quickly

"I saw him go in; it all comes to me now! But I must tell you quickly. Let me see; where was I? Ah! *mon Dieu!* can I have forgotten? No, I know! In the morning I was playing marbles in the Rue de Vigny. I saw M. de Carnoël arrive in a beautiful carriage; there was a gentleman with him—a gentleman with gold spectacles—and on the box with the coachman a man dressed like an office boy. The gate was opened, the carriage entered, and it closed immediately. I had thought M. de Carnoël had left Paris ; and then he looked so sad I

imagined he was carried off by force, and they were shutting him up as in prison.   Then I led off the boys to a
bastion where the Levallois lads come to play *bouchon.*
Ten minutes after I left them and returned to Rue de
Vigny.   I wanted to find out if M. de Carnoël had left
the house.   Ah ! then I got up some brass.   I rang and
asked the porter squarely :

"'Is my master here ?'

"'Who is your master ?'

"'M. the Marquis Robert de Carnoël.'

" I thought he would have swallowed me up.

"'Get out, you vermin,' and he slammed the door in
my face.

" I couldn't break it down, but I hid in the street behind a pile of masonry, and stayed there till night.   The
carriage came out again at the end of an hour, and M. de
Carnoël was not in it.   I said to myself, they have shut
him up to do him some harm, but I will get him out.
Just then I saw a child that I knew.   His father keeps a
gymnasium in the Avenue de Wagram.   I gave him ten
sous to bring me a good knotted cord with a hook at the
end.   When eleven o'clock struck there was no one passing on the boulevard.   The snow was falling heavily.   I
came to this spot.   I threw up my hook, climbed up on
the cord, and placing myself astride on the top of the
wall, I looked and saw—"

" M. de Carnoël ? "

" Yes ; he was standing behind the panes of a large

window, and held a candle so that I saw him distinctly. I recognized him perfectly, and think he recognized me, for he made signs."

"And then?" asked Maxime, quickly.

"Then I fell, and I remember no more; it is all gone —all is confusion in my brain. I want to go back to grandmother."

"Come, my friend," said Maxime, who knew enough to act on.

CHAPTER XII.

MAXIME INTERVIEWS THE COLONEL.

WHILE Maxime Dorgères was promenading with Georget, Col. Borisoff, reclining indolently on a divan, was conferring with his intendant, whom he had just summoned. The ci-devant M. Briare, the false representative of the false agency, the man with the sallow visage and the smooth tongue, was standing before his master, awaiting in a respectful attitude his lord's commands.

The colonel blew out a long puff of Turkish-tobacco smoke, let fall his narghile pipe, and said, somewhat languidly :

" What is the Frenchman doing now ? "

" He is asleep, your excellency."

" Or pretends to be. What has he talked about this morning ? "

" Of nothing, your excellency. He makes no reply when I inquire for his health."

" Is it good ? "

" Very good, excellency. He is scarcely altered. The man is sustained by an iron will."

" Say rather that he is headstrong ; that, having reflected upon the situation, he has determined upon silence at whatever cost. Of two evils that threatened he has chosen the lesser."

" It seems to me that if you dispatched him to Siberia his fate would be no enviable one. I hardly see what worse could befall him."

" Vacili, you have no common-sense."

. " I beg pardon, your excellency ; but it seems to me, if this young man could avoid this journey by delivering up the names of his accomplices, he would do well. He has sense enough to understand that it is the only way out of the difficulty." .

" Yes, but he has sense enough to know too that those he had betrayed would never forgive him. He knows they have no mercy for traitors. He cannot be ignorant of the history of Serge Lawrowski It happened only last year at Pultawa. Did you know this Lawrowski ? "

" Yes, your excellency. He was one of the most skil-·ful agents of the political police."

" Well, with all his skill he was ensnared by a priest's daughter, a child just seventeen years old, who looked like a saint. She drew him into a garden at night, where the Nihilists awaited him. They cut off his ears and nose, and the poor devil died in consequence of this ugly operation. My prisoner does not desire such an end as that ; he prefers the journey to Siberia, and that is the secret of his resistance."

"Perhaps, too, he does not believe you will carry out your threat."

"Yes ; these French always imagine it is impossible to treat them like simple mortals, and that one would not dare to act here as one would in St. Petersburg. But I charge myself with undeceiving him. You will get ready the rolling prison that serves for these transports, and when he sees it all drawn up he will decide, perhaps, to speak."

"The question is whether he has really anything to confess," said Vacili, timidly.

"Do you doubt it?"

"Your excellency, I should not allow myself to entertain a different opinion from my master, but if you will deign to hear my reasons—"

"Speak, I consent."

"First, is it likely that any one in league with Nihilists would so easily have fallen into the trap I laid for him? The rascals of that sect do not dream of embarking for America."

"I have not said he was a regularly enrolled Nihilist. Firstly, he is not Russian ; he is merely a simpleton whom one of their infernal women has seduced."

"Your excellency forgets that he loved the daughter of M. Dorgères."

"Did he not rob me of my papers on the very day he was dismissed by the banker? On that day he listened to the voice of a woman who had been his mistress. She promised him her protection in foreign parts, and he was content with the fifty thousand francs taken from the safe."

"Unless it was sent to him as he asserts."

"Bah! This person who suddenly remembers an old debt is a very improbable character."

"However it may be, your excellency, this accomplice of M. de Carnoël it has been impossible to find."

"Because the search has not been well made. The information I have recently received from the chief of the third section is very incomplete. There are obscure women whom no one has thought of as managing and arranging these plots. They knew that my casket contained the whole plan of my mission, all my correspondence with the general and the minister."

"What is extraordinary is that they should have been aware of the depositing of the casket with your banker."

"Informed by the secretary, no doubt."

"Your excellency, I have made a minute inquest concerning the life led by the young man, and it is certain that he did not associate with a single Russian I have gone so far as to obtain information concerning this Countess Yalta, who has funds deposited at M. Dorgères, and I am satisfied that he has never seen her."

"Oh, the Yalta has no connection with Nihilists. I have pointed her out to the department. She has been watched very closely, and it is certain thal she is not engaged in politics. Her father was a kind of Circassian prince, who sold his principality to the emperor for several millions of rubles. The daughter married some other dispossessed lord, who soon left her a widow. She left Russia in her childhood, and has since only thought of her pleasures. Let us leave her and return to the Frenchman. I must decide what course to take. His month of protection will end to-morrow. I must, before giving it up, make one more attempt. I saw the banker yesterday, and he told me that the time of his daughter's marriage was fixed. We shall see what the prisoner will say to this disastrous intelligence. It is the ruin of his last hopes. What do you say to my idea, Vacili ? "

"Your excellency, I confess another has occurred to me."

"Let us have it."

"I start from a principle you have just laid down, that the young man will keep silence to the end for fear of the vengeance of the Nihilists. I have more than once been disposed to regret his capture. Do you not think that had he remained free he would have compromised himself by some imprudent act ? "

"Yes," murmured the colonel, "we were perhaps too hasty. Unfortunately it is too late to retrace our steps. This Carnoël is forewarned. He would not be so foolhardy as to visit his accomplices, or rather his accomplice, for I am convinced it is only a woman."

"Your excellency," said Vacili, with embarrassment, "there is still time to have recourse to a means you have

overlooked. I believe it would be better to restore
M. de Carnoël to liberty."

" To release the Frenchman ! You are mad, Vacili."

" Pardon me, your excellency. I have reflected much
on the situation, and I see no other means of discovering
M. de Carnoël's accomplices.'

" You forget that his first care would be to avenge
himself on me. He would enter a complaint for arbitrary sequestration."

" Your excellency, I do not believe it. It would compel him to enter into explanations which he would rather
avoid. Besides, you could exact a promise of silence. If
he gave you his word of honor he would keep it."

" I admit that he will not complain to the authorities,
but if he sees Mlle. Dorgères or writes to her, which is
infinitely probable, he will naturally be led to explain
why he did not appear for a month."

" Your excellency, I know him, I have studied him.
If he promises you silence he will be silent even with
Mlle. Dorgères."

" But you forget there was some one who saw the
Frenchman enter this house."

" Your excellency alludes to the child who came to
ask for him the day I brought him here. The child's
conduct proved that he suspected something, and I
should have watched him closely, but I learned next
morning that there was nothing more to fear. He was
picked up half-dead on the boulevard. What happened

to him is not known, but I suspect he was trying to scale the garden wall and fell. What is certain is that he is an idiot and will never speak of what he knows."

"I am not too sure of that. He might get well. And it is very extraordinary that a groom should have risked his neck to ascertain what had become of the banker's ex-secretary. Who knows if this chap hadn't something to do with the theft. You ought to have made an inquest."

"Your excellency, it has been done, and I have ascertained positively that it was a mere chance. Fortunately he broke his head before he had time to babble. And the proof is that during this month no attempt has been made to deliver M. de Carnoël."

The door opened and a *valet de pied* entered, bearing a card on a silver waiter.

"Who is it?" asked the colonel, with a gesture of impatience. "I have said I should receive no one."

"Your excellency, this gentleman insisted, saying that he came on pressing business.'

M. Borisoff took the card, and read with astonishment the name of his visitor.

"Ask him into the salon" he said to the *valet de pied.*

When alone with his steward: "Do you know who asks for me? It is the nephew of the banker Dorgères. I do not know him What can he want with me?"

"Your excellency, perhaps the young man was sent to you by his uncle."

"Very likely; but for what? It is singular that he

appears just as we were speaking of the secretary. Say
to the head of the stables to make ready my travelling-
carriage at all events. It is by no means certain that I
shall decide to release our man."

The intendant bowed profoundly, and left the room
backward.

After dismissing him, M. Borisoff rose from the divan
and passed into the neighboring salon.

He found Maxime Dorgères standing by a window,
and by the expression of his countenance judged that his
errand was of a grave nature. It was not the first time
he had seen the banker's nephew, but had never spoken
to him, and their meeting would have been cold enough
but for the colonel

"Monsieur," he said, "before inquiring what has
brought you, permit me to congratulate myself on your
visit. M. Dorgères has frequently spoken of you, and I
have regretted that I had not the pleasure of your acquaintance.'

"I am obliged to you, sir," replied Maxime, coldly ;
"but when you learn why I have come—"

"Tell me something of M. Dorgères. I have not seen
him for some days."

"I do not come on his behalf, and I—"

"How is his lovely daughter ? Is it true that her mar-
riage-day is fixed ?'

"I do not know, sir, and I have something else to talk
about."

This was said in so dry a tone and so serious an air that the colonel immediately changed his attitude and language.

"Then, sir, be kind enough to explain yourself," he said, haughtily. "I thought you wished to pay me a friendly visit. It seems I was mistaken; but I cannot guess what you have to say to me."

"I have to ask what has become of M. de Carnoël," replied Mazime, looking fixedly at M. Borisoff.

It must have been that the colonel was gifted with a *sang froid* that was invincible, for he replied without betraying himself:

"You wish to know what has become of M. de Carnoël, who was employed, I believe, with M. Dorgères, my banker?"

"Yes," replied Maxime.

"Well, I wish to know why you address yourself to me, who had no relations with this gentleman. I saw him, I believe, once in M. Dorgères' office, and did not speak to him."

"It is possible, but subsequently you were much occupied with him."

"Be good enough to explain yourself more clearly."

"Willingly. I need not say that M. de Carnoël left my uncle's house the evening the safe was robbed. A casket was taken belonging to you, and M. de Carnoël was accused of the theft."

"It is true. But it was agreed that this should be kept

secret, and I am astonished that M. Dorgères has related it to you."

"No matter, I know it; and I know also that you charged yourself with discovering M. de Carnoël."

"I engaged your uncle not to lodge a complaint. It would be offensive to me to have my name mixed up with judicial inquests. M. Dorgères yielded to my view, and begged me to make use of my diplomatic relations for the discovery of the wretch who had robbed him. Unfortunately the researches ended in nothing. M. de Carnoël went into Brittany, and after his return to Paris could not be traced further. It is likely he has left France. But you know all this, since you are so well informed, and I cannot sufficiently express my surprise at such a proceeding. It is not, I presume, your uncle who has recommended it?"

"No, sir; I have consulted no one, but have acted with a perfect knowledge of the facts, and I demand once more an answer to my question: 'What has become of M. de Carnoël?'"

"Do you ask me this seriously?"

"Very seriously."

"It is so strange that I might take it in bad part, but I content myself with saying that I have already answered you. M. de Carnoël is in foreign parts, I have every reason to suppose."

"M. de Carnoël is in Paris."

"How do you know?"

"I have seen him."

"When?"

"A month ago."

"Very possibly ; but in a month he has had time to cross the frontier, and even the seas."

"I saw him pass near here in a carriage, which went toward Monceaux Park."

"It is to be regretted you did not follow it. We might have known where it conducted M. de Carnoël."

"I did not follow it, but some one saw it again afterward."

"Ah ! really ! and where did it go ? "

"It went to the Rue de Vigny, it stopped before your house, the gate opened, the carriage entered—"

"What ! here ! " cried M. Borisoff. " Ah ! this is too much, and I am amazed you should attach importance to so absurd an invention."

"It is no invention. The person who saw it made no mistake."

"So," replied the colonel, feigning to suppress a strong inclination to laugh, "you believe that this secretary, after having been sent off and accused of theft, has made me a visit. It was probably for the purpose of returning my casket."

"I do not suppose he came here voluntarily."

"Then I kidnapped him in the midst of Paris and in full light of day ? And for what purpose may I ask ? "

"I cannot say, sir, but I know that M. de Carnoël has

been brought to your house, and that he must be still there."

"He must be there," is admirable.

"Railing is not answering. If he is not here you know where he is, for you cannot deny that he came here."

"I do deny it on the contrary. I deny it absolutely."

"You deny it, I affirm it, and I wish to know what you have done with M. de Carnoël."

For a few moments the colonel did not reply, and when he did, it was in a serious and injured tone.

"Sir," he said slowly, "I should be justified in cutting short such an interview as this, but I have friendly relations with M. Dorgères, and I content myself with reminding you of the very singular nature of this summons which you have addressed to me in my own house. Assuredly you do not hope that I shall submit to you, and do not pretend to constrain me to answer you?"

"No, I shall take other means to attain my end. If necessary, I shall have recourse to the commissary of police."

"This passes all bounds," said M. Borisoff. "I have listened patiently to absurd questionings. I cannot tolerate threats, and beg you to leave my house."

"Is it your last word?" asked Maxime, red with anger.

"Yes, sir, and I should have spoken it sooner, for this conversation has lasted too long."

"Very well. I know what remains for me to do, and

have nothing more to say. You cannot tolerate threats ; I cannot tolerate offensive language. You have spoken of my questions as absurd. To-morrow I shall send you my seconds."

"I am ready for them," replied the colonel, turning his back on Maxime, who went out furious.

The calm which M. Borisoff had maintained during their interview was on the surface, and when Vacili saw his master again he discerned that a storm was brewing.

"Do you know what this scoundrel has said to me ? He has summoned me to render up M. de Carnoël. He affirms that he was seen to enter here a month ago—in a carriage. "He is, you see, well informed."

"It must have been that child—and yet no—since he has lost his memory. If he had told it immediately, M. Dorgères would not have waited so long to set these proceedings on foot."

"It matters little how he got his information. He has challenged me and threatened me with the commissary of police. I scoff at his challenge and his threats. However, we must take the subject into consideration. And first I cannot release the Carnoël, neither can I keep him here longer. I don't intend to run any risk of being brought before their tribunals. M. de Carnoël will leave here to-morrow evening. Let the carriage be ready at nightfall. Be sure and telegraph to our agents to have the relays ready as far as Strasburg."

"Your excellency, it shall be done."

"Now I am going to make a last attempt to induce him to capitulate. Go and announce to him my visit."

Vacili bowed and went out.

His master was decidedly in an ill-humor, for he walked up and down the room with long strides, gesticulating and even doubling his fist at his invisible enemies.

"Cursed be the day when I came to Paris to watch over the intrigues of a few undiscoverable knaves ! In Russia one has at least power, and is not afraid to arrest suspected creatures. If I do not succeed in my mission, the great chief will say I am a blockhead. I should like to see him here in my place. Come ! this Carnoël shall pay for the others," concluded M. Borisoff as he pushed open with violence the door of a gallery leading to the library in which Robert was confined.

Robert de Carnoël was not expecting a visit from his jailor—Robert de Carnoël had ceased to expect or to hope.

The first days of his captivity had been passed in fearful agony. He had frequent interviews with the colonel, who amused himself by torturing him with accounts of the project of marriage formed by M. Dorgères, and the progress which Vignory was making in the heart of Mlle. Alice.

The apparition of the first night was not renewed on the night following. Robert passed several hours uselessly before the window panes. The child did not reappear on the wall. But that was no reason for despairing.

If the brave boy proposed to deliver him either by force or stratagem, he must take time for the execution of so difficult an enterprise.

A week passed, then two, and then three, and there was no sign of Georget. Soon the colonel also ceased to visit him, abandoning him to the care and vigilance of his subalterns. And Robert, left to his reflections, confined in complete isolation, little by little came to believe that there remained to him not a single chance of safety. Abandoned by all, he had accepted his destiny, and had arrived at that stern resignation that is born of despair. He spoke no more, and forced himself to think no more.

It will easily be believed that in this frame of mind he received with indifference the announcement of the colonel's visit.

The intendant, Vacili, who brought it, received no reply, and when M. Borisoff entered M. de Carnoël did not deign to rise and receive him.

"It is a long time since I have seen you," said the Russian, taking no notice of the prisoner's attitude. " I have given you time to reflect on the proposition I made, and which I do not withdraw. I gave you a month for consideration, and this month will expire to-morrow. I come to know if you have decided to speak ?"

" I have nothing to say to you."

" I must remind you that if you consent to name your accomplice you will be free that very instant, and that I

will undertake to reinstate you in the eyes of M. Dorgères."

" It is very tempting, but I repeat that I am innocent,
consequently that I have no accomplice, and that I shall
not buy my liberty at the price of a lying confession."

"I know what restrains you. You believe Mlle. Dorgères to be irrecoverably lost to you. I am about to put
you in possession of the facts—to tell you how matters
stand."

"Spare yourself the trouble ; you will obtain nothing
from me."

" No matter, it is well you should know all. I told you
of the project of M. Dorgères to give his daughter to his
cashier, whom he had just made his partner. Now the
marriage is decided. Your friend Vignory has been
accepted by Mlle. Alice. To tell the truth, I did not
think she would decide so quickly. It was your prolonged absence which led to this result. Had you
listened to me it would have been in your power to reappear and cut short your rival's matrimonial campaign ;
to-day it would be more difficult. Early in February
Mlle. Dorgères will become Madame Vignory."

" Why, then, fatigue me with your solicitations ? Were
I free to-morrow the marriage would take place none the
less. I should not try to hinder it."

" You would be wrong. There is still time to do so.
Mlle. Dorgères has consented against herself. She has
grown weary of the war, when after days of waiting you

did not appear to confound your calumniators. It would be easy to explain your silence. You might say that you were ignorant you had been accused. It would be plausible, since the theft was known only to three or four persons. You might add that you had just heard these reports; you might have learned them from some one who was interested in you—this groom, for instance, who was in the waiting-room when the theft was discovered, an urchin named, I believe, Georges or Georget."

At this name Robert could not suppress a slight movement, which did not escape the quick eyes of the colonel.

"I mention this child because he took an interest in you," he resumed. "It seems he saw you when you were brought here by my steward, and came to inquire for you."

"If he knew I was your prisoner," said Robert, not without an effort, "he would not have kept it a secret, and some one would have been found to deliver me from your power."

"It is quite probable, but on that day he had a fall, from the effects of which he is and will remain an idiot."

This time Robert turned pale. He understood now why Georget had not reappeared.

"I tell you this," resumed the colonel, "that you may not build on the hope of being succored by this *gamin*. And that reminds me that I made a mistake in advising you to say that you were informed by him of the remarks of which you have been the subject. But you might designate another, M. Maxime Dorgères, for instance. He also is interested in your behalf."

" I scarcely know him," said M. de Carnoël, impatiently. "Listen to me, and when you have heard me through, I have not another word to say. You are convinced, are you not, that I have loved, that I still love Mlle. Dorgères ? "

" I am sure of it."

" And the offers you have made me are sincere ? You are prepared, if I accept your conditions, to restore my liberty, to support my cause with M. Dorgéres ; you will even go so far as to declare that you have discovered the real culprit ? "

" I have promised you that I am ready to do it," said M. Borisoff, quickly, satisfied that he was gaining the desired end.

" And you think that, given this new situation, M. Dorgères, to repair his wrongs toward me, would feel it his duty to accord me the hand of his daughter ; that Mlle. Dorgères, who has not ceased to love me, would be happy to become my wife ; that my rival would remember that he had been my friend, and would not seek to dispute with me the heart of Alice ? You think, in short, that it rests with me to pass from the depths of misery to the extreme of happiness ? "

" For this dream to become reality, you have only to name your accomplice."

" Do you think I should hesitate if I had one ? " asked

Robert, in a voice which vibrated. "You have, then, never loved, since you suppose that a man could sacrifice his love to some sentiment of keeping faith with conspirators. Had I stolen your casket for the purpose of delivering up your secret papers to the revolutionists of your country, I would go myself and recover it from them, if it was necessary, in order to marry the woman I loved. I would brave their vengeance and risk a thousand deaths sooner than refuse the happiness you propose to me. You see, then, that I know nothing, and that you will gain nothing by tormenting me further. Do with me as you please. You may kill me. You will extract nothing more from me."

The colonel knit his brows and bit his mustache. For the first time since he had secured the person of M. de Carnoël he asked himself if he had not made a false move in arresting him.

CHAPTER XIII.

THE COUNTESS ARGUES THE CASE.

IS there any one whose curiosity has not at times been aroused by some woman who has passed him? She is young, she is pretty, she is alone, and she walks with a hurrying step. She has an object, and she sees only this object. Is her walk to end in a romantic dé-nouement, or simply to conduct her to her dressmaker? This is the question that puzzles the curious who follow her with their eyes. Before the problem can be solved, she is already far off. She has disappeared without leaving any more trace of herself than a bird in its passage through the air.

The old Parisian recognizes quickly enough the Eng-lish or American girl who goes out without a chaperon for the pleasure of going out, of tossing her blonde hair in the wind, and laughing in the face of those whom she observes to mistake her for a seeker after adventure.

But the morning after Maxime Dorgères' attack upon Col. Borisoff, it was unquestionably a French girl who, toward twelve o'clock, passed up the Avenue de Friedland, and a French girl young and pretty. A thick veil was

347

drawn over her face, and she evidently did not wish to be recognized. At times she turned as if to see if she was not followed, and appeared uncertain of her route, for she stopped frequently to look at the houses and cross-streets. Evidently she sought for some indication which she did not care to ask of passers-by.

At length she observed an errand porter whom she decided to approach.

"Could you tell me where to find the house of a lady named the Countess Yalta?" she asked, in a scarcely audible voice.

"The Countess—Yalta? Ah, yes, the Russian princess who rides horseback dressed like a man? You are there, mademoiselle. There is a little door on the avenue fifty steps from here, but if you're not a friend of the house it's no use to ring; they wouldn't open to you. The great entrance is on Rue Beaujon, there—to the right. There is no mistaking it; it's gilded from top to bottom."

The woman murmured her thanks and entered Rue Beaujon, which branched off from the Avenue de Friedland at the point where she had been interrogating the porch.

She soon discovered the magnificent entrance to the Yalta mansion, and there her hesitation renewed itself. She began to walk slowly the length of the iron railing, behind which was stationed the majestic porter who had introduced Maxime the morning before.

This personage, doubtless, intimidated her, for the

nearer she approached him the more her footsteps relaxed, and she turned away her head as she drew the
brass knob near the lodge.

. The bedizzened Swiss advanced majestically, measured the visitor with a glance, and inquired politely what
she wished.

"I want to see Madame the Countess Yalta," she stammered.

"Madame the countess does not receive," replied the
colossus ; "but if you will give me your name and tell
me why you come—"

The girl started and lowered her head ; then conquer-
ing her timidity, raised it again, and said firmly :

"I am sure the countess will receive me if you will say
to her that Mlle. Dorgères wishes to speak to her."

The porter changed his tone instantly. He was not
ignorant that the head coachman had driven Madame
Yalta the day before to the house of M. Dorgères, Rue
de Suresnes.

"I beg mademoiselle to excuse me, and if mademoiselle will take the trouble to enter the waiting-room, I
will inform madame the countess. She is still much indisposed, and I had orders to admit no one."

This discourse was punctuated by the striking of a bell,
which resulted in the appearance on the stairway of a
valet de pied.

Mlle. Dorgères, introduced by the porter, was delivered
into the hands of this valet, who conducted her to the

apartments on the ground-floor in which her cousin had been received every day for a month past by Dr. Villagos.

She had not long to wait for the reply of the countess. The duenna who had introduced Maxime on his last visit came down stairs expressly to receive Mlle. Dorgères.

"Mademoiselle," she said smilingly, "my mistress is so happy to receive a visit from you that she will not ask you to postpone it till to-morrow, though she suffers much just now. She hopes you will excuse her for receiving you in bed."

Alice stammered a few words of thanks and followed the woman-in-waiting.

The duenna conducted her by the same stairway which ended in the superb apartments on the first floor through which she had conducted Maxime, but did not usher her into the oval chamber.

The countess was in her own room in an immense bed, a genuine specimen of the Louis XIV age, with heavy curtains of Gobelin tapestry. A faint light was diffused through the stained-glass windows.

Alice could scarcely summon courage to advance. Timidity took possession of her. How was she to approach the woman whose pale face was scarcely visible? How should she explain this strange visit? And if Maxime had exaggerated! If Madame Yalta had gone no further than to express a sympathy for M. de Carnoël, without having undertaken to defend him against his accusers!

All these discouraging thoughts came to her at once; but her apprehensions were quickly dissipated.

A voice which sounded in her ears like celestial music pronounced these words:

"I knew you would come. You guessed I had something to say to you."

Alice colored with happiness and advanced quickly.

"Thanks for him and for me," resumed the countess. "If you had not come it is impossible to say when I should have seen you, for yesterday evening a new crisis came on which has not yet passed. Pardon me that I do not offer you my arms, but my physician has ordered me to be absolutely motionless. Sit down and let us talk."

Alice took her seat in a low chair by the bedside, and said in an agitated voice:

"Madame, I am profoundly touched by your welcome, and cannot better' show that I am sensible of your goodness than by telling you the whole truth. I came without the knowledge of my father, because my cousin told me you were anxious to prove the innocence of M. de Carnoël. I wanted to know on what you founded your belief."

"You love him; is it not so?"

"I did love him," said Alice, with an effort.

"And yet you are betrothed to another?"

"I thought—they showed me that M. de Carnoël had

been guilty of something dishonorable. I yielded to the entreaties of my father, who begged me to marry. I am engaged in the eyes of the world, but my heart is my own."

" They have shown you that this young man has—stolen. Why not speak the word, since it is an odious calumny ? Before replying to this calumny, permit me to ask who informed you of what took place and what you have heard ? "

" My father. He told me that on opening the safe the cashier perceived the disappearance of a casket containing valuable papers belonging to a Russian. M. de Carnoël had left precipitately the night before at the very hour the safe was opened with a false key."

" And they concluded boldly that it was he. They did not stop to ask what interest this young man could have in possessing himself of a casket containing papers of nobody knew what sort, when the safe was full of gold and notes that were not touched."

" A sum of money was also taken," said the girl, in a stifled voice—"fifty thousand francs."

" It is not true," cried the countess.

" Alas, madame, it is too true ! The cashier counted the money in the presence of my father and this Russian. A roll of bank-notes was missing."

" It is impossible ! " said the countess, with an extraordinary confidence ; "but continue, mademoiselle. Your father has given you no other details of this affair ? "

" None, madame."

" He has not spoken to you, then, of a first attempt which failed, and which preceded the second by a few days only ? "

" No. Had there been a previous attempt to rob the safe M. Vignory would have told me ; it would have been spoken of in my hearing."

" Then he who gave me the information was mistaken."

" Georget, was it not ? "

" You know that ! Then you saw your cousin yesterday ? "

" Yes, madame. Maxime brought the poor child to the office. I met them as I was going out with my governess, and it was then I had this conversation with Maxime. You believe, then, that M. de Carnoël is in Paris ? "

" I am certain of it. You will be surprised when I say that the day you were awaiting him in the Bois de Boulogne he must have fallen into the hands of some powerful enemy."

" You knew I was expecting him ? "

" The day the great cold began I went to the lake in a sleigh with M. Maxime Dorgères. You passed near us in a carriage with your governess. Your cousin expressed a desire to follow you, and, pressed by me, confessed that he wished to be present at a rendezvous you had given to M. de Carnoël. Afterward I learned that M. de Carnoël had not appeared, and that he was accused of an infamy, —long afterward, unfortunately, for there was not time to avert what might have been prevented had I been better informed at first. But fate intervened. I fell seriously ill. Now the time has come to repair the evil I have unintentionally suffered. I want to find M. de Carnoël, and when I have done so will take him myself to your father."

" My father would refuse to receive him."

"He must receive him, when I bring him the proof that he has been calumniated and is entitled to reparation."

" The proof ? " repeated Mlle. Dorgères, doubtingly.

" Yes, the proof ; for if it is necessary in order to exonerate him the guilty party will denounce himself. I swear to you that it was not M. de Carnoël."

This reply was made in so positive a tone and with so much animation that the girl doubted no longer. Evidently the countess knew the author of the theft, and was resolved to denounce him to save the innocent one who was accused. Alice was blessing her, when a suspicion glided into her heart. Why did the countess undertake so warmly the defence of Robert ? Could it be supposed she maintained his cause out of pure love of justice ? She, whose life was the sport of her caprices ! It was much more probable that she was interested personally in M. de Carnoël, and this interest must be very lively, since she offered to sacrifice some one to him.

"She loves him, perhaps," thought Mlle. Dorgères, sadly.

"I hope now that you do not regret having come," said Mme. Yalta, "and that henceforth we are united in the effort to save M. de Carnoël."

"You have known him long?" she asked timidly.

"I do not know him at all; I have never seen him that I am aware of."

Alice's face brightened, and she was about to protest with warmth her devotion to the projects of the countess, but at this moment the lady-in-waiting entered, and said to her mistress:

"M. Maxime Dorgères begs to see the countess imme-. diately. He assures me that he brings news of impor- tance."

"Go," cried the countess, "bring him in."

The duenna turned briskly on her heels, and as soon as she was left alone with the countess, Alice rose and said with some agitation:

"Madame, I beg you not to compel me to see my cousin. I would not for the world have him find me here."

"If you were to follow my femme de chambre you would inevitably meet M. Dorgères. There is no way to avoid him but to go in there," she added, pointing to a door not far from the head of the bed, which opened in the midst of tapestry hangings.

"You will find it a very commodious prison, and, I

think, will not be detained long. It will be in your power to leave it should you change your mind as to the convenience of a meeting with M. Dorgères."

Alice ran to the point of exit indicated, and glided noiselessly into a vast apartment, a toilette boudoir filled with luxurious furniture, objects of art and curiosities in glass cases. She had no sooner disappeared than Maxime entered radiant. His joy was somewhat abated at being received, not as before, on a divan of state, but a real invalid's couch.

"What! you are seriously indisposed, and were out yesterday!"

"I did go out and I was wrong, having obtained nothing from M. Dorgères, and paid for my imprudence this morning. But that doesn't matter. Tell me of your expedition with Georget. First, how is he? Do you believe he will recover his reason?"

"I hope so. He has transient glimpses already, but is not yet master of himself. He allows words to escape him which he would not do ordinarily."

"What has he said?"

"I took him to the office where the theft was committed, and he mentioned that he knew the words that opened the safe, the defensive mechanism that protects it, —details of which no one is in possession but the cashier, and which Georget could have learned only by acting the spy on his chief. I beg your pardon for telling you frankly my opinion that your protégé was the accomplice of the rogues, that he furnished them information, and perhaps assisted them more effectively. He recognized a hiding-place in which he must have been lurking for the purpose of opening the door to them."

"It is quite possible," said the countess, indifferently.

"What! you are not distressed to learn that Georget has been implicated in this affair?"

"Bah! a political matter."

"Political! how?"

"Undoubtedly. What did they take? A coffer containing unquestionably state papers, since it belonged to a Russian diplomatic agent. The proof that they wanted only the papers, is that they did not touch the money in the safe. Georget is the grandson of a woman of high birth who has had relations with Polish emigrants. He has, perhaps, followed the counsels of his grandmother in giving aid to these people."

"He has none the'less been playing high, and if my uncle knew what this astonishing youngster has been doing, he wouldn't spare him—especially since money was taken as well as the casket."

"I have been told so, but can scarcely believe it. But I can answer that it was not Georget."

"Georget has merely connived at it. Moreover, in the remarks which he let fall, there was one which designated the thief."

"Designated him by name?"

"A name which will tell you nothing. It was Ladislas. But I know the man."

"Ah!" said the countess, tranquilly. "Who is he?"

"He is a foreigner, a Slav who led a mysterious life here, and suddenly disappeared. He lived in Rue Jouffroy, and had for companion a marvellously beautiful creature who vanished with himself. Dr. Villagos pointed her out to me at the Rink."

"And no doubt you made love to her?" said Madame Yalta, smiling.

"No. I accompanied her to her door, where I narrowly escaped being murdered. It was Georget who saved me from them. Being their accomplice he was aware of their plans, and manœuvred so as to deliver me from them without denouncing them."

"We see now that Georget knows better than any one what has transpired, since he knows the thief. Let us return, then, I beg, to M. de Carnoël. It is he alone who interests me, and whom I wish to find."

"I think I have discovered him."

"You have seen him?"

"No, but I know where he is. It chanced that, on returning with Georget to his grandmother, he recognized a certain wall, from the top of which he had fallen, and remembered at last why he had climbed it. He had in the morning seen Robert de Carnoël enter a house, the garden of which was enclosed by that wall, and having watched before it all day, ascertained that he did not leave the

house. An instant before his fall he saw him again, holding a torch which he waved as a signal. I shall give you
a surprise when I make known to you that this house is
occupied by the Russian whose casket was stolen from
my uncle's."

"Borisoff! ah, the wretch! He only would be capable of so infamous a proceeding!"

"Then you believe as I do, that the colonel has made
use of a ruse to get M. de Carnoël in his power, and of
violence in keeping him?"

"I think we may esteem ourselves fortunate if he has
not killed him. This man is a secret agent of the Russian
foreign police. He wishes at any price to discover by
whom his papers have been taken. M. de Carnoël was
accused. He began by obtaining possession of his person, and has made frightful threats with the hope of
inducing him to confess what has been done with the
casket. M. de Carnoël has not been able to say, since he
did not know, and Borisoff, having compromised himself
by this arbitrary arrest, cannot set him at liberty. Borisoff
will make an end of him if he has not already done so. I
have not a moment to lose in saving the unfortunate
young man, and it is I only who can. I beg you, therefore, to abstain from taking any step."

"But," said Maxime, "it is—I have already taken
one."

"What?" asked the countess, quickly.

"The most natural. After having taken Georget to his

grandmother, I returned quickly to Rue Vigny and asked for Col. Borisoff."

"It was folly.   He did not see you, I suppose?"

"I beg pardon, madame.   He received me immediately. He thought I was sent by my uncle."

"*Mon dieu!* what did you say?"

"I asked what he had done with M. de Carnoël."

"Ah!" murmured the countess, "all is now lost."   .

"What!" exclaimed Maxime, "if I had not gone directly to the point he would have had time to prepare his reply.   I hoped to surprise and embarrass him."

"Do you flatter yourself that you succeeded?"

"I cannot affirm that he seemed perplexed.   These Russians have a marvellous *sang froid.*"

"What was his reply?"

"He began by asking why I applied to him for news of the young man, and feigned ignorance.   Then I told him plainly that M. de Carnoël had been seen to enter his house, that he had not been seen to come out, and that he must be still there."

"And in proceeding thus you hoped M. Borisoff would confess what he had done and yield up his prisoner to you?"

"I confess I had not reflected much—I followed the first impulse—which I regret, since you disapprove of it," added Maxime, sadly, feeling conscious that his conduct appeared absurd in Madame Yalta's eyes.

"Oh, I do not reproach you ; you acted for the best ! Tell me how the interview terminated."

"The Russian denied the charge with disdain. I threatened him with recourse to the commissary of police."

" Nothing more was wanting— "

" I was irritated, else I should not have gone so far, especially as I have no idea of mixing the police up with this affair. And the colonel did not seem to attach any importance to this menace, for he assumed a haughty and contemptuous tone, which exasperated me. I re-doubled my urgency, he requested me to leave, and I went out announcing that I should send him my seconds.'

" But you have not done so, I hope ?"

" Not yet; I have not had time to look for them."

" And I hope you will not look for them."

" Borisoff expects them."

"Borisoff knows well enough that an affair entered upon in such a manner will have no consequences. And he has his reply all ready in case you send two of your friends. Forget, then, the false step you made yester-day, and let us consult as to the best means of repairing it."

" So," asked Maxime, timidly, "you judge me still worthy of seconding you in your generous enterprise ?"

"Do you doubt it ? If I had not an absolute confi-dence in you, do you think I should initiate you into my most secret projects ?   I have no other friend on whose aid I could rely :   Dr. Villagos least of all."

"He fears for your health, and he is right."

"Not only for my health.   You have never reflected on the danger attending an attack on Col. Borisoff."

"I confess I have not.   We are not in Russia, and in Paris I do not see how this Russian agent can exercise his occult powers."

"You have, however, under your eyes, a striking illustration of his mode of proceeding with a Frenchman who incommodes him."

"M. de Carnoël's case is peculiar.   He was accused of theft ; he had taken flight.   It was probable that no one, unless it were his accusers, would concern themselves to know what had become of nim.   The colonel would scarcely undertake such a game with you or me."

"He would find some mode of attack.   I tell you this man is formidable, for he shrinks from no means of vengeance, and in this affair he has a great vengeance to execute.   He has been overreached by those who have taken his papers, and if he could annihilate them every one he would not hesitate."

"You believe that this theft had only a political end. But by whom ?"

"By proscribed unfortunates, probably.   Europe is full of exiles who, having suffered from Muscovite despotism, make war upon it from afar   I have the good fortune not to be a Russian subject.   I have, therefore, nothing to do with persons of the Borisoff species. But I am always of the party of the weak, and therefore it is that I interest myself in those whom this spy persecutes."

"Then if M. de Carnoël had aided the persecuted in getting possession of this casket, you would defend him still ?"

"Yes, certainly; but it is not true. We know who committed the theft since Georget has designated a certain Ladislas. It is a Polish name—some refugee, doubtless."

"Before placing myself at your disposal, let me enlighten you further as to the history of the theft. It is well you should know all. One Wednesday evening, Vignory and I, who were going to pass the evening at my uncle's, observed a light in the office, and on going in made a frightful discovery. The safe is defended by an apparatus so constructed as to seize by the arm any one who shall attempt to open it without taking certain precautions. Well, a woman's hand was found remaining in the vice. To avoid being arrested, she had caused her hand to be amputated."

"Do you believe an ordinary thief would have done that?" asked the countess, in a quivering voice.

"Assuredly not. I thought from the first this attempt at theft had a special motive. Afterward, when I learned the disappearance of the Russian's casket, I was convinced of it. We conceived—Vignory and I—the unfortunate idea of keeping what we had learned, secret.

The attempt was not repeated by the woman, who must have been suffering the consequences of the amputation."

" If she did not die of it," murmured the countess.

" It is certain that she had an accomplice—this Ladislas mentioned by Georget—and the next day this accomplice succeeded without accident."

" You say that there were two attempts at theft, and that the first took place during a soirée at M. Dorgères'. M. de Carnoël was doubtless in your uncle's salon at that time ?"

" Yes, certainly ; he never missed the Wednesday reception."

" He was not, therefore, with the thieves. It might be said he had given them instructions. It is inadmissible. Information, furnished by the secretary of M. Dorgères, the intimate friend of the cashier, would have been more complete. The unfortunate woman, who was mutilated, would not have lost her hand. He who took the casket the next evening understood how to avoid its terrible embrace. Do you still maintain that in this interval M. de Carnoël might have warned them ? It would be an absurd supposition. The secretary, initiated into all his master's secrets, must have long known the existence of the trap, and had he been in league with the thieves, would not have waited for a grave accident before pointing out the means to avoid it."

" All that is very just," murmured Maxime.

"So just," resumed the countess with energy, "that I am lost in amazement at the blindness which struck you all at the moment the theft was discovered. To accuse a man for the simple reason that he is absent is something unheard of."

"It was not I,—I did not accuse him,—I was not present."

"No; Georget told me there were only this Russian and the cashier. The Russian was in the waiting-room. The cashier was alone when he discovered the theft."

"True; but he called Col. Borisoff, and sent immediately for my uncle. Vignory verified the contents in his presence."

"And they recognized the disappearance of the casket. The cashier also made known that a sum of money was taken—I don't know what, something comparatively insignificant,—and it was believed on his affirmation."

"But—unless it could be supposed he had taken it himself."

"No such question was raised. The case is simply this: Here are three men brought together by an event which touches them all in different ways; and without reflection, without investigation, these three men agree to impute the misdeed to a youth whose life hitherto had been irreproachable."

"Appearances were against him, his abrupt departure—"

"But they knew the cause of this departure. Your

uncle knew very well that he had dismissed M. de Carnoël, who was in despair. The cashier had received the
young man's confidence after the event took place, and
the Russian was made by them aware of the situation.
No matter—these gentlemen forthwith decide that M. de
Carnoël is the last of scoundrels ; that he has dishonored
himself to oblige an enemy of M. Borisoff and to appropriate a few bank-notes. And instead of delivering him
to the authorities, who would at least have allowed him a
chance to vindicate himself, they agree to abandon him
to the investigations and the vengeance of a man interested, and consequently partial. In truth, one appears to
be dreaming when he examines calmly the strange features of this affair."

Maxime, struck dumb as he listened, lowered his head
and spoke not a word, having no reply to make to the
close reasonings of the countess.

" That M. Dorgères should have suffered himself to be
carried away by his *bourgeois* prejudices," she went on ;
"that he should even have seized on the single pretext
which offered to break a project of marriage that displeased him, need not greatly astonish us. He wished at
any price to get rid of M. de Carnoël, and did not hesitate to dishonor without hearing him. Your uncle is an
honest man in the strictest sense of the word, but there
are sentiments he is incapable of appreciating. As to
the Russian, who is in truth only a spy, it might well be
expected that he would throw himself with ardor on the

first trail pointed out to him, and in default of any other victim pursue M. de Carnoël without respite or scruple. But there is one whose conduct in this sad case is absolutely inexplicable."

"Who?" stammered Maxime, more and more out of countenance.

"The cashier, Vignory," said Madame Yalta.

"Vignory!" exclaimed Maxime. I assure you his conduct has been unexceptionable. He defended M. de Carnoël warmly."

"Were you present when the scene occurred?" asked Mme. Yalta, coldly.

"No, but Vignory told me himself the same day, and he is incapable of lying. Besides, how could he do otherwise than defend M. de Carnoël, who was his most intimate friend?"

"And his successful rival."

"That is not exactly the word. He had long had an inclination for my cousin, but he perceived that Robert de Carnoël and Alice loved each other, and kept himself aloof. He is the most modest and also the most loyal of men. Had it been in his power to save the honor of M. de Carnoël, he would have done it."

"Really? He is, then, deficient in intelligence?" asked the countess, abruptly.

And as Maxime, stupefied, made no reply, she went on:

"He is stupid, then?"

"Stupid! why?"

"I did not think I should need to explain. Here is a man who hears his best friend charged with an infamy. He knows a fact which would change entirely the whole face of things. The accusers are ignorant of it. He has only to speak to modify their ideas. It was even probable that in bringing together and comparing different circumstances his friend's innocence would be apparent. And this man is silent!"

"What do you mean?" stammered Maxime.

"M. Vignory is cashier. On arriving one morning he finds the safe open. He sends for M. Dorgères, who cries out: 'It is M. de Carnoël!' And M. Vignory does not reply: 'No, it is not he. An attempt has been made before this to open the safe. A woman has left her hand there. M. de Carnoël had nothing to do with this first attempt since he was passing the evening with you; therefore M. de Carnoël took no part in the second.' What would your uncle have opposed to this statement? Assuredly he would not have persisted in accusing his unfortunate secretary on the pretext that he had ill chosen his moment for leaving the house."

"I do not know," murmured Maxime, feeling all the justice of the countess' reasonings. "My uncle is very determined in his ideas, and had resolved to get rid of M. de Carnoël. I doubt if his opinion would have changed. It is none the less true that Vignory would have done better to speak—to tell the whole truth. He

failed through want of presence of mind; it is pardon-
able under circumstances that must have so disconcerted
him."

"I do not believe it. It was through fear of compromising himself. He was afraid of being reproached—
for, between ourselves, he well deserved it; for the fact
of his having been silent as to the severed hand is inexplicable and unpardonable."

"I had something to do with the part Vignory took; I
had begged him to keep silence, and having always exer-
cised a certain influence over him, he consented."

"Once more, you were not M. de Carnoël's friend.
Moreover, you could not foresee that he would be accused. But your Vignory has only to open his mouth
for the affair to wear quite another aspect. With a word
he could put his friend outside the case, and this word he
took good care not to pronounce. The intention to injure is evident. In acting thus this man yielded to a base
sentiment—jealousy."

"I should be pained to believe it. I think that even
now if I asked him to relate to my uncle the adventure
we concealed he would not refuse."

"Take care you do nothing of the sort. This tardy
confession would not benefit M. de Carnoël, and it is of
great consequence to me to act without the knowledge of
the future son-in-law of M. Dorgères. If you persist in
your generous design to aid me to find M. de Carnoël, I
must exact of you a promise to make no sort of confidence to Vignory. "

"It will be very easy. He thinks only of his approaching marriage and recent elevation to the partnership with my uncle ; so much so, that when I took Georget there yesterday, he received me almost coldly. I understood, from his attitude, that this old story interested him no longer."

"He is not aware, I hope, that you know, or think you know, that M. de Carnoël is Borisoff's prisoner ?" asked the countess, quickly.

"No," replied Maxime, earnestly. "It was after a visit to the office that I passed with Georget by the Russian's residence. We parted almost angrily, and I have no need of your instructions in order to be reserved on this point."

"Thanks. I see that I may count on you. However, I shall not put your services too much under contribution, at least at present. The first point is that Borisoff should be reassured. He must hear no more of you. He will think you acted yesterday without consideration, and that you will not return."

"It is a painful enough rôle that you impose on me," said Maxime, with a smile that was rather forced.

"Why ? Your altercation with the man did not go far enough to render a meeting the necessary consequence. And you have certainly no cause to fear any provocation on the part of Borisoff. He wishes only quiet."

"Since you wish it I resign myself not to disturb him. But may I ask how I can be permitted to serve you ?"

"By abstaining from taking any measures."

"What ! you will not allow me to assist in the delivery of M. de Carnoël ? "

"If I succeed it will be to you I owe it, for without you I should not have known that M. de Carnoël was Borisoff's prisoner. But it is I alone who can act effectively—I alone in all the world."

"In the condition you are in ! "

"Some one will take my place. I shall not appear, but will direct all. You do not understand. It is, however, impossible for me to say more. Moreover, you will not remain long in uncertainty. At this moment, after the warning you have given, the colonel is making his arrangements to rid himself of M. de Carnoël. I cannot affirm that he will kill him, but assuredly he will not keep him at his house. I have not an instant to lose. In three days from now you shall know whether I have succeeded.

" How shall I know ? "

" By coming to see me. If my servants tell you I do not receive, insist on speaking to my *femme de chambre* who has always shown you in. She has my orders, and will admit you."

" At least if Dr. Villagos does not oppose it."

"Villagos ! yes, you are right ; he might do so ; above all if he suspected M. de Carnoël to be in question."

" And his authority would certainly be stronger than mine."

"I will indicate to you how to make him yield. You have the ring I gave you yesterday?"

"I shall never be separated from it until you reclaim it."

"Show it to the doctor in case he undertakes to hinder you from seeing me—in that case only."

"And like Madame Piriac, he will obey this talisman?"

"He will obey it. Perhaps he will ask some questions. Do not answer them. And now that I have said all," added the countess, "do me the favor to ring for my femme de chambre who will show you out. I am expecting this very Villagos, and do not care to have him find you here."

Maxime reached out his hand to the silken cord when a cry rang in his ears which proceeded from the chamber in which Alice had taken refuge.

"Do not ring," said the countess, quickly, who had started at this cry.

"It was, I thought, a woman's voice," said Maxime.

"It is a woman, but why she calls so I cannot tell."

"I did not think she called. It was rather a cry of fright—or of surprise. If she wanted aid she would have repeated it."

"There is nothing to hinder her from coming out. The door communicating with my chamber is not locked. Some one is concealed there who wished to avoid meeting you, but who will forgive me for disregarding a childish fancy. Enter, I beg, and bring with you the person you will find there."

Maxime, completely puzzled, obeyed without comment. He opened the door and found himself face to face with Alice Dorgères—Alice, pale, agitated, trembling.

He was undoubtedly the more astonished of the two, for he had no suspicion that his cousin was in the countess' house, while Alice, on the contrary, was very well aware of his presence there.

"Well, yes, it is I," he said, laughing. "You cried out so that Madame Yalta was frightened, and wished to know if you needed assistance. Speak. What has happened ?"

"Nothing," stammered Alice. "A nervous shock. Take me away."

Maxime took her by the hand, and led her to the countess' bedside.

"Mademoiselle," she said, in a voice serious and agitated, "you could not remain longer in that room, which I regret having made you enter. But it is better you should go out with your cousin than to be surprised by my physician, whom I am expecting, and who has forbidden me to see any one to-day. It is important to us both that your visit should remain unknown ; and it is probable that we shall not meet again unless the situation should be altogether changed. I have said all I had to say concerning M. de Carnoël. Your cousin knows more, and is in a position to advise you if you need advice. Soon, I trust, the truth will appear and M. de Carnoël will speak for himself. Before we part, mademoiselle, I ask only one thing, that you will speak to no one, under any pretext whatever, of what you have seen or heard here—to no one, you understand—neither now nor ever."

" I will be silent always," murmured Mlle. Dorgères.

" I rely upon you, mademoiselle," said the countess. " M. Dorgères, be so good as to ring."

The duenna appeared, and Maxime, leading Alice, followed her.

They walked side by side in silence until they reached the end of Rue Beaujon, when Maxime said abruptly :

" Why did you not confide in me ? Had I known you had decided to see the countess, I would have spared you the embarrassment of going alone."

" My resolution was taken last night, and I wished to execute it immediately. It was the conversation with you yesterday which led me to wish to interrogate for myself this great lady who comes so late to the succor of the absent. She swore to me that she would save him. What is her vow worth ? Does she even know whether Robert de Carnoël is in Paris ; whether he is alive ? "

" She did not know, when you arrived. She knows now."

" How is that ? "

" You did not hear our conversation ? "

" You do not ask that seriously ? "

"It is absurd, I confess. It is not your habit to listen at doors. Well, it is I who have just informed , the countess that Robert is not dead and that he has not left Paris."

"Where is he ? " Alice asked quickly.

"This morning I could have answered you, but I have just promised the countess that the secret should rest between us two."

"Of me also she exacts secrecy. That house is full of mysteries."

"I begin to think so. We will abstain from mutual questionings. But I may at least ask what course you mean to take. What will you say to your father, to Vignory ? My uncle is persuaded that all is satisfactorily arranged ; Vignory rests in absolute security. Do you intend to leave them to their illusions ? "

"No," replied Alice, "I shall tell my father to-day that I have changed my mind and do not mean to marry."

"*Diable !* your father might take you at your word. You will not marry Vignory, but neither will you marry Robert."

"It is my dearest wish not to marry at all."

"My dear Alice, I believe you do not say what you think ; but this is not a moment to discuss it with you. One word, however. Do not come to any decision for a few days, and above all do not declare yourself. It is more than will be needed to decide what course to take with respect to M. de Carnoël."

"You are then on his side?" asked Mlle. Dorgères, with emotion.

"Yes; I am even astonished that I should have given in for an instant to the foolish suspicions that were so easily admitted."

"Your friend Vignory does not think with you."

"I feel less sure of Vignory since the countess has touched on certain inexplicable points in his conduct."

"Ah ! at last !" cried the girl. "Then I may speak. You will understand me when I say that in a moment of anger and despair I engaged myself to this man, but I would die sooner than marry him. If he had any heart he would never have accepted what I had to offer—indifference and a large dowry. His resignation is but calculation ; his gentleness, baseness."

"You go rather far," said Maxime ; "but I have not the heart to blame you, and, I repeat, you may count on me. Here we are at the Boulevard Haussman. I do not know that I shall see you to-morrow. Write to me if anything occurs to make you wish for me ; and then, perhaps, I may be able to tell you what the countess desires me to conceal for the present concerning Robert de Carnoël."

"And I," murmured Alice, lowering her voice, "can perhaps tell you what I have just seen at her house."

CHAPTER XIV.

LAYING A TRAP FOR THE COLONEL.

AFTER the explosion that followed the inconsiderate visit of Maxime Dorgères, Col. Borisoff quickly returned to calmer sentiments. His fits of anger did not last long where grave interests were at stake, and such was the case now, for he had to determine a delicate question on which he felt himself very much in the dark. The proceedings of this hare-brained Maxime proved nothing, unless it were that an almost idiot boy affirmed that M. de Carnoël was retained by force in a house in the Rue de Vigny. The supposition was so unlikely, it could scarcely gain credence anywhere and need not give him very serious concern, and the seconds of young Dorgères not having shown themselves at twelve o'clock next day, there was no longer reason to expect them.

But concerning his prisoner, M. Borisoff's anxieties were great. He could not keep him indefinitely, neither could he release him without exposing himself to the danger of a publicity which he greatly dreaded. To send him to Siberia, the order for which had been given as a last resource, did not remedy anything. It was to cut the difficulty, not to resolve it,

377

Besides, in his last interview with him, Robert de Car-noël had spoken with so much energy and earnestness that he succeeded in casting doubts in the mind of his jailer.

In the capacity of secret agent, this Russian was accustomed to look at affairs from all points, and to change his batteries as often as necessary. He possessed a marvellous suppleness in turning when once he discovered himself to be on the wrong track. And he now began to ask himself if he would not do well to search elsewhere for the accomplice of the thieves That some one in the banker's house was in league with them was certain, but what proved this to be M. de Carnoël ? Why not some other ? Suspicion might rest upon the cashier himself as well as upon the secretary.

"What might not have been gained," said the colonel to himself, "if, instead of directing all our efforts toward this young man, we had carefully watched the clerks and valets of the banker ! Perhaps there is yet time. I am half tempted to think Vacili is right, and that he must be released on giving his word of honor to be silent concern-ing the past month."

These perplexities occupied Col. Borisoff all the evening and night after his conversation with M. de Carnoël. Their effect was to induce him to countermand the journey to Siberia. In truth, he feared being reproached for having taken a measure of this sort of such questionable utility. He decided to temporize and to connect himself more closely with M Dorgères, in order to study the habits and relations of those around him. And as he felt the need of distraction, he had·his horse saddled and went to the Bois attended by a groom, after announcing his intention to dine out and to return probably quite late.

His ride was marked by no incident and had the effect of enabling him to collect his ideas. He said to himself that he might at any time be released from an embarrassing position by liberating M. de Carnoël, promising him his support as the price of his silence. And confiding in his *savoir-faire* which had extricated him from more difficult positions, he returned to the city with a tranquil mind, proposing to pass the evening according to his fancy.

He dismounted at the door of his club, and intending to dine there, sent away his horse and groom.

He found what he sought, a place at a whist table, and that nothing should mar his satisfaction he had unusual good-luck, and when he rose to make his toilette for the evening had won a considerable sum.

It was his habit to make up a party here from four to six, and in that case his valet de chambre had orders to bring him his dress for the evening.

He was putting the finishing touch to this toilette, when a card was placed in his hand from a gentleman who wished to speak with him on urgent business. The man was unknown to him, and the card had a peculiar mark in the corner.

Quite surprised to see this sign, which was understood only by the attachés of the Third Section and by those only of a certain grade, the colonel decided that he could not dispense with giving audience to the man who made use of this sign, and could shorten the interview if the subject seemed not worthy of his attention.

On entering the parlor of the club, he found there a young man of fine presence and elegantly dressed, who welcomed him by a phrase in the Russian language,—a phrase more significant than the mark on the visiting card. There was no longer room to hesitate. The new-comer belonged to the political police, and occupied, too, a high place in it.

The question was, why had he come to Paris, and Borisoff experienced a vague disquietude.

"My dear Alexis Stepanowĭtch," said the unknown, addressing him, according to the national custom, by his first name followed by the Christian name of his father, "this is not a favorable place for talking ; let us dine together at a public house."

"Willingly," replied the colonel, who felt the necessity of putting on a good countenance; "which would you prefer, my dear—Mouriatine ?"

"Say Ivan Ivanovitch. Let us go to—Begnon's, Avenue de l' Opera. I arrived this morning after sixty hours of express train, and am in need of refreshment."

The colonel showed his compatriot the way from the antechamber, and hastened to don his overcoat.

As soon as they were on the boulevard, which in this locality was quite solitary, the newly-arrived began thus, still in Russian :

" You do not know me, and do not recognize the name of Mouriatine. That is not surprising. I was stationed in our Polish provinces while you were with the general at St. Petersburg, and I returned to the department when you went abroad. My wish is, my dear Alexis, to act with you as comrade. I shall not begin by showing you my written powers,—they are, however, at your disposal when you wish. Meanwhile, shall I give you the pass-word ? "

He leaned toward the colonel who, on hearing the word, said :

" It is useless, my dear Ivan ; but tell me, you are sent, then, on an extraordinary mission ? "

" So extraordinary that the general allowed me only two hours to make my arrangements."

" And what is its purport ? "

" Yourself, my dear Alexis Stepanowitch."

" Me ! of what am I accused ? "

" Of negligence, firstly, or rather imprudence. It seems you placed all your important papers in a casket and had the singular idea of depositing it with your banker."

" I could not but believe it a safer place than my own house. I was known to the Nihilists who have agents everywhere, and was uncertain of some of my people."

" It is not the less true that the box has been stolen,

and doubtless by those whose measures you apprehend."

"True ; and I was wrong not to render an account of
the affair to those who have a right to know. I had reasons for acting thus, which I will explain presently.
May I ask by whom the chiefs have been so well instructed?"

"You do not suspect? There is, however, a French
proverb which asserts that one is never betrayed but by
his own."

"Betrayed by my own ! I have here neither friends
nor relatives."

"You have an intendant, my dear Alexis Stepanowitch," said the *euvoyé*, laughing.

"Vacili ! what ; this knave has been acting the spy
on me and corresponding with the department ! "

"He was authorized to do so, that I can inform you.
You must be aware that, in foreign parts especially, each
one is watched,—sometimes by a comrade whom he is
himself charged with overlooking. It is a system of mutual observation, against which it is useless to recriminate.
And I enjoin you very earnestly not to let fall your anger
upon this subaltern who was, after all, simply exercising
his functions."

"I will beware of doing so. He would be capable of
inventing calumnies on me to avenge himself. Perhaps
he has already done so, for I suppose he was not satisfied
to narrate the story of the casket ? "

"He wrote that instead of opening an intelligent inquest you had set to work very clumsily."

"Then he has stated that I have laid hold upon a young man who was suspected of being the accomplice of the thieves ?"

"He has told all. He has exposed the means to which you had recourse to obtain possession of his person and the embarrassment in which you now find yourself how to dispose of him. He even declared that you were on the point of despatching him by the secret means that are made use of on great occasions. And I will not conceal from you that he animadverted warmly upon your course."

"Criticism is easy, but I should like to know what the rascal would have done in my place. It is true that, despairing of extracting anything from this Carnoël, I had thought of sending him to Siberia, but I have abandoned the idea. If you could indicate to me a method of disposing of him without compromising anything, you would oblige me infinitely."

"Well, we will talk over all this at dinner. And after dinner, if you will, we will go to the opera."

"I see with pleasure, my dear Ivan Ivanovitch," said the colonel, laughing, "that business does not hinder you from thinking of pleasure while in Paris."

"All goes together perfectly. You shall see. I have reason to believe we shall not lose our evening. But let us begin by preparing ourselves. My appetite is voracious, and I mean to do justice to the cuisine and wines of France."

Whilst talking they had reached the fashionable cabaret recently opened on the Avenue de l'Opera.

Borisoff desired nothing better than to enter, for he was greatly annoyed by this bombshell that had fallen into his life, and this desultory conversation unnerved him. Wine unties the most discreet tongues, and he hoped that at table this representative of the great chief would unmask his real purpose.

Ivan Ivanovitch spoke French as fluently as his own tongue, and ordered his repast with an ease which gained him the esteem of the waiters.

No one supposed him to be a Russian until the end of the first course, when the colonel, who had hitherto confined himself to current trivialities, in endeavoring to lead the conversation back to the interesting topic took the precaution to return to his native tongue. He first questioned Mouriatine adroitly with regard to the chief and certain employés of the Third Section, and if there had still lingered any doubts as to the authenticity of the mission with which said Mouriatine declared himself charged, they must have been dispelled by the first replies of that personage. The *envoyé* was thoroughly acquainted with the most secret machinery of the administration which he represented. Evidently he played an important rôle in the political police.

It was the new-comer who took up the thread of conversation where it had been dropped on the boulevard.

"My dear sir," he said, pouring the colonel out the dozenth glass of *cliquot*, "I must protest in advance against an intention which you might attribute to me. I did not come to Paris for the purpose of sustaining your steward against you. I do not even wish to see him, and you may count on his remaining ignorant of the nature of my mission. He need not suppose his denunciations have been listened to at St. Petersburg. But we will consult together whether something better may not be done. Important papers have been stolen from you ; that is unfortunate, but it is not an irreparable disaster ; and instead of concentrating ourselves on the discovery of the thieves, we must extend our operations. It is the chiefs we must reach and not the miserable subalterns who do not even know the real end of the execrable sect with which they are affiliated."

"These chiefs I hoped to arrive at by pursuing the simple soldiers, and I persist in the belief that if this Carnoël has been concerned in the theft of my papers, it was a woman who instigated him, and a woman occupying a high place in the association."

"Perfectly reasoned ; but you have not the slightest conception who this woman is. Between ourselves, my dear Alexis, since you have been in France you might have used more sagacity. Thus, we have known at home that you have been occupied with a number of Russians who reside in or pass through Paris, who are not worth observing. It is wellnigh certain that these Nihilist rascals are directed in this country by a French woman, and that this woman is—but what is the matter, my dear friend? You are not listening."

"Excuse me," said Borisoff, "a gentleman who entered just now distracted my attention for a moment."

"That tall young man at the other end of the hall?"

"Yes. He is the nephew of my banker, and took into his head yesterday to question me as to what I had done with M. de Carnoël. I asked him out of my house. He announced that he would send me his seconds. I have not seen them, but am not without anxiety with regard to that madcap."

"He seems little inclined to pick a quarrel with you. See, he has taken a seat at a distance, and does not appear to notice you."

It was true. Maxime Dorgères, whom chance had led there, true to his promise to the countess, was not thinking of resuming with the colonel the stormy conversation of the day previous. He did not look toward Borisoff, nor the latter toward him.

But the companion of the colonel had attracted his attention from the first, and whilst affecting to be absorbed in the *menu*, he cast stolen glances at Mouriatine.

"It is strange," he said to himself; "surely I have seen that face somewhere—and that not long ago either. I have a memory for faces, and this one is not commonplace. He certainly has not a French head. Probably he is Russian, since he is dining with that scoundrel Borisoff."

On their part, the two foreigners had resumed their drinking, and talking in Russian as before the arrival of Maxime.

"Let us forget this gentleman and return to the woman of whom we were speaking. We have reason to suppose that it is she who conducts everything in Paris, and I am firmly convinced that she organized the theft of your casket."

"You say she is French?"

"French by birth, but of Polish origin, and intimately connected with all the enemies of Russia."

"It is very extraordinary, if she lives in Paris, that she has not been marked out."

"She has only recently been denounced to the Third Section ; but you might have met with her, for she must have been revolving round you, so to speak."

"In the world in which I move?"

"No, my dear Alexis ; you move only in the true, and it is a mistake. Our chief said so to me the evening before my departure."

"What world should I frequent to satisfy him?"

"All of them, including the half which you have entirely neglected."

"Because there was nothing to be learned there. You know as well as I do that in this country the *femmes galantes* are not engaged in politics, especially foreign politics. They make the most of us willingly, we Russians, but they do not conspire against our government."

"There are exceptions, and the person whom I have mentioned is one."

"Then this person is a demoiselle—a *cocotte*, to speak more precisely ?"

"She is an irregular, but not one of the creatures whom one meets everywhere. She is very little known. It might be said, moreover, that she is intermittent, for she does not always reside in Paris. She is to be seen at Nice, at Monaco, at Geneva, and her journeyings have always one end. It was at Geneva that she was pointed out to me last summer."

"Ah ! you know her then by sight ?"

"Better than that. I got presented by one of my compatriots, whom she had bewitched and must have ruined. I had some suspicion that she was enrolled among the Nihilists, but there were no proofs, and I did not concern myself about her seriously. This winter we have received detailed reports of her proceedings. Thanks to her character of pleasure-seeker, no one suspects her, and she has every facility for connecting herself with those Russians from whom she hopes to extract valuable information. It was thus that two months ago she was here openly, under the protection of one of our generals, who was here on furlough."

"I must at least know her name," murmured Borisoff.

"She changes it frequently. When I met her it was Madame de Garches. Here she has assumed, I am told, some vulgar name. But had you been better informed of what transpires in the camp of adventuresses, this one could not have failed to attract your attention, to say nothing of her beauty, which is marvellous."

" I confess I had not even a suspicion of her existence," said the colonel, somewhat piqued ; " and until the contrary is proved you will permit me to doubt the fact of her having stolen my papers."

" She has not taken them with her own hand, but they were stolen by her orders and under her instructions."

" Then she knows me ? "

" She has possibly never seen you, but she must have been aware of the nature of your mission, of the importance of the documents in your casket, and of the deposit of this casket with your banker. Around her swarm agents obscure but well informed and always ready to do her bidding. She had but to make a sign and the casket was brought to her."

" You admit, then, that this Carnoël was of the band, and that I was not wrong to secure him ? "

" On that point I am not yet settled. It is possible that he gave indications, and may even have given them undesignedly. This lady is very skilful in making persons speak. The thing is to ascertain whether she had relations with the young man, and of that I can easily satisfy myself."

" I am curious to know how."

" Dear Alexis Stepanowitch, you shall see, and that shortly. I came to Paris to clear up this matter. If you wish, we will begin this evening."

" Where ? "

" At the opera.   The lady will probably be there.   She has returned to Paris without a cavalier, to spread her nets in the hope of capturing a Russian sufficiently high in place to serve without suspecting her.   Why should you not be this Russian ? "

" I ! you are mad !   You have just said that she knows what my occupation is in Paris."

" The more reason for her seeking to connect herself with you.   If she has not already tried it, it is because the occasion has not presented itself.   Remember, she is persuaded you will take her simply for a *femme galante*. She will not suspect that you know anything about her. She supposes herself to have all the advantage, and asks nothing better than to attract the man most formidable to her sect.   This is, as you must know, their method. These ladies ingratiate themselves by every means with the enemies of their sect, that they may surprise their secrets and hinder their action.   They have always one foot in the enemy's camp, and thus it is that they accomplish so much harm.   Now is the time to pay them back in their own coin."

" By suffering myself to be seduced by this woman ? " asked the colonel, ironically.

" Yes, and in profiting by your superiority over her. You can read her hand and she cannot read yours. You will go only so far as it suits you, and, however great her cunning, she will at last let you find out her vulnerable point.

" Besides, you have an ally in me. When I met her last summer in Switzerland I took care to assume the appearance of a liberal Russian, and it would be easy to make my liberalism still more pronounced until I have gained completely her confidence."

" If she saw you with me she would scarcely be ready to recognize you as a thorough partisan of her own."

" Oh, I shall not speak extravagantly. I shall be governed by circumstances. What I want is to discover whether this young man was really concerned in the theft, and if not, I have an easy way out of the situation, which will compromise no one."

" And you propose to begin operations this evening at the opera ? " said Borisoff.

" Yes, if we meet the lady, as I hope. But, tell me, don't you think that young man looks at us rather oftener than is necessary—the one who came to ask you about M. de Carnoël ? "

" He is a madcap, not worth occupying our attention."

" So be it, but if you take my advice we will raise the siege before he is through his dinner. The youth annoys me, and under other circumstances I should like to make him feel the point of my sword," grumbled Mouriatine, outlining the lunge with which he would be pleased to gratify Maxime.

At the same instant Maxime was struck by a sudden recollection :

" Ah ! *parbleu !* I recognize him now ; this man is the

fencing-master of the countess. Yet no—I must be
mistaken,—but that cast of feature. When once I have
seen a face I don't forget it—it was the change of costume that perplexed me. I even remember her calling
him by his name—a Polish name."

While Maxime Dorgères thus gathered up his recollections, Mouriatine shrugged his shoulders and said to
Col. Borisoff : "Bah ! I need not be disturbed about
him. The young man is not thinking of us. Let us ask
for coffee and light our cigars. We will take a smoke on
the boulevard."

"You said you expected to meet this woman at the
opera. May I ask on what you found this hope, having
come straight from St. Petersburg ? "

"I could not be expected to be so well informed as to
the disposition a Parisian demoiselle will make of her
evening. All I can affirm is that Wednesday is her day
for the opera ; there are then chances that we will meet
her there—if not, we will find her somewhere to-morrow
or next day."

"You are bent on presenting me, then ? " asked the
colonel, after a pause employed in sipping the coffee
that had just been served.

"I am—in your interest."

There was silence for several moments. The two
were observing each other. At the other end of the
hall was one who observed them both while apparently
absorbed in a partridge which had just been served.

"The more I look at that man," thought Maxime, "the more am I satisfied of having seen him, foil in hand, fencing with Mme. Yalta. How does it happen that I find him here dressed in the last extreme of fashion and dining at the dearest restaurant in Paris? This fencing-master must love good wines and have money in his pocket, and the countess must pay her professors better than generals are paid in France. But that he should be on terms of intimacy with Borisoff is indeed inexplicable."

Whilst Maxime was holding this monologue, conversation was renewed at the table of the two Russians.

"If you could succeed," said Mouriatine, "in suppressing this creature without disturbance, you would regain the reputation for skill which the affair of the casket has somewhat impaired. It is the damsel in question who must be sent to Siberia, not M. de Carnoël."

"*Parbleu!*" exclaimed Borisoff, "I begin to believe you are right. Let us settle and leave. It seems to me this Frenchman is watching us surreptitiously, and I want to throw him off the track."

Mouriatine was of the same opinion. He called the waiter to settle his bill.

"It is unheard of," growled Maxime, cramming down his truffles to make an end of them. "Borisoff and the countess' fencing-master are intimate friends. And this Borisoff is a secret agent of Russian diplomacy; a spy, to call things by the right name. She is no conspirator that I know of; but she knows, perhaps, those who are, or at least those whom Georget assisted to steal the casket. Is this pretty professor betraying his mistress? She also has secrets, perhaps. Who knows if he is not selling them to this man whom we believe to have confined Robert de Carnoël? *Parbleu!* I know what to be at. She made me promise not to act against Borisoff, but I am not engaged to shut my eyes when I meet him. I have the right to go where he goes, and even to follow a monsieur of his acquaintance."

He would gladly have sacrificed the remainder of his dinner, but could not break off abruptly from his partridge, scarcely yet touched, and precipitate himself into the street, without being remarked by the very persons whom he wished to watch unobserved.

So he resigned himself to suffer their departure, determining at the same time to cut short his sitting, and with that view taking double mouthfuls. He ascertained at a glance that they went toward the boulevard, and promised himself to follow them from afar up to the moment of separation, when he would give all his attention to the fencing-master. The colonel was now the countess' business, but he might and must study the proceedings of a hireling of the countess surprised in familiar intercourse with Borisoff.

It never occurred to him that this fencing-master acted, perhaps, on behalf of the countess, and in truth there appeared little probability that a subaltern of this class would be entrusted with the private confidence of a great lady of the Avenue de Friedland.

"The Frenchman is distanced," said Borisoff, on reaching the boulevard. "We have time to finish our cigars before going to the theatre." ·

"Especially," replied Mouriatine, "as I have taken the precaution to procure chairs just below the lady's box."

"I see you have thought of everything. However, if you had not found me, which might easily have been, since I was not anticipating your visit— "

"In that case I should have gone to the opera alone, for I am bent upon making use of this opportunity to meet the lady in question. But on going to your house I was told you would dine at your club, so I found you without difficulty. Is it in that beautiful Rue de Vigny mansion that you have shut up your prisoner?"

"Yes," said Borisoff, "and I beg you to believe that he is out of the reach of all pursuit. The house is large and completely isolated. I have made interior arrangements to facilitate watchfulness and prevent flight. My prisoner is as well guarded as if he were shut up in a fortress at St. Petersburg."

"But," resumed Mouriatine, "you have been obliged to take your domestics into your confidence."

"Oh, my servants are all old soldiers or subalterns attached to a lower order of the Third Section, and accustomed to passive obedience. They are as mute as fish, and always ready to act promptly. Had I wished to get rid of the Frenchman I had but to speak the word."

"But you have contented yourself with shutting him up in a cellar."

"That would have been useless. I have installed him in a large hall which serves me for a library. The doors of this apartment are all made fast and guarded. The windows look out on a garden, and are thirty feet from the ground. To fly, or to communicate with any one would be impossible. I have no neighbors."

They had just arrived at the Place de l'Opera. Had either of the two turned back, he would have seen Maxime, who had just set foot on one of the shelters illuminated by the electric light. Having finished his dinner, he had darted off in a chance pursuit of the two Russians. He had sped in every direction and perceived them at last, just as they were turning the corner of the Place de l'Opera.

"They are going to the opera," he murmured. "Decidedly they are intimate. I am not dressed and shall be taken for a provincial or usher, but I must know what these foreigners are about."

Maxime was a subscriber to the opera, and did not need to provide himself with a ticket. He suffered the couple he was in pursuit of to pass on in advance, and, five minutes after they had entered the door, presented himself at the comptroller's office, not without having pulled up the collar of his overcoat to disguise his black cravat.

The dress he wore suggested to him an idea.

Instead of taking his seat as usual, he would remain in

the passage-way of the orchestra until he discovered the colonel and his companion, and when he had ascertained in what part of the hall they were seated, would place himself so as not to lose sight of them.

This manœuvre was successful. From his ambuscade he discerned them installed in the orchestra, and he would remain in the post he had chosen till the curtain rose.

The two were engaged in inspecting the boxes with their glasses, and, having taken a rapid view, Mouriatine said to the colonel :

" She has not yet arrived."

" Are you certain she will come ? " retorted Borisoff, not sorry to find his companion's sagacity at fault.

"Certain ? no. One is never certain what a woman will do ; above all, a woman of this sort. But it is not late, and I do not despair of seeing her appear during the second act."

" And you think she will come alone ? "

" Very likely. At Geneva she went everywhere without a cavalier. They called her the Solitaire."

" Does the lady understand Russian ? "

" She pretends not, but I do not believe it. And I need hardly say that I shall not make use of our national tongue to speak to you confidentially in her presence."

" Ah ! " said Borisoff, " there is a woman entering, on our left, and a pretty woman, truly."

" It is she, my dear sir," murmured Mouriatine. " I

should recognize her anywhere, were it only by her eyes."

"They are wonderful, truly; I have never seen such before."

"Then you have not met with her?"

"Never; and it astonishes me. If this marvel is a *femme galante*, I do not understand why I have not re-marked her, or why she has not been pointed out to me."

"I have already said that she is an apparition that only appears in Paris now and then, and is not disposed to ex-hibit herself."

"She is examining the orchestra chairs with extraordi-nary persistency,—now she is directing her glass to the passage-way on our left."

"Ah! she ceases to inspect. See her now in all her splendor."

The new-comer now appeared in the forepart of the box, and her striking beauty attracted all eyes. Maxime, hiding himself in the depths of the orchestra, had taken no note of the star that had just risen. It was only when the lady set down the double opera-glass which had concealed the upper part of her face, that he recog-nized her. He still hesitated, unable to believe his eyes.

"She!" he murmured, "she here!"

"Madame Sergent! ah! it is too much. After the trick she played me, this rogue dares to appear openly at the opera—and in the first boxes still! And here have I been searching for her in vain for a month! She doubtless returned to Paris supposing I would think no more of her. Only she has not brought with her the Carpathian bear. She has left him in his own country and replaced him by another animal of the same species. Certainly," concluded the young man, "I was happily inspired this evening. At the restaurant I surprised one of the countess' hirelings in great intimacy with Borisoff, and here, at the opera, I discover a rogue who has tricked and robbed me. The thing is to determine what I had best do. *Parbleu!* my choice cannot be doubtful. It doesn't matter very much how this man finishes his evening with Borisoff, whilst if I let slip the occasion for laying hold on Madame Sergent, it will never present itself again. The safest plan would be to go up to her box and have an immediate explanation with her."

It was a favorable moment. The three strokes had just announced the second act.

Giving a last glance at the box before going out, the most surprising spectacle presented itself.

Col. Borisoff and his companion, both standing, were preparing to leave their places, and Madame Sergent was smiling to them.

Maxime fancied he must be mistaken, but as the two foreigners passed near her box he saw distinctly that they bowed to her, and that she returned the bow.

"They know her!" he murmured, and he stopped in utter consternation.

On one side, the countess' fencing-master exchanging gracious looks with the accomplice of those who had taken the casket, and, by excess·of marvels, the owner of this casket on pleasant terms with the friend of the thieves, and these two personages with one accord going to join her.

"I was astonished awhile ago," thought Maxime, "but this is beyond belief."

The more he reflected, the more the reunion appeared to him monstrous.   He seemed to see in it mysteries of iniquity, criminal alliances, unfathomable abysses of dissimulation.

He asked himself whether all these people were banded together to play a wicked comedy to the prejudice of Robert de Carnoël and himself.   He even went so far as to suspect the intentions of Madame Yalta—this countess who knew so many things, and loved secret intrigues.

"Is this man betraying her, or is she fooling me?"

He answered this question by a violence which he formulated thus :

"*Au diable!* the Russians, the Poles, and the great foreign ladies.   I have had enough of their intrigues, and can trample on their spider's webs.   I am afraid of no one after all, and have the right to call Madame Sergent to account."

This was a project easier to conceive than to execute. One does not rush into a lady's box in the midst of a performance to summon her to answer for her past conduct in the presence of two men who are not responsible for the doings and exploits of this woman. An inroad of this sort could end only in a quarrel, and quarrels never elucidate anything.

There was nothing for him but to observe and wait.

Whilst from the passage-way of the orchestra the invisible witness followed up the movements of the three whom some inexplicable chance had brought together, the adventure sketched by Mouriatine began to take shape.

The lady recently from Geneva, the ex-marvel of the Rink, had at length deigned a glance at the spectators nearest her.

Her sparkling eyes had encountered the gray eyes of Mouriatine, and smiles were exchanged.

Then ensued a pantomime which invited him to her box, followed by a movement on his part indicating his neighbor in the stall, answered by a sign from the lady which might be interpreted thus :

"No matter; bring your friend. I should be pleased to see him as well as yourself."

Nothing more was needed to induce the acceptance of an invitation repeated with such gracious persistency.

The box-keeper ushered them in, and the lady, with eyes of fire, began thus, extending her hand to Mouriatine :

"You can't think how happy I am to meet you. I arrived from Monaco alone, and have not yet seen a familiar face. You recognized me immediately, did you not?"

"You are not of the number of those whom one forgets," replied Ivan Ivanovitch.

"Oh, after six months' absence one has the right to forget anybody. But be good enough to present to me monsieur, who has been so kind as to accompany you."

"Col. Borisoff, one of my compatriots. My dear colonel, we are in the box of Madame de Garches."

"True ; it is very necessary that you should present me also, for your friend does not know me, I presume."

"No, madame, and I am truly astonished not to have remarked you, however brief may have been your sojourns in Paris. Beauty such as yours cannot pass unobserved anywhere."

"You flatter me, colonel, and I warn you that I do not love compliments. Sit down, and we will talk of everything you please except myself. Your friend will tell you that last summer, in Switzerland, I had established this rule, and that all my little world submitted to it. I seek friends, but flee from lovers."

"It seems to me that last year—excuse my frankness—one of my compatriots knew how to please you."

"Who ? Ah ! that blockhead of a general. That doesn't count. It was one of my errors. Only think, he gained my confidence by proposing extraordinary ascensions ; he talked about climbing Mont Blanc, scaling the

Yung Frau, and I could never induce him to leave the Royal Hotel of Chamounix or the promenades of Interlaken. I don't like prudent people, so I disposed of him."

"My friend Borisoff is temerity itself," said Mouriatine, with a burst of laughter.

"Take care," said the lady, "you will set me to putting his temerity to the proof."

These words, addressed directly to the colonel, embarrassed him visibly. He had, in truth, since his entrance into the lady's box, cut an awkward enough figure, though ordinarily it was not assurance that he lacked. Presented to a strange lady by a friend fallen from the skies like an aerolite, Borisoff did not feel certain of his ground. He was a skilful diplomatist, but accustomed to proceed methodically without trusting anything to chance. Furthermore, and above all, he was submitting, in spite of himself, to the ascendency of a pair of beautiful eyes ; eyes the like of which he had never seen before, and which were fixed on him with a disquieting persistency.

Mouriatine came to his assistance.

"To what proof would you subject my friend? What peaks do you mean to require him to scale?"

"Oh," replied the ex-marvel of the Rink, "the question is not one of perilous ascensions now. We are not in Switzerland ; we are in Paris, in a city where courage consists in mocking prejudices and braving public opinion. You both entered my box in the midst of the opera. That was a fine example of it."

"One which cost me very little," replied Mouriatine. "I am proud of being seen with you."

"My dear friend, you are a bird of passage. You come to France simply for amusement. You owe no account to any one and may act as you please, while with Col. Borisoff, not being in the same situation, there is more merit in attaching himself to a *déclassée.*"

"What do you call *déclassée?* Do you suppose I confound you with the demoiselles who make the tour of the lakes every day ?"

"No, but neither do you take me for a woman of the true world, and you are right. I was born in that world, and it is perhaps in my power to return to it, for I am free, and better still, I am rich ; but it was my choice to leave it, and it is my choice to live as an irregular. Therefore it is that you met me last summer exploring the glaciers and lakes in company with a lord, whom I dismissed when the fancy took me ; and thus, that having passed a fortnight at Monte Carlo, where I broke the bank, I arrive in Paris alone and unoccupied, uncertain whether I shall remain all winter or leave to-morrow."

"Your programme is charming—nothing fixed, everything to caprice—that is the motto of us Russians."

"Let your friend speak," said Madame de Garches, fixing her eyes on the colonel.

"I agree with my compatriot," said the colonel, who could no longer remain silent. "Pleasure is the great concern, and I also am free to choose my associations."

" Really ? "

" Do you doubt it ? "

' I doubt it no longer since you say so, but they have assured me that you were entrusted by your government with a secret mission. 'They' means this general by whom I was nearly bored to death last year. Don't ask me his name ; I don't wish to recall it."

" You remember at least what he told you about me ? " asked Borisoff.

" Oh, perfectly. I am glad you should know how it happened that you occupied my attention whilst exploring the beautiful valleys of Helvetia. I had inhabited in Paris the same neighborhood with yourself and do still."

" You know where I live ? "

" Yes. In going to the Bois I have often passed your house in Rue de Vigny. I have seen you sometimes driving yourself in a beautiful phaeton, and being curious, naturally I made inquiries about you. I learned that you were a Russian gentleman, very rich, and very agreeable."

" Why did I not know that you condescended to think of me ? " said Borisoff, gallantly.

" Oh, I was only passing through Paris. I came from London and was going to Geneva, where the most tiresome of generals awaited me. It came into my mind to ask information about you, because I had remarked you. You see, I am frank."

" You overwhelm me. But I fancy my illustrious compatriot took the trouble to dispel your illusions."

"He tried to do so. After having intrenched himself in prudent circumspection, he ended by a mysterious revelation that you belonged to the political police."

"It was a joke, I suppose," said the colonel, a little disconcerted by this abrupt declaration.

"A silly joke," seconded Mouriatine. "Did he accuse me also of being enrolled in the secret service?"

"No," replied the lady, somewhat scornfully, "but I can assure you he was not joking at all. He explained the colonel's mission to me, and entered into a number of details."

"Then I have a mission?" inquired Borisoff, forcing a smile. "I am charmed to know it. It has enhanced my importance in my own eyes."

"You are, it appears, charged with watching over the Nihilists."

"*Diable!* I execute my mission very imperfectly, then, for they have created much talk of late."

"In Russia; but you are concerned only with those who reside in France, at least according to the general."

"I believe," said Mouriatine, "my friend Borisoff has really a mission in Paris, and no very difficult one. He has a revenue of a hundred thousand roubles which he consecrates to the study of the pretty women of this country, where all types are to be met with."

"If I were certain you were telling me the truth," murmured the incomparable brunette, "I—but your friend should be the one to protest, and it is you only who speak."

"To protest!" exclaimed Borisoff, who had recovered his *sang froid.* "I shall do nothing of the sort. I should be glad to have you believe me the grand master of the police of all the Russias, and to prove to you that my greatness would not hinder me from following wherever you might lead."

"*A la bonne heure!* That is language that I understand. I believe you, my dear colonel; you are no political agent. The general was a fool, or not a fool either. Perhaps he had reasons for calumniating you. He knew I had observed you and was jealous. Now that I know just what ground we are on, I may profit by the chance that has brought us together this evening. I shall be in Paris only a few days, and wish to enliven my dulness as much as possible. If the colonel now had been really the formidable representative of a formidable police, I should be, to my great regret, deprived of the privilege of receiving him."

"You would have had nothing to fear from him, for you do not conspire against our government."

"How do you know?" asked Madame de Garches, with a smile that might have melted all the glaciers of Mont Blanc.

"Eyes like yours do not conspire. They love."

"You are right. Love is better than politics, and I care little about overturning governments. But I can't help pitying the proscribed,—the exiles, and should not wish to live on friendly terms with those who persecute them."

"If you only knew them—these people whom you compassionate—"

" I do know them, or to speak more exactly, I have known some of them."

"Where ?   In Switzerland ? " asked Mouriatine.

" In Switzerland and in Paris," replied Madame de Garches.

" What ! at Paris too ! I thought the headquarters of these people was Geneva."

"I supposed so, but I met some one here last year who was certainly working for your Nihilists."

" She made you her confidante ? " asked Borisoff, with an air of doubt.

" No, chance made me acquainted with a secret which I did not try to penetrate, and this secret I have intentionally forgotten.   Let us talk of something more lively."

" Willingly," said Mouriatine," and we would do well to lower our voices.   They are murmuring against us in the neighboring boxes."

The prudent Ivanovitch was, moreover, of the opinion that it was not expedient to attract attention at the theatre when treating of certain subjects.

" You are right," murmured the lady, with eyes of fire; " we are scandalizing our neighbors, and, moreover, not listening to a note of Meyerbeer's music. It is real sacrilege."

" Are you very anxious to listen to this divine music ? " asked M. Borisoff, who began to think Madame de Gar-ches worth more than all the operas in the world.

" Exceedingly, though I know it by heart," replied the incomparable brunette, turning toward the stage.

The change was not acceptable to the two messieurs. Borisoff especially was enticed by the indiscreet words she had let drop ; moreover, he thought her ravishing. He could never remember to have met with a woman who charmed him so much, and at the same time excited his curiosity. He was devoted body and soul to the govern-ment he served, but he had not given in his resignation as a man of intrigue—this skilful and gallant colonel. To please an adorable creature and make use of his con-quest to regain the esteem of the chief of the Third Sec-tion, what a dream ! But the point was not yet reached. To arrange his batteries so as to profit by the situation, would not be very easy even for diplomatists, and he al-most despaired of success. But Ivan Ivanovitch, who had no misgivings, encouraged him by look and gesture ; while Madame de Garches, leaning on the front of her box, was absorbed in a musical revery.

The subtle Ivan was unconscious that Maxime Dor-gères was prowling in the corridor like a lion waiting for his prey.

Maxime had decided to come out from the depths of

the orchestra, that he might watch more nearly the suspicious creatures who occupied his thoughts. He was
revolving in his mind a crowd of contradictory projects.
He wished not to lose sight of Madame Sergent, and at
the same time to avoid being seen by her. A police
agent would have been perplexed how to attain this
double end, much more Maxime, complete novice that
he was in such matters, who had always come off worsted
in his encounters with the thief of the bracelet,—even
with Col. Borisoff.

Mouriatine, far from thinking of him, was seeking to
recover the thread of an interesting conversation, and the
colonel meanwhile admired the Greek profile and golden
complexion of Madame de Garches.

Suddenly she changed her attitude and turned toward
her adorer.

"Do you know what I am thinking of?" she asked
abruptly.

"I only know that I am thinking of you."

"I was thinking of the tragic scene of the fourth act
of this play, and that it is sometimes enacted under another form in real life."

"Hum!" sneered Mouriatine, "the passions have
much calmed down since the days of St. Bartholemew."

"Do you think so? For my part I fancy nothing has
changed. Bring together love and politics, and a tragedy
as exciting as 'The Huguenots' will be the result. Suppose, for example, one of the Nihilists of your country in

love with an officer—an aide-de-camp of the Czar, for
instance. She knows of a plot soon to be developed—
the palace is mined and is about to be blown up. Her
lover is called there on duty. He is with her—is about
to leave. She holds him back—he questions her. And
there she is reduced to the alternative of leaving him to
perish or betraying the secret of the conspirators."

"That would recall to mind the famous fourth act,"
said the colonel, smiling, "but permit me to say that you
have much too romantic an idea of these partisans in petticoats. They are the most prosaic people in the world on
all subjects, and would sacrifice every sentiment to their
interest or their pleasure. You are not aware, perhaps,
that they have gone so far as to steal. The Russian
papers gave only yesterday an account of the condemnation of half a dozen young and pretty women who took
part last winter in an expedition directed against a bank-
ing-house. Their friends had made an underground passage-way to reach the vaults of this bank, and obtained
possession of four or five millions of francs. All these
rascals of both sexes will end their days in Siberia, and
the men no more resemble Raoul than the women do the
Valentine of Meyerbeer's opera."

"It is true," murmured Madame de Garches dreamily,
"they do steal—but only on behalf of their cause."

"What do you know about it?"

"One of them told me so."

"Had she a lover?"

"Yes, and I think there passed between them something analogous to the great scene of 'The Huguenots.'"

"Really? If you would let me have the story I should be glad to know if I have slandered these people in declaring them incapable of elevated sentiments."

"Oh, the situation was not the same as in the opera. He was not a conspirator, nor had his brothers been massacred. But his mistress exacted of him the sacrifice of his honor, and he yielded."

"In other words, to make himself agreeable to her, he stole."

"Something of that sort, and the unfortunate young man was cruelly punished. He was compelled to flee, or at least he has disappeared, and the woman concerns herself no more about him."

-"Was he Russian?" asked Mouriatine with an indifferent air.

"No, he is French. But I left Paris and do not know the end of the story. I should be glad to hear the dénouement."

"Nothing prevents you from instituting inquiries now that you have returned."

"The woman has probably left France. Besides, it was a sorrowful adventure, and I came to Paris for amusement. I should like for a few days to lead the life of a young man. You laugh. I am quite serious. I have an insane desire to sup, to get intoxicated, to frequent public balls."

" Not alone, I hope ? "

" Why not ? It would be the true way to amuse myself. But I do not know that I shall venture."

" Should you like to be accompanied by two discreet
cavaliers ? "

" You and your friend, you mean ? "

" Precisely. I assure you, you could not do better.
We seek only amusement and will act as your escorts,
with that view only."

" If I was sure of it—"

" Doubt nothing. When shall we begin ? This evening ? "

" This evening there is no masked ball anywhere.'

" We may sup, nevertheless, and if it suits you to sup
in that house in Rue de Vigny, that you have observed—"

" Thanks. I sup only at a restaurant or at home."

" At home ? I thought you were only here in passing."

" That is true, but I have a house furnished as if I
resided in it all the year round. It is not far from yours.
Are you familiar with Rue Jouffroy ? "

" Rue Jouffroy ? " repeated Borisoff.

" Yes, between the Boulevard Malesherbes and the
Avenue de Villiers. I have there a lodging not equal to
your palace in Rue de Vigny but which suffices for me,
alone as I am."

" And the general ? " asked Mouriatine, laughing.

"The general has never set foot there, thank heaven. I tolerated him as a travelling companion. I should not endure him in Paris."

"And you have given him no successor ?'

"Never. I have declared my independence and wish no master even temporarily. I am alone, I repeat, and if you doubt it, I invite you to supper this evening at my house."

"Do you know that I have a great mind to accept ? " said the colonel, laughing.

"If you refused, you would disoblige me exceedingly. I should think you were distrustful of my *cuisine*. I assure you it is excellent, and the wines I shall offer you will not be improvised. I am expected every evening, and arrangements are made to include a few friends. I must add that I am a horrible gourmande."

"Then you are perfect," said Mouriatine ; "a pretty woman who loves a good table is so rare."

"I am going to excite your enthusiasm. Know that I have a cellar of the first order. I hope you will no longer hesitate to come and try my wines."

Borisoff said not a word, though his companion consulted him with his eyes. He desired nothing better than to sup with the incomparable brunette, but would have preferred it should be at his own house.

"Well," she said, after a short silence, " I see that my proposition does not please you. We will say nothing more about it."

"But if," said Mouriatine, "I should agree to accept it and gladly?"

"Your friend is not so inclined, and I cannot resent his reserve. He scarcely knows me, and considering the progress Nihilism is making he does well to be prudent."

"What has Nihilism to do with the pleasant party you propose?"

"How do you know I am not one of that sect? Have I not just acknowledged that I know a woman who is,— and a thief if you please. From thence to conspiring is but one step."

"Why do you take pleasure in making game of us?"

"I speak very seriously."

"Then you wish to convince us that if we went to pass our evening with you we should run the risk of falling into a den of revolutionary bandits?" said Mouriatine, with a burst of laughter. "Why not try to persuade us that we should share the fate of those who sat down to the table of Lucrezia Borgia?"

"The Nihilists in petticoats are capable of anything— the colonel himself has said so—anything—even to serving their enemies with poisoned wines."

"Dear madame," said Borisoff, who had just determined on his line of action, "you attribute ideas to me that have never entered my head. I am yours too entirely for discretion. I should be delighted to follow you anywhere, and for the pleasure of supping with you, no matter where, would sup with all the conspirators in the universe were they guilty of the blackest crimes."

"Good ! I take you at your word."

"It is I who take you at your word, and to prove that I do not fear the company with which you are trying to frighten me, I will declare that I should be delighted to have you invite this evening your thief and her young associate."

"Come, I give you back my esteem, and if I knew where to find the persons you speak of I would beg them to join us. Unfortunately they are fled I know not where. The woman, perhaps, has fallen into the claws of the Russian police, who have most likely sent her to Siberia. The lover must have crossed the seas, if he has not blown his brains out. We need think no more of them and will sup without them."

"At what hour ?" asked Mouriatine.

"After the theatre—is it not, colonel ? "

"Certainly," said Borisoff, bowing.

"You will think me very indiscreet," said Mouriatine, "but I have just asked a very insidious question. You must know I am nearly famished. I arrived this evening at five, and had only time to make my toilette and look for my friend Borisoff at his club. We found so much to talk about that we forgot our dinner."

"To come to the opera ? What a lover of music you are ! "

" I had telegraphed from St. Petersburg to reserve two

seats,—the fancy of one at a distance who wishes to enjoy a thorough Parisian life without losing a minute. I counted on the company of my faithful Borisoff, but did not calculate on the train being two hours late."

"Good ! I understand, and it would be a poor reward for your frankness to compel you to suffer the tortures of hunger till midnight. We will leave whenever it pleases you, messieurs."

"What ! you would sacrifice to our appetites the remainder of this play ?"

"Willingly. The act is about to conclude. We will leave before the third."

"You are as good as you are beautiful. But it will not be for your house, I suppose ? You will not be expected so early as this ?"

"My servants expect me always. I have sent away my coupé, it is true."

"And I have not given orders to my coachman," said Borisoff.

"No matter. A hack will take us to Rue Jouffroy in twenty minutes, and in ten other minutes, my famished messieurs, you will sit down to table."

"Adopted unanimously," cried Mouriatine, gaily.

The colonel thought no more of opposition. He approved of the fable of the neglected dinner, for his opinion now was that it was expedient to penetrate at the earliest possible moment the house of this woman who deserved to be studied more closely.

She turned toward the stage and appeared to be absorbed in the last airs of the act that was concluding.

Suddenly, however, she took up her opera-glass and directed it toward one of the boxes on the same side. Two women occupied the front of this box, in the back of which was a gentleman who was scarcely visible.

"Strange!" cried Madame de Garches. "I could swear it was he."

"Ah!" said Mouriatine, jocosely, "is your general of last winter here?"

"I am not thinking about that personage, but I fancied I recognized a young man whom I little expected to see here."

"The friend of your Nihilist, perhaps?" said Mouriatine, still in a bantering tone. Nothing can be seen of him but the end of his nose; and as for the two women, I can only say they are neither young nor pretty."

"They are *bourgeoises*," said Borisoff," very rich and very common, who have taken a box for the winter in the hope of being seen and espoused by some ruined princes."

"The resemblance is strange," continued the brunette to herself, "but if it were he it would be stranger still."

"Surely, madame, this youth may flatter himself with having inspired an interest on your part. If he knew you were at so much pains to identify him, no doubt he would hasten to show himself."

"I doubt it very much," murmured Madame de Garches.

"You think then he has a reason for concealing himself?"

"My dear sir, you are too curious."

"I confess it and am silent."

"You would do better to wait until he leans on the front of the box, and then tell me if you have ever seen him."

"Ha! I come to Paris too rarely to know the habitués of the Opera."

"It would in truth be better to ask the colonel if he has ever met with the young man whom I fancied I saw in that box. His name is M. de Carnoël."

At this name spoken by the charming mouth of Madame de Garches, the colonel involuntarily started. Anything might sooner have been expected than inquiries from her concerning M. de Carnoël.

Nevertheless he must answer without evasion, must reply by yes or no. His professional instinct suggested the thought that it were better not to cut short all possibility of further investigation by a negative reply.

"Is not M. de Carnoël the son of a former attaché of the embassy?" he asked.

"Yes, I think his father was formerly engaged in diplomacy. Then you have met with the young man?"

"Often enough to recognize him if he were here."

"Do you suppose it possible that he could be at the Opera in company with the widows in that box?"

"I should see nothing surprising in it. He has, I believe, no fortune, and seeks, no doubt, an advantageous marriage."

"He! marry one of those vulgar upstarts! I could not believe him capable of such a thing. Besides, I was insane to imagine he would appear at the opera in an un-covered box."

"Why?" asked the colonel, assuming an astonished air.

"Because he cannot be in Paris."

"One would infer from your words," said Mouriatine, " that the gentleman in question was forced to hide him-self. Has he been guilty of any crime?"

"Madame," resumed Borisoff, who began to get a clear view of the situation, "I can certify that you are mis-taken. M. de Carnoël has not left Paris as far as I know."

" He may have done so without your knowledge."

"Then he must have left this morning, for I saw him yesterday."

In acknowledging that he held intercourse with M. de Carnoël, the colonel was burning the bridge behind him, but it had become apparent that Madame de Garches knew a great deal about the prisoner, and the best means of extracting what she knew appeared to be to assume the attitude of a friend of the young man who interested her.

" You have spoken to him!" she exclaimed.

" Yes; I met him on the street this morning."

"And he did not try to avoid you?"

."Not at all. We have not been intimate, but have held the most courteous relations. Why should he have avoided me?"

"I thought he must have reasons for not wishing to meet with former acquaintances, and am delighted to learn that I was mistaken. Did he speak to you of his present circumstances?"

"Yes; but with considerable reserve. He told me, however, that he had abandoned a situation he had held and proposed to embark for America. I offered him a recommendation to our consul-general at New York."

"And he accepted?"

"With gratitude. That reminds me that I have not sent him the promised letter. I shall repair my negligence to-morrow."

"It is very singular," said Madame de Garches, still directing her glass to the box occupied by the matrimonially-inclined widows. Then suddenly laying it down, she said aloud : "I was sure of it. The young man has just risen, and his full face does not resemble M. de Carnoël in the least."

"He is very fortunate, this M. de Carnoël," laughed Mouriatine ; "he absorbs all your thoughts. Might we know when and where he made your conquest?"

"Dear monsieur," said the brunette, with eyes of fire, dryly, "your question is an impertinence. No one has made my conquest. If I am interested about this young man it is because one of my best friends, who is residing in Florence, has charged me to find out what has become of him, and to deliver a box—"

"Containing love tokens ? "

"I know nothing about that, but I know that you are insupportable, and I beg you not to interrupt my conversation with the colonel."

" Madame," said Borisoff, " I will with pleasure undertake to forward the box to M. de Carnoël."

" He has given you his address ? "

"It was necessary he should do so that I might send him the letter, and if you would like at the same time to have my valet deliver the box—"

"Thank you ; I promised to place it in his hands myself. I confess it embarrasses me a little, for I can scarcely go to him ; but I can write, and suppose he will not refuse to come to see me at my house."

" Assuredly not, but it would be well not to delay too long, for he may leave Paris at any moment."

" True ; he must be in haste to depart," murmured Madame de Garches to herself. "What is to be done, then ? "

"Is it really important that you should see M. de Carnoël ? " said Borisoff, after a short silence.

" Undoubtedly."

" Will you receive him this evening ? "

"Why not ? Our interview would not be long and need not interrupt our supper."

"Well, I can pass by his lodging. If I find him there, as is quite likely, I will bring him to you ; if not, I will leave my card, with a word to signify that I am awaiting him in Rue Jouffroy. He will suppose it to be on account of the letter and will certainly come."

"My dear colonel, if you would do that you would be the most amiable of men."

"There is a compliment which I hasten to deserve. Permit me to leave you for an instant. We must make sure of a carriage. The sooner we arrive at your house, the sooner I may go in quest of M. de Carnoël."

"Perfect. I shall be ready on your return."

The two Russians hastened from the box and reclaimed their overcoats, without having perceived Maxime, who was promenading at the end of the corridor.

· "Hey !" said Mouriatine in his companion's ear, "was I right in advising you to approach this lady ? I caught your idea of confronting the Carnoël with this jade. It is bold, but a masterly stroke."

"A stroke in which I might be the loser, did I not take precautions. I must first see the house, how it is guarded, and what servants she has under her orders. If I scent a trap, I shall make a feint of going in search of Carnoël, and shall return saying I have not found him. The affair will be ended for to-night, but I shall resume it after another method. If, on the contrary, I find that force could be employed with any chance of success, I shall bring Carnoël in a carriage with an escort of three good blades. I shall drive myself and will conduct him to the mistress of the house. That will be the psychological moment, as M. Bismarck says. With a glance we may detect whether there has been any complicity between them. My three old soldiers will enter with me ; three others will guard the door and the street. We will search the house from top to bottom, and I hope will make many discoveries."

"Your casket very likely," said Mouriatine, "and as to this pretended Madame de Garches—"

"We will bring her to my house with the Carnoël, the femme de chambre, the cook, and the men servants, if there are any. We will empty the house in a few trips, and will then see what is to be done with our prisoners."

"It is spirited, but if well conducted it must succeed, and in that case the great chief will approve it."

"It will succeed. I shall not act without being sure of my ground."

'Oh, I feel confident of it ! Chance has been on our side ; let us make the most of it."

"Come, let us look for a hack," said the colonel, pushing Mouriatine toward the great stairway.

CHAPTER XV.

EXCITING SCENES IN RUE JOUFFROY.

MAXIME had not lost sight of his prey. He had followed the two foreigners, and was holding himself in ambuscade in the first turn in the corridor.

He had sworn not to leave the place until the brunette left her box, and to keep close in her footsteps so soon as she appeared. Further than that his plan was unsettled. Whether he should approach her as soon as she left the theatre, or follow her unobserved, he had not yet determined. The great point was not to lose sight of her, and to find out where she lived.

As for Borisoff and his companion, satisfied that they had left not to return, he thought no more of them, and was not a little surprised to see them reappear after an absence of a few minutes, and direct their steps toward the box where Madame Sergent still remained. Already he had ascertained that the box-keeper had brought her a superb fur pelisse and hood trimmed with swan's down, which recalled unpleasant recollections. Evidently she had begun her preparations for departure, and might be expected to leave the box every moment.

But Maxime had not anticipated that her two cavaliers would return to seek her. The door was opened, and the lady all wrapped up appeared on the threshold and took the direction of the stairway, escorted on each side by two personages whom Maxime was sending to all the devils.

"They are accompanying her," he said, between his teeth; "this is the climax. Where are they going? To supper, perhaps, but no—there is a mystery in the re-union of these three creatures who have no right to know each other, and I shall find out the answer to the enigma if I have to pass the whole night on my feet."

Talking thus to himself, Maxime followed from afar the ill-assorted trio, and arrived almost at the same time under the peristyle. There he took care to conceal himself behind a gathering of talkers, and from his post of observation saw Borisoff separate himself from the little group, push aside one of the doors separating the exterior flight of stairs from the vestibule and beckon to some one. Maxime understood immediately that he was ordering a porter to advance a carriage,—a hack to all appearance, for the servants of the boyard were not there awaiting their master.

It is vain to set one's good limbs and twenty-five years against a pair of horses, even hired ones, and Maxime understood that not a minute was to be lost in making his arrangements to follow them. It so happened that, just as he darted out, an uncovered victoria was passing

the square at slow pace, driven by a freebooter in search
of prey. He would have preferred a close carriage, but
there was no choice, and he jumped into the one that
offered, with a few very intelligible words to the coachman. In his character of experienced Parisian, he knew
well how to speak to this class in the language that
makes them move. Moreover, this coachman was one
who took in half a word. He drew up against the side
of Rue Halèvy, and awaited further orders.

Turning toward the theatre, Maxime saw the brunette
of the Rink and the two foreigners get in a large hack
with four seats, which turned toward the Chaussée d'
Antin. His only object now was to follow this hack
which proved easy, as the peaceable beasts which led it
travelled at a moderate speed.

"Where are they going? They are leaving the boulevard, consequently the night restaurants; then they do
not intend to sup—that is, unless they are going to sup
at Borisoff's. Yet, no; they would have taken Rue
Scribe. It is true that all roads lead to Rome."

The proverb found this evening its application. Arrived at the cross-street whence might be seen the
church of la Trinité, the hack turned to the left and filed
along the Boulevard Haussman, which ended in the
Boulevard Malesherbes.

"One would swear Borisoff is taking them to his own
house," murmured Maxime.

The victoria maintained its distance without difficulty, the coachman, an old stager, humming in a low voice Fahrbach's polka.

It was not the first time he had aided a citizen in watching a woman, and he knew that such expeditions were always well paid.

Before the doorway of Saint Augustin the situation began to define itself.

"There is no longer room for doubt," growled Maxime; "they are going to the Rue de Vigny. What are they going to do? To make an end of Carnoël—get rid of him? A spy, a valet, and a knave of a woman are capable of combining to murder a man who incommodes them; at least—that idea has never occurred to me, but it is not more inadmissible than all the rest—at least, if they do not all understand each other, and the Lord Robert does not make one of the band. I mean to set my mind at rest, and shall stick close to them till I have cleared all this up."

Unfortunately, it was not long before the problem became still further complicated. Instead of taking the Boulevard de Courcelles for the Borisoff mansion, the hack continued to roll in the direction of the fortifications.

"Can it be that they intend to leave Paris?" he asked.

It did not occur to him that Madame Sergent imitated the manœuvre of the hare, who returns to its home after having given a long chase. And when he saw the hack stop at the corner of a certain street, he had much difficulty in believing his eyes. It was the same through which he had conducted Madame Sergent one beautiful November night,—that in which was a house that had been abandoned six weeks ago by its strange tenants.

"Shall I stop?" inquired the intelligent coachman. "They are unloading yonder, the two gentlemen first and then *la particulière.* They are paying ; seems they've arrived."

"Go on further," answered Maxime, "only take the other side of the street, and put your horse into a brisk trot."

This manœuvre was not ill contrived. Just as he reached the rising ground of Rue Jouffroy the brunette and her companions entered it on foot, having sent away their hack.

The victoria continued its route, but as soon as it had passed the corner of the street which the trio had just entered, Maxime rose, put his hand on the coachman's shoulder, and said, in a low voice :

"Quick ! To the right ! Stop near the other side, and do not budge till I return. Here are twenty francs in advance. It is possible I may keep you here all night."

"Good !" sneered the sly coachman. "I understand. You are after *la particulière.* This sort of business always amuses me. Have no fear. I was fresh when you took me, and my horse will hold good till morning. And if you have need of me, call me in."

"I don't say no," replied Maxime, as he set foot on the ground, and he ran to gain his ambuscade on the corner of the street.

He arrived just in time to see the lady ring at the door formerly guarded by the cerberus with the red mustache.

The door opened immediately, and closed behind Madame Sergent and her friends.

Maxime was stupefied, astounded, petrified.

This dénouement was the only one he had not contemplated, and the more he reflected the less capable did he feel of explaining it.

But he must act, or, at least, try to penetrate this strange mystery. How was he to go about it? Happy ideas are sometimes born of great perplexities.

"*Parbleu!* I cannot do better than consult my old acquaintance, the porter opposite. He must have a pretty good recollection of me. I gave him twenty francs every time I talked with him, and this evening will willingly give him forty if he will consent to serve me. I even think he would not refuse me his lodge as an ambuscade. Provided my man has not gone to bed!"

He looked at his watch, and saw it was half-past ten.

"No," he resumed, "these tenants cannot retire so soon. But no time is to be lost.

The street, well lighted by the city gas, was silent and deserted. Not a passer-by, not a sound. Maxime glided

the length of the wall, as he had done before on his first
expedition to this quarter, and arrived without encoun-
tering a living creature at his wished-for haven.

From this well-chosen site he discerned, in full, Madame Sergent's mysterious habitation, and ascertained that
no light was visible from the windows. All was sombre
as on the evening he had escorted her from the Rink.
Evidently the receiving rooms did not look on the
street.

On the other hand, he observed, with a lively satisfaction, that from a window on the ground-floor of the
dwelling confided to the surveillance of the porter he
was seeking, shone the unobtrusive light of a lamp.

This curtainless window must be that of the lodge, and
looking in he saw the porter, his elbows on a table and
spectacles on his nose, reading from the evening's paper,
which one of his tenants was, perhaps, awaiting with impatience.

He was alone with a big cat and a featherless parrot.

Maxime, having to enter upon delicate negotiations,
could not have been more fortunate. Not being dupli-
cated by a companion whom he would have been compelled to make the confidant of his projects, there remained nothing but to approach the porter frankly and
enlist him as an ally.

Unwilling to quit even for a moment his post of observation, he concluded to strike on the window of the
lodge. At the sound the porter laid down his paper,

turned his head, and seeing the outline of a figure through the panes, went bravely to open it.

"Fear nothing," said Maxime, in a low voice; "I am the person to whom you gave some information last month about the Prussian opposite."

"How, sir, you!" cried the man, "at this hour!"

"Yes; I came to ask you to do me a service. Can you let me in—immediately?"

"With pleasure; and remain as long as you please."

"That is what I was about to ask. There is something new—over there. But do not leave me longer in the street. I don't wish to be seen over yonder."

"I come, sir; I am running," and having closed the window and drawn the cord, M. Bidard went himself to receive his unexpected visitor.

"Quick!" said Maxime, gliding into the alley. "Let us go in; and put out the light, I beg, or hide it in a corner if you can't put it out. And to indemnify you for disarranging you, here are two louis."

Bidard pocketed them, and thrust the lamp under the table, muttering:

"Monsieur, I thank you all the same, but can assure you that what I do is not from calculation."

"I am sure of it. Now station yourself as sentry with me behind the window, and let us talk."

The man hastened to follow a man who gave princely *pourboires*, and had ways as mysterious as a hero of romance.

"When did the tenants over there return ?" asked this munificent stranger.

"Return ! Monsieur knows the Prussian left six weeks ago, and nothing has been heard of him, and nothing ever will." ·

"Either by him or by some other the house is occupied now."

"By rats and mice, then. Everything is shut up, as monsieur may see, and nothing has budged since the Prussian decamped."

"You must be mistaken."

"Oh, no, sir. I pass half the day on the door-step since the weather is fine, and no one has been in the house. I answer for it with my head, and I beg monsieur to believe I set store by my head."

"A woman and two men are there at this moment. I have just seen them go in."

"And the Prussian is one ?"

"No ; they are foreigners whom I know, and do not resemble the bear. It is not the first time the woman has come here in the night. I escorted her to the door the night before I came to you for information, and on that day I told you the name she gave me—Madame Sergent."

"I recollect. Monsieur thought she was a *cocotte*. And monsieur is certain she is within with the gentlemen ?"

"Absolutely certain."

"Then that house is the Tour de Nesle," cried the

porter ; "there must be horrors going on there. Suppose I go for the police."

"No ; I have reasons for not having recourse to the police. Besides, what ground should I have? This woman has undoubtedly the right to enter a house of which she carries the key in her pocket, and to take there whoever she will. What I want is simply to find out what these people are about."

"Monsieur may act as if at home, and nothing can escape him here."

" Has the house another outlet ? "

"I don't know of any. There is a garden behind, but it is enclosed, and there is no gate on the other side."

" How is the house arranged inside ? "

"First there is the ground-floor, with a dining-room and billiard-room ; on the first floor a large salon ; on the second, two bedchambers ; on the other front a small salon on the first floor ; on the ground-floor—"

" Look ! " interrupted Maxime, " there is a light in the first story."

" True, they are lighting up the large salon ; two lamps—and wax candles. See how it is lighting up everywhere, quicker than the Champs-Elysées on illumination days ! The dining-room's turn has come now— one light—two lights—ah, the *cocotte* is going to give a ball and supper ! And the *larbins*, where do they come from ? See how they pass and repass before the windows. 'Pon my word if a body was superstitious he might believe the devil was making a feast there, for since the house was built nobody has seen the end of a candle burning in it."

"And you declare that for some days past you have seen no one enter?"

"Not a cat. Monsieur may ask all the tenants in the neighborhood. If they hadn't gone to bed they'd be at the windows, and would make such a stir people would collect in the streets."

"It is amazing," thought Maxime, "evidently they have brought a squad of servants in the night to prepare for the reception of the master and his guests. Who has done that and for what purpose?"

"It is my notion the *cocotte* has brought two rich foreigners to spend the night at play and get their money."

"I don't think play has anything to do with it. You say there is a small salon on the side next the garden?"

"Not so small, and richly furnished. It looks like a lady's boudoir."

"That is where she has taken the two men, while she gave orders to have the apartments for reception made ready."

"That's what I said to monsieur. ' They will begin by sitting down to table, and certainly it will not be to make way with the leavings of the Prussian. But where did they get decent provisions? Not a carriage from Potel or Chabot has been seen to enter Rue Jouffroy. Ah!

the illuminators are disappearing. They are coming to supper."

" Look ! " said Maxime, laying his hand on the arm of M. Bidard, " do you see those three shadows outlined on the curtain of the salon ? "

" Certainly, the woman and the two messieurs, *parbleu !* Must be that supper isn't ready, or they are expecting some one ; they don't appear to be going to the dining-room."

" They are standing though."

" Yes, or bowing and scraping. See ! the tallest bows, and the *cocotte* gives him her hand ; it's amusing like any thing, 'pon my word. One might believe himself at Seraphin's Chinese shadows."

" Ah ! ah ! the one that bowed is going out ; there are only two silhouettes to be seen now."

" Likely he's gone to bed. The other is the *cocotte's* gentleman. The friend who came with them has said good-night."

" No, if that was so they wouldn't have lighted the salon and dining-room. But we shall see."

Five minutes passed without incident. The two stories were brilliantly lighted, but the shadows had disappeared. Suddenly the little door through which Madame Sergent had disappeared the evening of the Rink was opened softly. A man appeared on the threshold followed by a servant bearing a light with two branches. By the brightness of this light Maxime recognized Borisoff and redoubled his attention. He held a short colloquy with the *valet de pied* which by means of the gestures the observer interpreted for himself.

"He says he will return," thought Maxime, "and the servant explains that he has only to ring and they will open to him."

The door closes again. Borisoff goes toward the Boulevard Malesherbes. And now the fencing-master and the thief reappear behind the window of the salon. From thence they observe the colonel. They are awaiting his return.

"Shall I follow their example or risk a sally to see where he is going?" Maxime determined on the latter.

"Listen," he said to his ally Bidard, "I want to find out what that man is going to do. I am going to follow him to the end of the street and return."

"That is easy. I will open to monsieur and resume my post. Monsieur has only to knock on the window when he returns."

Maxime glided into the street and saw Borisoff fifteen steps in advance, and at the same time a man whose feet were pattering on the square at the entrance of Rue Jouffroy. This was no other than the coachman of his victoria.

"Good!" he thought, "I may let my Russian pass on. My coachman will tell me which way he took." So he disappeared in the shadow of the wall to watch events from afar.

The colonel walking quickly soon reached the Boulevard Malesherbes ; there he stopped, and observing the coachman, went straight toward him. This surprised Maxime, who began to look with all his eyes, wondering, with a certain anxiety, what Borisoff had to say to this man. The conversation prolonged itself for an unreasonable length of time, more than could be needed to ascertain from a coachman whether his carriage was free. But at length Borisoff passed on his way and was lost in the darkness. Maxime after waiting awhile went toward the boulevard. Arrived at the end of the street he stopped to look around, then turned to the right and rejoined the coachman, who recognized him immediately and began to laugh.

" Ah, monsieur," he said, "*la particulière's* gentleman wanted to pump me, but I turned him off nicely. Fancy that seeing my coach drawn up here he mistrusted me at once, and asked if I had brought somebody to Rue Jouffroy. I knew what was up and told him I was waiting for a doctor who hired me by the month, and was on a visit in that big house yonder—on the boulevard."

"Really !" exclaimed Maxime, " you have put him off the track. That was a good idea of yours, and I shall remember it when we settle."

" Oh," said the coachman, " I'm not uneasy about my *pourboire ;* I know my man. That's why I could tell that tall one there was the husband, and a husband jealous as a turkey, and I see well enough that you mean to play him a trick."

"Perhaps, but did he not ask you to drive him somewhere?"

"Yes; it vexed him to see my carriage drawn up at the end of the street where he had just left his *particulière;* he knew I wasn't there for nothing. He has a sharp scent. He asked me first if I would drive him home—only two steps,—and I should have a hundred sous. He might have offered me a louis, and I'd have stayed by you. And when he saw I didn't bite, he filed off. I would lay a litre he's already at the Boulevard de Courcelles."

"You did well, *mon brave*, to send that man off to walk, and I promise you shall lose nothing. He will return, the animal, and as I want to watch him, I am going to station myself as sentry at a place below. You will remain here and keep your eyes open, and when I return tell me what you have seen. If by chance I should need your services, may I count on you?"

"Fully. You have only to call out, Auguste, and I come at a gallop. If any thumping is to be done, I can prove that I am not one-handed."

"Thanks, and *au revoir* to-night or to-morrow, according as events may determine."

Auguste, flattered by the confidence in him exhibited by his monsieur, made a magnificent gesture, which signified: "Be easy; I am here."

And having thus arranged his affairs, Maxime hastened to regain his ambuscade.

The porter awaited him and opened with great alacrity, anxious to learn the result of the sally.

" Is monsieur satisfied ?   Has monsieur discovered anything new ? "

" The man sped away by the Boulevard Malesherbes, but I am satisfied he means to return."

" Oh, that is clear as day.   They are not going to table without him.   All is lit up and nothing moves in the house.   Proof that they are waiting for him."

" Hush ! " said Maxime, in a low voice.   At this moment a carriage stopped a hundred metres from Madame Sergent's house.

To Maxime's great amazement, Robert de Carnoël descended from the carriage and advanced toward the house, flanked by two tall men who pressed him closely, but did not hold him as policemen do a prisoner.   They had even the appearance of talking with him, and it could be seen he walked of his own free will.   The door was open and a *valet de pied* stood there with a light.   Evidently he waited to receive Carnoël.

" Monsieur," said Bidard under his breath, " I believe they are going to commit a crime.   They are bringing the young man to the Tour de Nesle.   Surely it is to strangle him.   I have a mind to call for help."

" Not yet," replied Maxime, quickly, " see first what they will do."

"Look, sir! above there—in the salon—those two shadows behind the windows—"

"It is the lady and her friend, the one who remained —they are expecting the other. They heard the carriage and have come to the window."

"I lay a wager they don't open it. My two, tenants of the third story have opened theirs, and the brigands don't care to show themselves.

"See! the shadows disappear! It is the street we must watch."

Nothing extraordinary occurred. The carriage did not move—neither did the three men who had come as scouts. They had well chosen their places, for they seemed to make part of the wall, and to discern them it was necessary to know they were there.

The coachman remained motionless on his seat. Robert de Carnoël reached the little door escorted by two persons suitably attired, and followed by a third who left the berlin after him. A chance passer-by, whom a nocturnal promenade had led to Rue Jouffroy would have thought it all quite natural. Four gentlemen, arriving in a beautiful carriage before a house whose master gives a soirée is to be seen often and anywhere; but this very ordinary spectacle excited Maxime to the highest pitch. Robert de Carnoël falling in the midst of these people was stranger than all the rest.

"Where did he come from? Had he been the colonel's prisoner, and if so, why had he let him come out ? Why did he bring him to the so-called Madame Sergent's ? "

Just as the ci-devant secretary reached the door, where a servant armed with a torch awaited him, a strange noise pierced through the silence of the night. It was the crowing of a cock, or rather the counterfeit of it, proceeding from a human throat.

"It's up there," whispered the porter; "the clerks on the third floor are at the window. One is a comical fellow—likely he'll make us laugh."

Maxime had little inclination of that sort, and the persons on the street still less. They looked up to see who had uttered this mocking appeal—all, including the coachman on the box,—this singular coachman with a tall hat on. The one who paid least attention to this successful imitation of the reveille chant was undoubtedly Robert de Carnoël. He appeared in haste to enter, and the valet who held the candelabra made way for him to pass.

One of the three escorts passed the threshold immediately after the prisoner, and the two others were about to do the same, but the torch-bearer held a brief colloquy with them, during which they paused, standing on each side of the door their comrade had just entered. The coachman in citizen's dress tied the reins, left his seat precipitately and handed his whip to one of the individuals pressed against the wall. This man left his post and placed himself at the head of the horses,

"Monsieur," said the porter in a low voice, "look! the lights are put out in the salon. Droll idea that! to blow out the candles just as the guests arrive—the dining-room, too! They must intend to spend the night playing hide-and-seek. Look! it seems to confound the man who has just gotten down from the box—he looks at the windows—he retreats a little to get a better view— yes, ogle as you will, my child, all is black up there; you must go in without a light."

Borisoff standing in the middle of the street appeared to hesitate. He turned and looked up, probably to see if the persons who had imitated the cock were still at the windows. He then went straight to the door guarded by two of his subalterns. They moved aside to make way, and just as he was about to push it open, it was closed violently by some one on the inside.

"Ah! they have slammed the door in his face," exclaimed M. Bidard; "what was that coachman after? Did he suppose himself invited too?"

"It is no coachman," said Maxime, who had recognized Borisoff.

"He is queerly dressed for holding the reins, that's a fact. But if he is a monsieur, why was he on the box? Oh! oh! he is angry; he knocks at the door,—beats with his feet and fists. Good! there are the two others taking part in it. If the door was not pretty firm they would break it down. What an uproar they make! They will rouse the neighborhood, I am astonished the two clerks up there haven't cried out wolf."

"Hush! the dining-room window opens; a man appears there. It is one of the two who entered a minute ago. I recognize his square shoulders. Ah! there is the amateur coachman approaching; they are having a talk. I want to hear what they say. Open the casement a little way—softly."

"It is imprudent, perhaps—but if monsieur wishes it—"

The complaisant Bidard ended his sentence by opening the window with great caution, and Maxime listened.

A lively colloquy was taking place between the person who had appeared at the window and the colonel in the street. Both spoke loud enough to be heard, but at the first words that reached his ears Maxime discovered that they spoke in Russian.

Bidard, who was also listening, said:

"What a language! It must be Chinese. I thought those scamps were not French. *Dame!* the friends of the Prussian! and see how they are carrying on,—what gestures they make."

The talkers were making signals, which Maxime strove to interpret. Evidently the question was one of mounting or descending.

The dining-room was on the ground-floor, an elevated ground-floor, it is true, but the window was not more than ten feet from the ground. An adroit man might risk the leap, nor did it seem impossible to scale it. The valet leaned on the balcony, measuring with his eye

the distance from top to bottom. The master, on the pavement, measured it from bottom to top. The men who guarded the door, and those placed against the wall, approached the colonel and formed a circle around him. The little troop disposed itself as if for assault. The man who held the horses brought forward the berlin and placed it under the window.

"They are about to invade the house," Maxime cried out; "two of them are climbing on the box; the carriage is to serve them for a ladder."

"Ah! verily," exclaimed Bidard, "that is too much. Right here, in the finest neighborhood in Paris, to have these brigands acting like they believed it was the forest of Bondy. I am going to give the alarm—if monsieur does not oppose it."

At this moment the cock-crowing sounded out still more clearly, accompanied by a rattling noise. A falsetto voice cried out: "Cut-throat!" A base voice roared: "Scaling a wall—in the night—occupied house—band of malefactors—galleys for life."

These words, taken from the penal code, had a prodigious effect. The two men hoisted on the top of the berlin were about to assist each other in climbing the window, where their companion was holding out his arms to them, when the menace, hurled by an invisible witness, made them hesitate. At the same moment was heard the opening of the casements to all the windows of the house guarded by the porter Bidard.

"All my people are astir," he said, rubbing his hands; "the female tenant of the second floor, the druggist of the first, and now we shall have a play for nothing. The druggist raves like anything, and the female tenant dreams of murder every night."

"Ah! a thousand thunders!" vociferated a masculine voice, "what's all that? Robbers pillaging the house over there! Concierge, look for the police—the guard!"

"Murder! fire!" shrieked a female voice.

"Ah! rascals, wait awhile," resumed the man; "my revolver! where is my revolver?"

Maxime determined not to show himself, but to act according to the course Borisoff should take. He never lost sight of the boyard, who showed unmistakable signs of perplexity, even of fright. Evidently his attempt had failed, and nothing remained for him but to beat a retreat. He appeared, however, still to hesitate before decamping with his troops, and moved about uneasily, shaking his fist at the people who threatened him, reassembling his subalterns, and gesticulating violently.

By his order, doubtless, one of the men on the box dismounted hastily, and the other took the whip and reins. The man who had entered the house with Robert de Carnoël jumped from the balcony to the berlin and thence to the sidewalk.

The defeat turned into a rout. At this moment a pistol was fired by the terrible tenant of the first floor. The effect was not deadly—no one fell—but the explosion gave the signal for the rout. Borisoff hustled his men into the carriage, where they crammed themselves with some difficulty, and jumped in after them. The driver struck out his horses in the direction of the Avenue de Villiers.

"They fly, the cowards!" exclaimed Bidard, willingly showing himself now that all danger was past. "They don't get off like that. Come, sir, this is the moment to cry 'Stop thief!' There's a station down there on the avenue. The soldiers will stop the carriage."

As he said this he precipitated himself into the street. Maxime made no effort to abate his ardor, and willingly followed.

He had little hope of capturing the berlin. Indeed, it was a small matter to him whether or not they captured Borisoff, but he was greatly concerned to know what had become of Robert de Carnoël, Madame Sergent, and the countess' fencing-master. They must be in the house, and he counted on the tenants to assist him in forcing them out of their nest.

Just as he put his feet outside the door the victoria arrived at full speed.

Auguste, the faithful coachman, attracted by the pistol-shot, was hastening to the assistance of his monsieur.

"Stop!" cried Maxime, and Auguste stopped short.

"Good!" said Bidard, "we will jump into the milord and follow after the brigands."

"If the brigands are in the berlin which filed away

down yonder, it's no use to start my mare after them ; she couldn't catch up with ten-thousand-franc horses. I heard a pistol-shot. Was it monsieur that fired it ? "

"No, and no one was hurt. I believe it was fired in the air."

"Who is it undertakes to say I fired in the air ?" cried a rough voice.

Turning, Maxime found himself face to face with a grotesque personage ; a coarse, little old man enveloped in a dressing-gown, and armed with a cavalry revolver.

"I beg pardon, monsieur," said Maxime. "I thought you wished simply to give the alarm."

"No, sir ; I aimed for the chief of the robbers, and am sure I touched him. If I'd had cartridges I would have killed them all, but unfortunately I had only one load."

"Fortunately, Papa Pincornet," said a young man who had just come out of the house; "if you had fired oftener you would have done mischief. I was at my window, just above you, with my friend Galopardin, and your ball passed right under our noses."

"Monsieur Falot, I have told you before that it dosen't suit me to joke with you."

"Upon my word it is true. Ask Galopardin."

"I swear it," replied the clerk who answered to this absurd name. "I swear it by the concierge and by this house ; and here is Mlle. Saint Grès who will bear witness to having heard the hissing of this projectile."

. Mlle. Saint Grès was a person of ripe years, of a spare figure, and a pimpled face ; the female tenant of the second floor.

Maxime was not sorry to see all the tenants collected together.

"Gentlemen," he said, " I have not the honor to be known to you, and since chance has led me to be present at a singular spectacle— "

" I beg pardon, monsieur, who are you ?" asked the old druggist, gravely.

Maxime was wishing to send to the devil this ridiculous individual who assumed the airs of a magistrate interrogating a prisoner. But his situation was one in which he had need of everbody, and he did not disdain to conciliate the good-will of Signor Pencornet.

"I entered," he said, " to make some inquiries of the concierge, when I saw arrive, in carriage and on foot, the bandits who have attempted to climb into that house. Naturally, I remained to give assistance to honest people. I am the nephew of M. Claude Dorgères, banker."

" Good house, monsieur," said the bass voice of the old druggist. " House favorably known on change."

" Wait," said one of the young tenants of the third, " I know your uncle's cashier."

" Really ? " asked Maxime, a little surprised.

" I was quite intimate with him before he was such a grandee. We ate in the same restaurant ; soup, two dishes, half a bottle and dessert, thirty-six sous. His name is Jules Vignory. Galopardin knows him too."

"Yes," affirmed clerk number two, "would you like a description of him ? Vignory (Jules), called the *rosière* of the Upper Saône, because he was born at Vesoul and because he is virtuous, twenty-six years old, round chin, oval face—"

" I know the rest," said Maxime, laughing. " Vignory is my intimate friend, and I am pleased to meet two of his comrades. But suffer me to remind you that we all have a duty to fulfil, that of warning the occupants of that house that rogues have attempted to force an entrance."

"Not worth the trouble. The box is empty. The Prussian has gone home."

" His friends have come back, M'sieu Falot," said the porter. "For a quarter of an hour a woman and two men have been there, without counting the servants. If you hadn't stayed so long at Café Cardinet, you'd have seen 'em go in as we did—monsieur and me."

"And me too," cried the coachman. "I wasn't so near, but I've a pair of good eyes. And the husband offered me a hundred sous to take him to his house. I'd lay my life on it, he's just murdered his wife."

"A murder ! Ah, *mon dieu !* " groaned the female tenant.

" The tragedies of jealousy," sneered Galopardin.

"It would be well to enter and search the house," said Maxime. " If a crime has been committed the victim has need of assistance perhaps."

" Enter ! How ? The doors are locked."

" By the window, then," said Falot. " Bidard must have a ladder ; who hasn't ? "

"What's a ladder for ? " asked Auguste. " I'm going to put my carriage under the casement."

" Like the berlin a while ago ? It's a good idea," said Maxime.

" Good ! " cried Galopardin. " There is, perhaps, a corpse or two in there, and we are called upon to make a search. Falot and I will climb in with you. Bidard and Pincornet will guard the door, and Mlle. Saint Grès will pray for us."

This programme was laid off in so decided a tone that no one objected, and Auguste hastened to lead his horse by the bridle to the spot indicated. It was less adapted for the purpose than Borisoff's berlin, but the intrepid Falot found that by standing on tiptoe he could lay hold of the window with his hands, and Maxime, following the example of the two clerks, raised himself by the strength of his wrists and leaped the balcony after them.

" We can't see a jot here," said Falot. " Wait, I have some matches in my pocket."

He struck a light which was sufficient to enable them to discern on a table a candelabra filled with wax candles, and in another minute the darkness gave place to an illumination.

It was, as Bidard had said, the dining-room. The cloth was laid on a table, in the middle of which was a chalice of old Saxony filled with rare flowers. But it did not appear that any guests had been seated at the table, and in the great empty hall the silence was profound.

"One might suppose it was the castle of the Sleeping Beauty of the woods," murmured Falot.

"Let us search," said Maxime. "First let us see what way this door leads—hold—it is locked on the outside."

"Let us begin by calling," exclaimed Falot, striking with his feet against the door.

"Hallo !"

No one answered to this appeal, but a murmur of voices in the street attracted the attention of the explorers. They hastened to the window and saw the tenants and porter in conference with two policemen, who had been attracted by the report of the pistol.

Maxime saw that the moment had come for his intervention. Together with the two clerks, he had in a few seconds joined the group, and was in a position to add his word to the somewhat confused conversation between the occupants of the house opposite and the guardians of the peace. He recounted briefly what had taken place, and so told his story as to lead the policemen to believe that a crime had in all probability been committed, and that it was imperative to search the house immediately.

All the doors were locked. The commissary of police alone had the right to have them opened, and one of the policemen went in search of him.

This magistrate resided in the neighborhood, and in

twenty minutes he arrived, followed by a locksmith armed
with all the implements of his profession. He listened
attentively to Maxime's recital, the discourse of M. Pincornet, and, above all, the report of M. Bidard, who, in
his quality of concierge of the house opposite, was in a
position to certify to what had taken place for six months
past ; and finally concluded it was expedient to have a
legal search of this singular abode, whose occupants
showed themselves at intervals and disappeared like
phantoms. By his order one of the policemen rang several times, and no one answering, he commanded the
locksmith to operate.

It was the work of a moment, and they found themselves at the foot of a stairway, plunged in complete
darkness. But the knowing Bidard had foreseen this
case, and arrived with a lantern, which he hastened to
place in the hands of the policeman, for he was not bent
upon being the first to penetrate this dangerous castle.

The stairway led the visitors to a billiard-hall, an
apartment which had three doors, including the one
which opened from the stairway. One of them was
locked, but the key was in the lock, and it was only necessary to turn it to pass into the dining-room, where the
wax candles, lit by Galopardin, were still burning. The
third communicated with a cabinet containing a large
amount of plate and glass. The commissary remarked
that the window of this cabinet was open, a window
which opened on a stairway composed of six steps, descending into a garden or rather court.

"I see a ladder there placed against the wall!" exclaimed Maxime.

A policeman mounted the ladder and saw that there was one also on the other side. The two portable ladders joined at the top. To mount and descend by this route was easy enough. This precaution proved that the inmates of the house anticipated the necessity of taking flight. At the foot of the ladder the moist earth preserved the prints of their feet. They were many and of all sizes. Five or six persons had passed that way. The fugitives who arrived *pell-mell* had pattered their feet several minutes before ascending the ladder in file, and Maxime could recognize the boots with sharpened heels, which marked the passage of Madame Sergent.

Maxime accompanied the commissary to the end of his search.

The house underwent a thorough inspection from garret to cellar, as well as the grounds adjoining. They found nothing.

The commissary contented himself with taking down the names of those present, in case they should be required as witnesses, a case that appeared very improbable, for he began to believe in a hoax.

Maxime had to give his address, and mounted immediately in the vehicle of the faithful Auguste, not without having generously rewarded Bidard and taken leave of the two clerks, whom he even invited to dine with him, an invitation which they accepted in chorus.

CHAPTER XVI.

LOOKING BLACK FOR M. DE CARNOËL.

"Night brings counsel," says the proverb.

WHEN Maxime awoke next morning the scenes in Rue Jouffroy presented themselves under a new aspect. Now that he had come out from the hub-bub and could reason more calmly, he began to extract a few certainties from among all these obscurities.

The marvel of the Rink was not the friend of Borisoff. On this point there was no possibility of mistake. She had directed a plot for the deliverance of Robert de Car-noël, and the plot had succeeded. But by what miracle of address had she come to deceive Borisoff and induce him to bring his prisoner to her house? And who was this Madame Sergent who showed herself only to vanish immediately, who skated at the Rink like an adventuress, who was enthroned like a great lady in the first boxes at the opera, who supped with a Bertha Verrier, who had at her disposal a house peopled with liveried servants, who exhibited herself one evening in company with a suspi-cious boyard, and a month after was brought home by the most authenticated of Russian colonels? To all this he

455

was prepared with a reply. The pretended Madame Sergent could be none other than the agent of the conspirators who had stolen Borisoff's papers, an intimate friend
of the thief who had left her hand in the claws of the safe.
But if Madame Sergent were this, what was to be thought
of Carnoël ?   Either he was her lover or her accomplice.
This melancholy conclusion forced itself upon Maxime.
And in these cases he had betrayed poor Alice ; he was
unworthy of the love of the girl who persisted in believing in his innocence.

"So," thought Maxime, "those who accused the Lord
Carnoël were right, and I for my part acted as foolishly
as Don Quixote when he undertook to deliver the bandits who were being led to the galleys."

But he could not forget that it was not he alone who
had undertaken the defence of his uncle's secretary.
The Countess Yalta affirmed vehemently that Robert de
Carnoël was the victim of atrocious injustice. She it was
who had cast doubts into the mind of Alice just as the
poor child had begun to believe in the guilt of her lover.
It was she who had fired the zeal of Maxime, who had
launched him into a senseless enterprise. Her interest
in him drew its inspiration from a feeling of chivalry, a
natural propensity to defend the weak and succor the
oppressed.   But this nocturnal adventure proved that
her pity was ill placed. Maxime proposed to relate this
history to her and hoped to convert her to more rational
views.

He was impatient also to denounce the conduct of the

fencing-master who had shown himself the ally of Madame Sergent, and had certainly acted without the knowledge of the noble woman in whose service he was engaged.

In the last interview with Madame Yalta, she had clearly explained herself on the subject of the Nihilists and their adherents.

" I have the good fortune not to be à Russian subject," were her words ; " I have therefore nothing to do with these people, but I belong by instinct to the party of the proscribed, and am not of that of thieves and murderers."

But it was not surprising that a hireling had betrayed his mistress, and it might even be that Madame Yalta was surrounded, unknown to herself, by scoundrels affiliated with a sect whose dream is universal destruction.

These wretches were known to be everywhere, and to establish themselves from choice where no one suspected they would have the audacity to enter. If the fencing-master, Kardiki, was one of them, as it appeared, he had well chosen his post. The superb mansion of the Avenue de Friedland was a sure asylum where no one would think of looking for a socialist conspirator.

He hastened to dress, and had only to put on his overcoat and hat, when his valet presented him the card of a gentleman who asked to see him.

He was about to be excused to this early visitor, when to his great surprise he saw on the card the name of Dr. Villagos.

What could be the Hungarian doctor's object in this visit to a small apartment of Rue de Châteaudun where he had never set foot before? Concluding he had been sent by the countess, he refrained from excusing himself, simply resolving to be very cautious and beware of letting him into his confidence.

The doctor entered smiling. "Dear monsieur," he said, "you must be a little surprised at seeing me so early. I should not have disturbed you at this unusual hour had I not brought you news of a person in whom you are interested."

"The Countess Yalta? How is she? I was sorry to find her suffering yesterday."

"She received you, then?"

Maxime bit his lips. He saw too late that in spite of his sage resolutions he had committed an indiscretion.

"Yes," he said with embarrassment, "she was good enough to do so—but I remembered your orders and made my visit short."

"Oh," resumed the doctor, laughing, "I shall not scold her. You have proved very agreeable to her and she asserts that distraction will do her more good than my remedies. But it is not of my dear patient I wish to speak with you."

"Of whom, then?" asked Maxime, his curiosity beginning to awaken.

"Of a woman who perplexed you very much six weeks or two months ago. You remember the marvellous brunette whom I pointed out to you at the Rink?"

" Yes, certainly," he replied with some agitation.

" Have you seen her since ? "

This unexpected question disconcerted Maxime, but an immediate reply was necessary, and he answered evasively :

" I have seen her once at the theatre." ·

"And you spoke to her ? "

" No, she was in a box with a gentleman."

" A foreigner, was he not ? "

" He had that appearance."

The doctor reflected for a moment. Maxime more and more confused by this singular questioning could not long remain silent.

" You know her, then ? " he asked, looking with a certain uneasiness at Villagos.

" One of my friends knows her, and he was with her when day before yesterday I passed her in the street."

" And he has told you who she is ? "

" Yes, and it is so curious a history that I came expressly to relate it to you. This creature who amuses herself with skating on casters like a simple *cocotte*, and who looks like an Andalusian ; this girl with eyes of fire is a Russian and a Russian Nihilist—one of those lunatics whose dream is to abolish everything."

" It is astounding ! " cried Maxime, feigning astonishment, though the doctor told him nothing new. "And your friend is sure of his facts ? "

" Very sure. You will see, presently, that he is well

informed. The evening you escorted her from the Rink did she not take you to a house in Rue Jouffroy ? "

" Yes," replied Maxime.

" And when you went next morning to enquire for her the answer was that they did not know her ? "

" You know that ! "

" No, but I guess it. You 'were so much excited about this marvel of a beauty that you would not be put off by the first check you received. Moreover, my friend told me that the lady had there a temporary lodging, which she never occupied two nights successively."

" Did your friend tell you why she has returned ? "

" Yes, and it is to speak to you of that, that I came. She arrived there yesterday and is there now."

" Your friend is mistaken. She is not there," said Maxime, heedlessly.

"She was yesterday evening, and unless she can have decamped last night—but prepare yourself to be thunderstruck. Do you know why she has resumed temporary possession of this mysterious abode ? That she might receive there one of the accomplices whom you know better than I—your uncle's ex-secretary."

"You see that your dear countess was wrong to interest herself about that young man."

"Good ! good ! " said the doctor, laughing. " I know she has recommended silence. She is a little distrustful of me because she knows I do not approve her romantic fancies, but she ended by confessing that she had launched you into the insane enterprise of finding this

Carnoël. I do not know what you have done, but I am going to aid you with a piece of valuable information. I think Madame Yalta was wrong to embark you in this foolish expedition, but the evil is done, and I wish only to serve you. She is bent on fishing up this youth who has fallen into the sea ; well, we will fish him up together. I shall not be sorry to deliver him from the toils of this worthless woman, which it is in my power to do, and once withdrawn from her, we will facilitate his embarking for America. I suppose you no longer think of reinstating him that he may marry your cousin ? "

"Oh, no," said Maxime, "my mind is made up about him."

".Good ! we are agreed, then, on one point. It is what we are to undertake at the lady's house that concerns us now ; but we must know at what door to knock. These female Nihilists are marvellously skilful in eluding researches—this one especially. We should fail unquestionably if we went to seek for her where she is not, and the check would be irreparable. Now she can be in only one of two houses, either the house in Rue Jouffroy or—"

" I affirm that she has left Rue Jouffroy."

" Very well, I take your word for it. You assert that she has gone ; it would almost seem as if you had assisted in the moving. We have, then, nothing to do but present ourselves at a certain house to which they have transferred their nest."

"When?"

"This evening, if you will; or rather to-night, for it is just as well we should not be seen entering the house of a woman whose mysterious ways must have attracted the attention of the neighbors."

"Is it like the other?"

"No, it is a lodging meanly furnished in the faubourg St. Honoré near St. Philippe du Roule."

"It is very astonishing, and I wonder, above all, that you should be so well informed," said Maxime, to whom a feeling of distrust of the doctor now and then returned.

"Nothing is simpler," said. the doctor. "My friend has been intimately connected with her. He was madly in love with her, but had the courage to separate from her when he discovered that she was an active Nihilist. She does not hide from him, however. In France she incurs little or no risk, and he still possesses a certain influence over her; first, because he knows her secret, and secondly, because toward the end of their liaison he drew her from a very dangerous predicament. Now I am going to explain to you how we shall proceed if you agree to accompany us."

"Gladly. Where shall we meet?"

"Would you object to joining us at midnight in the Champs-Elysées?"

"Not at all."

"Well, from there we will go to the part of the city she lives in. My friend knows the house in which she hides and will know how to make it open to us."

"We will go armed, will we not? It would be more prudent. There is no telling what might happen."

"Armed! why? You fancy the brunette will receive you with a pistol? Make yourself easy; she will take care not to create a disturbance; and as for this M. de Carnoël, he is as anxious as any one to avoid publicity. For my part, I shall take only a cane, and I recommend you to do the same."

"But," said Maxime, after a little hesitation, "this woman may be surrounded with persons who are capable of doing us harm when once we are in her lodging."

"What! you suppose she has domestics in such a place as that?"

"I don't know; but I know she had three or four in her service in Rue Jouffroy."

"These lackeys must have dispersed when she abandoned her house, for she has abandoned it; you are certain of this?" asked Villagos.

"Yes," replied Maxime, with embarrassment.

He regretted having said so much in the beginning of the conversation, for it almost amounted to a confession that he had seen Robert de Carnoël and Madame Sergent the night before, and the countess had enjoined him to say nothing about Col. Borisoff's prisoner.

"I went yesterday to Rue Jouffroy to make inquiries, and was told that the woman when she occupied it was never alone. Her servants wore a livery, and had the appearance of foreigners."

"Nihilists, doubtless.   They have returned to Russia until they are needed here.   These sinister birds travel incessantly from east to west and west to east."

"*A propos* of servants," asked Maxime, suddenly, "is Madame Yalta sure of the fidelity of hers?"

"Absolutely sure.   All have made part of her household for years, and they worship the countess."

"Even those who are not domestics—the professors, for instance?   I know only the fencing-master, whom I saw on one occasion fencing with Madame Yalta.   He is a Pole, I believe?"

"The greatest Pole in the world—a political refugee. But Poland does not consort with Nihilism."

"Then you do not admit that he knows the brunette of the Rink?"

"How, *diable!* could he know her?   He never goes out."

"Nor M. de Carnoël either?"

"Still less.   May I ask, my dear Dorgères, the meaning of all these questions?"

"Oh, nothing.   I fancied I had seen him, a long time ago, dressed as a gentleman, and escorting Madame Sergent.   I was mistaken."

"Assuredly," said Villagos, who had listened with close attention while affecting indifference.   "I might lay a wager you were thinking of this reiter when you alluded to the possibility of a battle at the damsel's.   You thought he had followed her to her present abode."

"I confess I had some such idea, but I have it no longer," said Maxime, quickly.

A sudden flash passed through the eyes of the doctor, and from the change in his countenance a physiognomist would have divined that he had just come in possession of a proof long and skilfully sought of a fact which had for him great importance.

"Then," he said gaily, "you relinquish the intention to arm yourself to the teeth for our expedition to-night?"

"Oh, I am not afraid," said Maxime, who had caught the somewhat satirical meaning of the doctor, "and shall go unarmed, even should this Kardiki constitute Madame Sergent's body-guard."

"I do not cast any doubt on your courage, believe me, but when one carries a revolver he is always tempted to make use of it, and I do not wish to create a disturbance. It is agreed, then, I will meet you at midnight at the *rond point* of the Champs-Elysées. Permit me now to take leave of you; I have ten patients to see this morning."

Maxime extended his hand to the doctor, and made no effort to detain him.

"*A propos* of patients," resumed M. Villagos, "the countess has gone into the country to-day. It is cold and raining, but it matters nothing to her. I have done my best to deter her, but without success."

"It is strange," murmured Maxime, "she said nothing of her intention yesterday."

' Because this beautiful idea came to her in her sleep, and this morning she wrote to announce to me that she should start at nine o'clock."

This unforeseen absence of Madame Yalta deranged Maxime's plans. He had, however, enough to occupy the day—three persons to see, his cousin, his friend, and his uncle.

He made straight for Rue de Suresnes, and was not a little surprised to be informed by the concierge Doulevant that M. Dorgères had sent for him, and was awaiting him in his office. He found the banker promenading the room in evident agitation.

"Ah! here you are. I have heard pretty things of you."

"What have I done, my dear uncle?" asked Maxime, but slightly intimidated.

"Very wrong, I can tell you. You have assured my daughter that the scoundrel she dotes upon has been unjustly accused. Do you know what has been the result of this foolish talk? She has declared that she will not marry Vignory, and, moreover, that she will not marry at all. If she persists in this resolution, you may boast of having embittered her existence and mine. I will not speak of your friend, whose hopes you have dashed with the same blow. But I ask why you have, with reckless levity, destroyed the future of your cousin? Is this your gratitude to me for having always treated you like a son?"

·· " I was wrong, I acknowledge it, and I came this morning to tell you of the steps I meant to take to replace things where they were when I spoiled them by my folly."

" It is too late. It would be useless to retract before Alice. She would not listen to you."

" She will be compelled to yield to the evidence. I have the proof that M. de Carnoël is the accomplice, and perhaps the lover, of a woman who took part in the theft of the safe. I begin by a confession that will astonish you. The theft of the colonel's casket and the fifty thousand francs .was preceded by another, which Vignory and I ascertained."

" And you did not tell me ! "

" Vignory wished to do so. I opposed it. One Wednesday evening we had dined together, and came to pass the evening at your house. We saw a light in the office, and went in. You will be amazed to learn what I found there—the hand of a woman caught in the mechanism which defends the safe."

" A hand ! What absurdity are you telling me ? "

" Yes, a hand which the accomplice of the thief had cut off. I took into my head to discover alone the owner of the hand."

" That is just like you ; but how could Vignory countenance this folly ? His duty was to give me warning, and his silence was inexcusable."

" It was that I almost forced him to it."

"A beautiful reason.   He was my employé, and has proved false to me.   I shall never forgive him."

At this moment an office-boy appeared, who announced that Col. Borisoff wished to speak with M. Dorgères on very urgent business.

"I have not time," replied the banker, impatiently.

"I beg pardon, uncle," said Maxime.   "Will you do me the favor to receive Col. Borisoff, and to allow me to be present?   I shall not be *de trop*, for I am sure he comes to speak of your former secretary."

"The colonel has an important account with me.   It is more probable he comes on business."

"The business that occupies him just now is not an affair of money," said Maxime, with confidence, "and I answer for it the conversation will turn solely on M. de Carnoël.   If you will permit me to remain you will learn much more quickly what I have yet to tell, and I, perhaps, shall find out some things of which I am still ignorant."

"Very well, if I am compelled to ask you to go out, you will wait for me in my chamber, and we will resume our conversation.   Ask Col. Borisoff to walk in," he said to the office-boy.

In another moment the door opened and the colonel entered.

"Pardon me, sir," he said, "if I have insisted upon being received.   I leave this evening for Russia, and must speak with you before my departure."

"At your service, colonel. Monsieur is my nephew, but if you desire to be alone with me—"

"I have had the honor to meet M. Maxime Dorgères," said the colonel, slowly, "and congratulate myself upon finding him here. If I had not I should have begged you to send for him. You guess, perhaps," he went on, "the cause which obliges me suddenly to leave Paris?"

"I confess I do not," replied the banker.

"You have not, then, read the morning papers?"

"Not yet. I have been busy this morning."

"Then you do not know that rascals at St. Petersburg have attempted the life of the emperor, my master?"

"What, again?"

"This time they tried to blow up the Winter Palace. The emperor escaped miraculously, but brave soldiers have perished."

"It is abominable," said the banker, earnestly. "I suppose this crime was the work of those bandits whom you call Nihilists."

"There is no doubt of it. The sect has declared war on the government and on society. It is the right and duty of the government to defend its sacred interests, and it calls upon all its servants upon whose devotion it can count. I am of these, and I go."

"My best wishes accompany you, colonel. I execrate the enemies of family and property," said M. Dorgères, with visions of the red republic before his eyes. "You wish, doubtless, to withdraw the funds entrusted to me.

I will make arrangements for you to do so this very day."

"Thank you, sir. But I have something more interesting to speak of than the regulating of an account."

"Speak, colonel. I cannot guess its nature, but—"

"Have you ever wondered why I have resided in Paris for two years past?" asked Borisoff, abruptly.

"I supposed it was for your pleasure."

"You are mistaken, sir. I was sent here to watch over the Nihilists."

"We have them amongst us!" exclaimed the banker.

"Almost as many as in Switzerland. Their chiefs keep themselves prudently beyond our frontiers, and it is in foreign parts that they organize the plots which endanger our country."

"Then the Russian government has good reason to have their criminal procedures watched by its diplomatists."

"The diplomatists do not suffice for the task. I am not attached to the Russian embassy. I represent the political police of the empire."

"The police!" repeated M. Dorgères, somewhat nonplussed.

"Yes. I have no further reason to hide it, since I leave France never to return. The casket which I deposited with you contained papers of the highest importance,—the list of those associated with Nihilists, reports of the proceedings of certain persons who emigrated after the last insurrection in Poland. You have not, I suppose, forgotten that it was stolen, and the singular circumstances that accompanied the theft ; and you believed with me that the accomplice of the thieves was your secretary."

. " I think so still. My nephew has the proof."

" Ah ! " said the colonel, looking fixedly at Maxime, who remained unmoved.

" I, too," he resumed, " have the proof that M. de Carnoël was in league with the thieves. I have searched for, have found him, arrested and retained him for a long time at my house."

" Without letting me know ! " exclaimed the banker.

" It was useless. You had given me *carte blanche*, and I was free to act in my own way. I endeavored to extort a confession from him, but your *ci-devant* secretary knew that his friends would not abandon him, and preserved an obstinate silence."

" But what are you going to do with him ? If your intention is to deliver him up to the French police, I have nothing to say, but—"

" I shall not deliver him up to any one, for the excellent reason that he has escaped."

" *Ma foi !* " exclaimed the banker. " I shall not be sorry for him to go elsewhere to get hung."

" He will not be hung anywhere, for they do not hang in France, and he has, I believe, no intention of quitting it. He is in Paris, and perhaps not far from the Rue de

Suresnes. It was to make this known, that I called upon you."

"I am very much obliged to you, colonel," stammered the banker. "I shall take my precautions."

"You would do well to do so, for I am satisfied he will attempt to introduce himself into your house. I received yesterday the visit of a Russian who represented himself as sent by the chief of the political police, and who succeeded by a gross stratagem in effecting the liberation of M. de Carnoël. This morning a letter from St. Petersburg enlightened me as to the events of the night. The man was a Nihilist in disguise."

"I was sure of it!"

This exclamation escaped Maxime unguardedly.

"You know the man, then? Would it please you to tell me where you have seen him?"

"I saw him dining with you yesterday in a restaurant,— Avenue de l'Opera."

"How do you know that the man of whom I speak is the one who was dining with me?"

"I know it because I followed you."

"You were acting the counter-police as it appears."

"It is admissible when one is dealing with a spy."

"Maxime!" exclaimed the banker, with a severe glance at his nephew.

"Oh, let monsieur speak," continued the colonel, unmoved. "His estimate touches me very little, and I have several questions to ask him."

"You wished to know where I followed you? I was in the orchestra of the opera when you entered the box of that woman. I rode in a carriage behind the hack that took you to Rue Jouffroy. I established myself in a house opposite the one you entered, and remained there until you took flight, and even a little later."

"My best compliment, monsieur. The Nihilists have in you a valuable auxiliary."

"I am not with the Nihilists, you know very well," retorted Maxime, bluntly.

"You say so, and I wish to believe it," replied Borisoff, "but I am driven to think the contrary, for if you passed a portion of the night in watching me, it was not for the purpose of seconding me in my conflict with these people. May I venture to ask what is now your opinion of M. de Carnoël?"

"I can answer without the least embarrassment. M. de Carnoël is evidently the friend of the woman who delivered him."

"You admit also that the woman belongs to the sect which steals, burns, and assassinates."

"I admit it the more readily, as I am in possession of the proof."

"And this proof, would you furnish me with it?"

"To what purpose? You are about to leave France. The plots which are being carried on in Paris do not concern you. Besides, my conviction rests on facts which are personal to myself. As for M. de Carnoël, he has been delivered by a vile creature assisted by a false police agent, and has taken refuge in an asylum prepared for him by this pretty couple. It follows that he makes a part of the band."

"You are wonderfully well informed," said the colonel, smiling sarcastically. "But I did not come to see your uncle for the purpose of entertaining him with the political aspect of this affair. It matters little to him, I suppose, that his former secretary does or does not conspire against the Russian government, but it concerns him, perhaps, to acquire the certainty that this gentleman is a thief. When M. de Carnoël fell into my hands, I made use of means which the police of all countries employ with prisoners. He was searched, and was found to carry on his person five packages of bank notes of ten thousand francs each."

"Just the sum taken from me. It is perfectly clear."

"Here is the amount," continued Borisoff, drawing the notes from his pocket.

"Fifty thousand francs are very easily obtained when one has the funds of a government at his disposal," muttered Maxime.

"I cannot receive this money, at least without being certain where it came from," stammered the uncle, also uncertain of the sincerity of the colonel.

"If you refuse, I shall feel compelled to give it away in charity, for it does not belong to me," said Borisoff. "But I shall prove to you that I did not bring it with me

to effect the ruin of M. de Carnoël. When I asked him
to account for this sum, his reply was that it had been
sent to him by some one who had owed it to his father."

"That could not be," said M. Dorgères. "His father
did not leave a sou or credit of any sort. I was entrusted
with the settling of his affairs, and if fifty thousand francs
had been owing him I should have known of it."

"That is about what I said to the son. This son then
showed me the letter accompanying it, and you may
judge of the value of this justification. Here it is."

"It is not signed," said M. Dorgères, glancing over it ;
"an anonymous restitution ; such a thing is inadmissible.
What do you say to it ?" he added, passing the letter to
his nephew.

"I think," said Maxime, "that this letter has every
appearance of having been fabricated to meet the neces-
sities of the case ; by whom, I cannot tell. The paper it
is written on is the kind employed by men of business."

"And the father had no friends engaged in commerce.
Besides, a merchant would not reimburse to the amount
of fifty thousand francs in an anonymous letter."

"From whence it follows," said Borisoff, "that the son
had the letter written in case he should be under the
necessity of explaining the possession of the money. I
think, gentlemen, you must now be satisfied as to the
morality of this agent of the Nihilists."

"Oh, completely !" exclaimed M. Dorgères.

"Then," continued the colonel, "allow me to hand

you the sum and the letter.   I shall have no further business with M. de Carnoël, since I am recalled to St. Petersburg.   The same despatch announces the attempt against the Czar and my disgrace,—for this unexpected recall is a disgrace.   I shall no longer be employed except in Russia, and there is little probability that your *ci-devant* secretary will show himself there.   If his accomplices, less prudent, should ever fall into my power, I shall not fail to transmit to you whatever may come to light through these wretches concerning the theft.   And in any event I carry with me the satisfaction of having edified you concerning a young man who has sought to bring trouble into your family.   Should he renew his audacious attempt, I leave you the means of confounding him."   M. Borisoff had placed the notes on the table and handed the letters to M. Dorgères.   "There remains nothing now, gentlemen, but to take leave of you.   My steward will come to-day to withdraw my funds.   Adieu, monsieur.   Present my best respects to Mlle. Dorgères, and believe in my best wishes."

Before leaving, he turned toward Maxime and tossed him a bit of advice : ·

"Believe me, monsieur, you would do well to abstain from pursuing the rescuers of M. de Carnoël.   They would kill you."

With these words he disappeared just as the valet Joseph entered and said :

"Mademoiselle sends me to say to M. Dorgères that she is waiting breakfast for him."

" Very well. Say that I am coming."

The valet went out and the banker was left alone with Maxime, who was much less agitated than his uncle.

" May the devil take this Russian with his revelations and his restitutions," he said ; " I have a mind to run after him and return these cursed bank-notes."

" Why ? " asked the nephew. " Do you suppose he has taken them from his own property for the pleasure of dishonoring M. de, Carnoël ? I can scarcely believe it."

" Then you think he spoke the truth ? "

" Yes ; thus far that the fifty thousand francs were found in the pocket of your former secretary. It remains to be seen who wrote the letter."

" Do you doubt that it was this unfortunate young man ? "

" Not exactly, though that would upset the ideas I had conceived of his character. But between the act of stealing money and that of which we believe him guilty, the difference is small enough. To associate oneself with rascals who break into safes under the pretext of politics is more than enough to dishonor a man. Let me go on with the story which the colonel interrupted. I placed in my pocket a bracelet that was found on the hand, and kept it as a means of discovering the admirable person who had abandoned it to the claws of your safe. One evening, after having exhibited it at a public ball, I met with a woman, very pretty and not at all shy, who permitted me to act as her escort, and drew me into a spot

where four scoundrels, posted by her, were lying in wait
to murder me and recover the bracelet.   The jade after
this disappeared, and I saw no more of her until some
time after, when she appeared in a box at the Variétés.
She gave me a cordial greeting, and accepted an invitation to supper, during which she found means to fly, carrying off the bracelet.   It was then quite clear that this
creature had been despatched by the thief to recover possession of a means of convicting her.   Thereupon a new
eclipse of the damsel.   She became invisible, undiscoverable.   Meanwhile, I discover that Carnoël is a prisoner in
Borisoff's house.   Yesterday I met Borisoff with a person
who appears to me suspicious.   I attach myself to them—"

"I know the rest ; the colonel has just told us."

"Yes ; but the colonel did not tell you that the woman
who fled with Carnoël was the same who twice made an
attack on me because of the bracelet—the *chargé d'*
affaires of the one-handed.   And now that you know all,
am I right in affirming that Carnoël is the associate of
these rascals ? "

"*Parbleu !* I have no doubt of it.   I am not the one
to whom you must say that in order to repair the mischief you have done."

"But I intend to say the same to my cousin also."

"When ?   Will you wait until she dies of grief, or flies
into a convent ?   My life is intolerable.   Alice neither
speaks nor eats.   Vignory looks like a funeral.   It is
enough to drive one mad."

"I ask for twenty-four hours to make a declaration which will produce a decided effect on my cousin."

"Why this delay? She is waiting for me now. Breakfast with us.".

"I will do so to-morrow if you wish, and as I am going this evening to lay hands on M. de Carnoël and his mistress—for this woman is his mistress—"

"What! you are going to arrest them. What is your profession, then?

"Oh, I am not yet enrolled in the prefecture of police; but I wish to know finally where I stand in regard to your former secretary, and I know some one who will introduce me into the house in which he is hiding."

"*Diable!* it would be a hazardous expedition. Remember the words of the colonel: 'Take care, these people would kill you.'"

"I am not afraid of them."

"You will be always the same—going straight on, doubting and suspecting nothing. They have just blown up the Winter Palace; to murder you would be a much smaller matter."

At this moment Jules Vignory entered. He had an anxious appearance, and seemed surprised at seeing Maxime.

"Monsieur," he said, "I have just been notified that Col. Borisoff will withdraw his funds at three o'clock. May I settle his account?"

"Yes. I have just seen the colonel. But I wish to

speak with you. Why did you not tell me of the first attempt at theft? Oh, do not assume the astonished! I know all. Maxime has just given me the history of the hand."

"He ought to have done so sooner," replied the cashier; "it was he who urged me to silence."

Maxime said nothing, but he knit his brow. He found Vignory over-prompt to vindicate himself at the expense of a friend.

"I know that, and I am not displeased with you beyond measure, though it seems to me that your situation imposed upon you duties to which you have been wanting. But we will leave the past, and be kind enough to examine these packages of bank-notes," added the banker, pointing to the files which were still spread out on the table.

Vignory took them up and began counting them over.

"There are fifty," he said.

"That is not what I ask. Where do you think they came from?"

"From my safe, undoubtedly. I recognize the way the pin is stuck in: a little more to the right and a little lower down than the packages made at the Bank of France."

"Very well. My rogue of a secretary can no longer maintain that he has not stolen them."

"What! it was—"

"We hold in our hands the sum that was taken from me, and it rests with me to have this Carnoël arrested."

"He is in Paris !" exclaimed Vignory.

"Yes, and I have in my hand the proof of his infamy. Would you believe that he has had the audacity to assert that this money was sent to him by a debtor of his father ! He had a letter written. Read it, and tell me what you think."

Vignory turned pale and took the letter with a hand that trembled visibly.

"The imposture is evident," he said, after having glanced at it ; "it is even very clumsily done ; this letter must have been dictated by M. de Carnoël."

"Dictated to whom ?" asked Maxime, abruptly.

"To one of his friends, no doubt. I do not know the handwriting."

"But intimate as you were, you must know the friends of Robert de Carnoël."

"Friends—he had few," stammered Vignory. "A few college chums, and those he saw very rarely."

"Then," said the banker, "it is useless to try to find out who wrote the letter."

"I believe so, monsieur—however, if you would entrust it to me I may perhaps—"

"No, it would be waste of time ; my mind is entirely made up, and I desire only to impart my conviction to— to all those who doubt still. This letter is a proof and I shall keep it."

The door opened softly, and Alice's face appeared, but seeing her father was not alone she made a movement to go out.

"Come in!" exclaimed M. Dorgères. He concluded to profit by the presence of Maxime to strike a great blow, but reflecting that that of his cashier would embarrass his explanations with his daughter he took him aside and said :

"Be so good as to leave us. You were wrong to follow the advice of my hare-brained nephew, but it is not a hanging matter. Go, my friend, and return to dine with us."

Alice avoided looking at him as he went out somewhat discomfited and crest-fallen, but exchanging a quick glance with her cousin, she read in his eyes that he was not the bearer of good news.

"Your arrival is opportune," said M. Dorgères; "I even regret that you did not come sooner. You would have found Col. Borisoff here."

"Then I did well not to come. That man inspires me with horror."

"Yes," said the banker, mischievously. "You detest him because he believed with myself that M. de Carnoël had been meddling with my safe. It is time to put an end to the false idea you persist in maintaining. This man is unworthy of you."

"You have told me so before, and I have refused to believe it. And Maxime does not, either," she added.

"Maxime! ask him what he thinks of M. de Carnoël."

Alice said nothing, but her eyes sought her cousin's

face, questioning. Maxime colored and made no reply.

"Come! speak!" cried his uncle. "Assure this foolish girl that my former secretary is associated with a band of rascals. You have just told me his exploits and drawn your own conclusions from them. I hope you do not mean to retract before my daughter."

" No," murmured Maxime, "for, unfortunately, I have advanced nothing but the truth."

"What!" murmured poor Alice.

"You, too—you abandon him—you, who declared to me only yesterday—"

"Yesterday I was pursuaded he was innocent. To-day I am obliged to recognize that I was mistaken."

"What has happened since yesterday?"

"I saw M. de Carnoël taking flight with a woman who was certainly a thief."

"A woman!" repeated Mlle. Dorgères, sorrowfully.

"Yes, a woman, my dear Alice, and what a woman! one who is engaged in the service of revolutionaries of the lowest order."

"And you affirm that he fled with her? Fled! why should he fly? He has, then, been arrested?"

"I beg you, my dear Alice, not to insist in knowing all the details of this affair, but be satisfied when I tell you on my honor and my conscience that M. de Carnoël has been guilty of acts which create between him and you an impassable abyss. You may believe me, for I defended him when I believed it possible, and I have no interest in ruining him."

"It is well," said Alice, with effort, "where is he?"

"Where is he!" exclaimed M. Dorgères. "It is not your intention, I hope, to run after him?"

"I want to know where he is."

"You are absolutely bent upon it?" asked Maxime, decided to make an end of this; "well, he is at this woman's."

"Prove to me that you are not lying."

"How shall I prove it? I cannot take you there, can I? But I shall see him myself this evening—I shall see his contemptible accomplice—and to-morrow, if you wish to hear the confessions I shall force from him—"

"Enough!" interrupted Mlle. Dorgères. "There is nothing left me but to die."

"To die!" exclaimed the father. "You love me no longer that you talk of dying. What have I done that you should break my heart?"

"No," said Alice, throwing herself into her father's arms, "I have not ceased to love you; but forgive me if I have not the courage to live."

She burst into tears and sobbed aloud.

Her father received her in his arms, and Maxime, almost as much moved, bent his head to conceal his agitation.

"Speak," cried M. Dorgères. "Help me to make her understand that she is wrong to afflict me so; that she has not the right to grieve my old age by refusing to marry—"

"Never," said Alice, disengaging herself from her father's arms. "I may promise to force myself to be resigned; I cannot promise to forget. But I swear to you never to pronounce the name of the man I have loved; and I ask it of you, my father, of you, Maxime. It is not much to exact."

"Do not fear that we will revert to this sad subject," replied M. Dorgères, who had recovered a little his composure, and felt the necessity of putting an end to a painful scene. "You will remain mistress of your own will, my dear child. Wisdom will return to you, perhaps, and I will wait for it. And now will you wait for me in the dining-room? I have a few words to say to your cousin."

Alice offered him her forehead, and went out without pressing the hand of her cousin, who understood well why she treated him less affectionately than usual.

By way of compensation, she had no sooner disappeared than her father exclaimed:

"My boy, I give you back my esteem. You have been firm, and without you I do not know what I should have done with that wayward girl."

"Alas! I fear my firmness has not changed the situation."

"You are mistaken. The blow has struck home. Time will do the rest. If you can finish what you have so well begun—"

"Cure her! I should ask nothing better. However, there is, perhaps, one means. Will you allow me to see Alice when I wish, and with whom I wish?"

"Certainly."

"Then I am going."

"When shall I see you again?"

"When I have succeeded."

And he descended the stairway, saying to himself:

"It is only the countess who can convert Alice."

CHAPTER XVII.

VILLAGOS, THE NIHILIST CHIEF.

MAXIME left the house of his uncle a little more perplexed than he had entered it.

On his arrival he fancied he was going to set everything to rights, overwhelm M. Dorgères with joy, bring Alice to right views, and reassure his friend Vignory. And M. Dorgères had just been subjected to a heart-rending scene, Alice talked of dying, Vignory went away anxious.

But there remained one last card to play.

Maxime was not the dupe of the sentiments his cousin had expressed with so much violence. Hope was still living in the bottom of her breaking heart, and she was resolved to cherish her liberty, because she believed the hour would come for the reinstating of the betrothed of her choice.

It was only necessary to tear from her this last illusion. And Madame Yalta alone could do that. He was impatient to see her, to acquaint her with what he had discovered concerning Robert de Carnoël, and if he could have hoped to find her at home would have run. But Dr. Villagos had told.him the countess would be absent for twenty-four hours, and he must postpone his visit to the next day.

Where should he go? He hardly knew, and took mechanically the route to Rue de Châteaudun, when, in turning into the Boulevard Malesherbes, it occurred to him to go and inquire for Georget.

On reaching Monceaux Park, he turned aside to take a look at Colonel Borisoff's house. He ascertained that the Russian agent had spoken truly. His servants were engaged in storing away baggage in a wagon.

"A pleasant journey to him," murmured Maxime, "and may he never return."

He followed Rue de Vigny to its terminus, and, plunged in his reflections, was crossing the Boulevard de Courcelles when a cry met his ears and roused him from his revery. Raising his head, he saw a horse whose breast nearly touched him—a horse attached to an elegant victoria and driven by a woman who, with rare skill, had just succeeded in arresting a blooded animal in full speed. Maxime sprang aside quickly, and was about to apologize when he recognized Madame Yalta bent backward and pulling on the reins to restrain her trotter. She had very nearly crushed a man who would willingly die for her, but in another fashion.

"You!" she exclaimed, turning pale at thought of the danger he had escaped.

"You!" exclaimed Maxime, amazed at this unlooked-for meeting. The two monosyllables crossed each other.

"I will take you," she said in an agitated voice; "jump in, quick! Nedji is impatient."

Maxime did not require a second invitation. He took his place by Madame Yalta's side, and the fiery animal filed off like a cannon ball.

"I was so terrified," said the countess; "a step more and you would have been under the feet of my horse."

"I owe you my life, and the joy of seeing you again would have consoled me if I had been wounded. I resigned myself with difficulty to postponing my visit till to-morrow and here you are back again!"

"Back again! what do you mean? I went out for an hour only and was returning to wait for you."

"You did not leave Paris this morning for a château some distance in the country?"

"Why, no."

"How was it, then, Dr. Villagos told me—"

"You have seen him?"

"Yes, he came to see me this morning for the first time, at my house."

"What did he say? speak! tell me!"

"He—I hardly know where to begin," stammered Maxime, astonished that the countess showed so much impatience. "He said so many things."

"About me?"

"He repeated that your state of health required great

care, and recommended me as usual not to abuse the interviews granted me."

"He asked you not to speak to me of M. de Carnoël?"

"Not positively, but from certain words he let fall I understood that he was aware that you were interesting yourself in his behalf."

"I hope you diverted him from the idea."

"I tried," replied Maxime, with embarrassment, "but I fear he persists in believing it. He has reasons that—"

"What reasons?"

"In walking with one of his friends he met this woman of whom I spoke to you—the associate of the woman who lost her hand in trying to open my uncle's safe."

"Well?"

"His friend knew, it seems, that this creature had been the mistress of Robert de Carnoël."

"It is not true. Villagos has lied."

"He asserts that he has proofs."

"What proofs?"

"Last night, events took place which I have been impatient to relate to you. I was witness to strange scenes which took place in this very Rue Jouffroy, and M. de Carnoël played the principal part."

"You were present, you say?"

"By a concourse of strange circumstances I saw all, and am certain that M. de Carnoël is the lover and accomplice of a worthless creature."

"And you told Villagos what you saw?" asked the countess, in a husky voice.

"No. But whether he saw it himself, whether his friend informed him of it, or whether he divined what I wished to hide—I believe he knows all."

"And I—I know what awaits me," murmured the countess. She had spoken low, nevertheless, Maxime caught the words which revealed that a danger menaced her.

"What do you mean?" he cried.

"Nothing. Go on, I beg. You have just asserted that M. de Carnoël is a wretch. The doctor is of your opinion, I suppose."

"Yes, or rather I am of his. After having seen this Carnoël rescued by a knave I doubted still. It pained me to recognize the fact that you were interested in an unworthy man. The doctor removed my last doubts. He informed me of what this Carnoël did after quitting Rue Jouffroy. I should have begun by telling you why he was in the house and by whom he was brought there, but—"

"It is useless, tell me the rest."

"Well, madame, since you wish first to know the end of this sad story, know that Carnoël followed his mistress and she has taken him to a house where he still remains with her."

"And Villagos knows the house?"

"Perfectly."

"You believe it?"

"Why should I not believe it? The doctor has offered to take me there. We are to go with his friend this evening—or rather to-night. I am to meet them in the Champs-Elysées."

"You shall not go. I forbid it."

"May I ask why? said Maxime, surprised and at the same time charmed at the countess' tone. She would not have spoken in the imperative had she been indifferent to him."

"Because you would be rushing to your death," she replied quickly.

"To my death!"

"Villagos wishes to draw you into a trap. You will not return alive if you follow him this night."

"What interest has the doctor in making away with me?" he asked, smiling.

"The same which he had in preventing you from seeing me. He went to your house expressly to persuade you that I would be absent till to-morrow. This falsehood had an object. If I had not met you by a miracle, I should not have seen you to-day, and Villagos calculated that to-morrow you would no longer belong to this world."

"What! Villagos who boasts of his devotion to you; Villagos conspire against you! I dare not say against us, though you do me the honor of including me in the proscription you accuse him of meditating."

"Do not jest. Nothing is more serious ; I will prove it to you presently. In the meanwhile let us talk of something else. Have you seen your cousin since the events of last night ?"

"I have just seen her."

"Alone ?"

"No ; her father was present. The scene was a very painful one. I did not conceal from her what I thought of M. de Carnoël. Alice did not contradict me, but she declared positively that she would never marry."

"That signifies that she does not believe a word of your allegations, and that she intends to be constant to the absent one until his innocence shall appear. She is a woman ; she has faith.".

"You approve, then, of her persevering in her illusions ?"

"Assuredly."

"And I have been counting on you to make her listen to reason ! "

"Not a word more. We will resume our conversation in a few moments, for here we are."

The Russian trotter had vanquished the distance, and though Madame Yalta had taken the longest route, they were entering the Avenue de Friedland by the Place de l'Etoile.

She stopped Nedji before the little gate by which Maxime had first entered with Dr. Villagos. This private entrance opened at a stroke of the bell by the *valet de pied,* who took the reins and received from his mistress an order in a foreign tongue.

The countess passed in first and took a side walk which wound through a lawn and ended in an immense conservatory.

"Here," said Madame Yalta, "we may speak freely; no one will interrupt us."

"Not even the doctor?" asked Maxime, laughing.

"No; if he comes he will be told I have not returned."

"Do you intend never to receive him again?"

"I shall see him once more for the last time."

"He has, then, decided to pass over to the enemy?"

The question to which Maxime attached no importance made the countess start.

"No," she replied, slowly; "it is I who wish to separate from him."

And as Maxime seemed astonished, she added

"Come, you shall know all."

At one of the extremities of the conservatory, was a rendezvous furnished in a manner appropriate to a sylvan boudoir; divans covered with Japanese stuff, rocking chairs and a bamboo table.

"So," said Madame Yalta when they were seated, "You saw M. de Carnoël last night?"

"I had a glimpse of him, for he simply appeared and disappeared. Borisoff brought him in a close carriage, which he drove himself under a good escort, to the house where his accomplice awaited him. He left it almost immediately by scaling the garden wall. What means the woman took to draw him from the clutches of this Russian, I cannot tell, but I am anxious that you should know that her associate and auxiliary in this enterprise was your fencing-master."

To Maxime's great amazement, this revelation was received with perfect indifference.

"Ah!" she said tranquilly, "you recognized Kardiki?"

"Yes, though he was dressed as a gentleman. He dined at Bignon's with M. Borisoff who treated him like a comrade, and never suspected, certainly, the trick that was about to be played on him."

"Kardiki is very adroit."

"But do you not think that he is betraying you?"

"Why? He is a Polish refugee and has a right to counteract the designs of a Russian spy."

"Then you do not take in bad part that he should have aided a pair of rogues, for this creature and this Carnoël have been associated with the people who opened my uncle's safe with a false key."

"You are mistaken. M. de Carnoël does not know them, and he saw last night, for the first time the woman who rescued him."

"But she at least is, beyond doubt, a thief."

"No more than he is."

"You are not aware that they found on this wretch the fifty thousand francs taken from the safe."

"It was M. Borisoff who found them, was it not?"

"He has just placed them in my uncle's hands to-gether with a letter written by Carnoël to account for being in possession of this sum. It was sent to him, he claims, by a friend of his father, an anonymous friend."

"Or by an enemy who invented this ruse to ruin him. One of the two explanations is true, I grant."

At this moment a sound attracted Maxime's attention, and turning he saw a gardener approaching, a rake on his shoulder and watering-pot in his hand.

The height and broad shoulders of this man attracted his attention, and on looking at his face, he recognized him immediately as the person who had been success-ively porter in the house in Rue Jouffroy and protector of the false Madame Sergent.

This singular apparition drew from Maxime a cry of surprise, which made the suspicious gardener raise his head.

"What is the matter?" asked the countess, quietly."

"That man!"

"He has the charge of my flowers. He came to make the round of the conservatory, and is going off for fear of disturbing us."

In fact, the man with the rake, after respectfully taking off his straw hat, was retracing his steps.

"But he—he too knows the thief. It was he who for-merly kept the house in Rue Jouffroy, and afterward played the rôle of foreign lord, protector of this jade. I quarrelled with him, and we were to fight next day."

"You see it is well you did not do so.* You would have crossed swords with a domestic."

"And you are not astonished to learn that your gardener is also the accomplice of this worthy friend of M. de Carnoël?"

"I am astonished at nothing; but I understand that everything will be a surprise to you, and the time has come to make known what I should have preferred to keep from you. Learn, then, that I know by whom and why this theft was committed."

"You knew it, and you did not tell!"

"Listen before you judge. And first remember that they took from your uncle's safe only a casket belonging to a Russian spy. You will object that they took also a sum of money. I will come to that presently, and will prove to you that things were not as has been supposed."

"Then the thieves were Nihilists?"

"The government which employs Col. Borisoff has other enemies than Nihilists. All the proscribed, all who defended the independence of Poland, and who live in exile far from their conquered country. This Borisoff's mission was to watch and denounce the Nihilists, whose aim is to destroy everything, and the oppressed who still struggle against their oppressors. The casket deposited with your uncle contained written proofs of a vast conspiracy against Russian tyranny. The papers had been given up by a traitor, who has met with his deserts, and the patriots whom they compromised wished to regain them at any cost."

"And they could do no better than steal them."

"In their eyes the end justified the means. Two of them resolved to make the attempt."

"And one of them was a woman."

"Yes; a woman devoted to the cause she served—devoted even so far as to sacrifice her life, and even more than her life—her honor. The other was a Polish refugee, who had passed ten years in the mines of Siberia, to which Russian despotism had condemned him, and was prepared to do anything for the sake of vengeance."

"Prepared to do anything; that is just the word," said Maxime, between his teeth.

The misfortunes of the Polish insurgents affected him very moderately, whilst he had true tradesman-like ideas of the sacredness of a banker's safe.

"They went together one evening," resumed the countess, "and reached your uncle's offices without difficulty. Some one awaited them there who had procured a key, and indicated the word to open it. The woman wanted to operate herself, and you know what it cost her. He who gave her the information was ignorant of the terrible mechanism, whose claws seized her hand as she introduced the key into the lock."

"I had no difficulty in guessing the beginning of the story, and I know the end. But I have often wondered what came to pass when the thief found herself caught."

"She whom you call the thief tried to extricate herself," replied the countess." Her friends tried to deliver her. They could not discover the spring that had to be touched to withdraw the apparatus. Time was passing; some one might have come in, and if she had been surprised all was lost. She did not hesitate. She commanded the man who accompanied her to cut off her hand."

"And he consented to render this frightful service?"

"He was under her orders; he obeyed. He had a poniard, large and sharp; with one blow the hand was severed."

"And this strange heroine did not die? She did not fall fainting on the floor?"

"She had strength to stand, and conquered her pain. Her companion, who had served in war, knew something about wounds; he tied up the wrist, and led off the wounded woman, who was scarcely able to stand."

"She was dressed as a man, was she not?"

"Yes."

"Then it was she and her accomplice whom Vignory and I met in the gateway. We saw the light, and entering the office—"

"Where you found the hand. To remove it your friend Vignory touched the spring. You believed yourselves alone, but some one saw you—heard you. This thief, as you call her, knew that you had taken her bracelet, and that it was your intention to search for her, to conduct by yourself an inquest which belonged of right to the agents of the prefecture of police."

"Good ! the traitor heard my conversation with Vig-nory and made his report to her who paid him.

"You are partly right. Only he was not paid, but he told what he had heard, and she whose destruction you swore, swore to regain possession of the bracelet. She had all the forces of the association of the proscribed at her disposal, and to recover the jewel which might have betrayed her, she made choice of a woman skilful and bold."

"The woman of the Rink !"

"It was, I believe, at the Rink that she arranged her meeting with you. Having failed in that, she tried not long after a less violent and surer means. You were fol-lowed step by step. You were observed one evening en-tering the Variétés. She came there. You invited her to supper. I need not tell you the rest."

"No, I have not forgotten the sequel. Then this crea-ture did all by order of the one-handed ?"

"Yes."

"So I supposed, for she possesses her two hands and is very skilful in pilfering with them. But this brunette with the golden complexion cannot be Russian ?"

"No, she is French and married to a Pole."

"I pity him. And now may I ask how it is that your gardener has been associated with her in the several plays in which she has acted ?"

"You told me that he passed for her protector, did you not ?"

"Yes, when he appeared with her at the theatre; but in Rue Jouffroy he was taken for porter of this house, which appears to have served as headquarters of the band. —I have seen him there."

"Not last night, I suppose, for yesterday evening quite late he came to me for orders for some changes I wished to make in my conservatory, and this morning, quite early, I found him at work."

"He was not of this expedition; but why had he served her before?"

"He is her husband."

"Her husband! and he tolerates the life she leads!"

"You are mistaken with regard to Justine. Her conduct is quite irreproachable. She obeys no one but her husband, whom she loves—and a woman who protects her."

"Yes, the woman of the bracelet. But, why did she give asylum to this Carnoël? To save him from Borisoff was well, but to hide him at her house—that hardly accords with her great love for her husband."

"That is absolutely false. Justine carried M. de Carnoël to a house where he is in safety, but she is not with him."

"Then M. Villagos—"

"Has lied. He invented this fable to draw you into a trap. You incommode him. He wishes to be rid of you."

"I incommode him! How?"

"You have meddled with his affairs."

"Without suspecting it, certainly. What affairs has he? Is he also a conspirator?"

"The chief of them. Villagos directs all the intrigues against the government of the Czar; and he has not the same grievances as the proscribed Poles. He is Russian. His name is not Villagos, it is Grisenko. He has no country to avenge. He is a Nihilist."

"Nihilist! this amiable doctor! Then he was concerned in the theft of the casket?"

"It was he who organized it."

"Ah! now I see why he pointed out to me the brunette who skated on rollers. He was in league with her. But why does he reproach her now for her connection with Carnoël? I am lost in inconsistencies."

"They are only apparent. I have not told you all. Villagos knew from the first that M. de Carnoël had disappeared, and that he was suspected of the theft. It mattered little to him that the innocent should be accused. He even rejoiced in it, for it diverted suspicion from the real culprits. Now it happened that the woman who played the principal rôle in this affair was interested for this young man who was accused, and who was not there to defend himself. She took into her head to repair the wrong that had been involuntarily done, and to attain this end, it was necessary to find M. de Carnoël. This project did not suit Villagos, who feared she would compromise herself, and, above all, the Nihilists. And

he had reason to fear it, for M. de Carnoël had fallen into
Borisoff's hands, and could not be delivered without coming in conflict with a man sent to Paris for the express
purpose of watching over the enemies of Russia."

"The lady confided her design, then, to this Satanic
doctor?"

"No, but he guessed it. She allowed herself to let fall
expressions of sympathy for the misfortunes of M. de
Carnoël. It was all that was necessary to make him
divine that she would seek to save him."

"Did she know that Carnoël was a prisoner in the
house in Rue de Vigny?"

"No one knew it, but the lady suspected it and acted
accordingly. Villagos only learned it afterward. How,
I cannot tell. You saw him this morning. He certainly
made an effort to surprise your secrets. Are you certain
you did not let him do so?"

"I! deliver up a secret you commanded me to keep!
I listened to the doctor, but told him nothing—or almost
nothing."

"Little as you may have said, it was too much. Villagos is sagacious and cunning. He has to appear the false
to discover the true. I fear you have, unknown to yourself, given him the information he was in search of."

"You have a sad opinion of me. Is it my intelligence
or my fidelity you mistrust?"

"Neither; but you are hardly the rival in cunning of
a man whose life has been spent in conspiring, and who

possesses in the highest degree the art of reading the thoughts of others whilst concealing his own.   Try to remember.   Did you not let fall some imprudent word? Did you not say, for instance, that M. de Carnoël was taken last night to a house in Rue Jouffroy ? "

" It was he who said so.   I told him that he was mistaken."

" And that he was there no longer, did you not ? "

" It is true," answered Maxime, reddening a little. " But he knew it already.   I told him nothing new."

" And no doubt you spoke to him of Kardiki ? "

" I—no—I believe not."

" Be frank, and hide nothing from me, I pray.   It is important I should know."

" I only told him that I fancied I had recognized your fencing-master dressed as a gentleman and seated in a box beside the woman of the Rink, but that I was not quite certain."

" Thank you," murmured the countess, who had become quite pale.   " I know now what to think of the consequences of your conversation with that man."

" But," resumed Maxime, quickly, " he replied that I must be mistaken ; that this Kardiki was a poor devil of a Polish refugee, and had no acquaintance with Mlle. Justine."

" And it was after having given you this assurance that he told you that I would pass the day in the country ? "

" Yes.   What connection was there between this falsehood and the mistake I made of mentioning the name of Kardiki?"

"If Villagos endeavored to deter you from coming to see me, it was because he did not wish me to know that he was aware of the conduct of Kardiki. I will explain to you why I know, as I told you, the woman who protects Justine, and who undertook the campaign to draw M. de Carnoël from the claws of Borisoff. In acting thus, this woman disobeyed the orders of the Nihilist committee, represented by Villagos, and has incurred a terrible punishment. Villagos thought you would speak to me of your conversation with him; that I would foresee the danger which menaced my friend, and would hasten to warn her of it. If he has engaged you to defer your visit till to-morrow, it is because he has resolved to act before you have seen me."

"Well, his Machiavellian plan has miscarried, and now that we both understand perfectly the situation, I charge myself with bringing M. Villagos to reason. Shall I begin by boxing his ears, to teach him to fool me as he did this morning?"

"No," said the countess, quickly; "to play your life against his would be too unequal a game. It is for me to act, for I alone can save those who have been exposed to the vengeance of the Nihilists. But first I must convince you of M. de Carnoël's innocence. I have not yet spoken to you of the second attempt—the one which succeeded. It was made by one man alone—the same who accompanied my friend on the first expedition, in which she lost her hand. I knew this man, and I swear to you that no one assisted him in opening the safe ; that he took only the casket, and that he was ignorant of the existence of M. de Carnoël."

"It remains to be explained how M. de Carnoël had on his person the fifty thousand francs which were certainly taken from the safe. Vignory explained to us that the packages of notes were pinned in a particular manner, and is certain of having pinned them himself."

"M. Vignory is mistaken, or he lies."

"My uncle would scarcely admit that, if the question were submitted to him."

"He would admit it, I\ suppose, if my friend should appear before him to confirm the statement I have just made to you."

"I doubt it.   Besides, she could not do that without confessing her own guilt."

"Without confessing that she has conspired against the oppressors of her country."

"It would be a generous action—too generous ; for if M. de Carnoël is innocent, why does he not come forward himself ?"

"He would already have done so if my friend had not restrained him," replied the countess, with confidence.

"Your friend !   He has, then, taken refuge with her ?"

"Where else would he go after the events of last

night? Justine carried him to her protectress, and he has remained with her."

"That is natural enough; but the asylum is ill chosen for a man who claims to vindicate himself of the charge with which he is accused, for the person 'who receives him has attempted to open the safe, and one of her accomplices has succeeded. It will not fail to be said that these people all understand each other."

"My friend will request M. Dorgères to examine all those who took part in the affair of the casket. They will declare unanimously that M. de Carnoël knew nothing about it, and as they will be compelled to accuse themselves their testimony need not be suspected."

"Well, let him appear and plead his own cause if he has nothing to reproach himself with. I do not say that he will win, but in any event he has little to lose."

"And had he everything to lose he would not hesitate."

"You have, then, seen him?"·

"Yes."

"Will he go alone?"

"No. In all probability he would not be received."

"Will it be more likely if he goes with your friend?"

"'I shall go with him, and I count on your assistance. Your presence would be indispensable to me."

"I am at your service, but my situation is a difficult one. I have just sworn to my cousin, sworn on my honor, that Robert de Carnoël was unworthy of her."

"You spoke according to your conscience. You will speak differently, now that you have more light. And your cousin will believe you now that you have proved to her that you have never disguised your opinion."

"Perhaps. But I doubt whether my uncle will let us see her."

"I have foreseen that, and made arrangements for an interview with your cousin. I have written her that I was in possession of the entire proof of M. de Carnoël's innocence, and begged her to come immediately by the little door on the Avenue de Friedland. After a brief interview, I will return with her myself to her father, and he must receive us."

Maxime would have had more than one objection to urge, but it was now too late. He knew Alice; he knew that she would catch at this last hope, would find means of escape and hasten to the stranger who promised to restore to her the betrothed of her heart. He was roused from these reflections by the sound of a light step approaching through the shrubbery. Madame Yalta, absorbed in her reflections, seemed to hear nothing. Soon a white hand put aside the leaves, a head appeared between two camelia bushes, and Maxime rose, uttering a cry of surprise. He had recognized a face which shone an instant like a ray of sunlight, to be eclipsed almost immediately.

"She !" he exclaimed.

"What do you mean?" asked the countess, raising her head.

"The woman of the Rink—the woman who delivered Carnoël!"

Madame Yalta started. Evidently she was not expecting this visit, and found it inopportune. But she soon recovered herself, and called :

"Justine!"

The branches were put aside again, and the brunette with the golden complexion reappeared. She was beautiful as ever but had changed her toilette. The skater of the Rink, the elegant lady of the opera was modestly clad as became a lady-in-waiting. The butterfly had returned to a chrysalis.

This enigmatical creature came forward deliberately and appeared not at all surprised at seeing Maxime, who, on his part, looked at her in stupefaction.

"What is the matter?" inquired Madame Yalta.

"The person whom Madame the Countess was expecting has just arrived."

"Where have you taken her?"

"Into Madame the Countess' boudoir."

"Villagos has not yet arrived?"

"Not yet ; but a box has been brought from him. Madame the Countess will find it on the lacquer table in her sleeping chamber."

"Very well. Leave us."

Justine bowed and went out quickly.

"This girl has just informed me that Mlle. Dorgères is here," said the countess. "Do you wish to see her?"

" But—I do not know whether I ought," stammered the cousin.

" Yes.   Better that you should be present at our inter-view.   Come."

" But—"

" What ? "

" The brunette—the accomplice of the thieves—she whom you call Justine—"

" Is my *femme de chambre*," replied the countess, quietly.   " Come, the moments are precious."

And cutting short any further explanations, she rose to leave the conservatory.   Maxime followed without a word.   He was in a state of extreme agitation.

" Her *femme de chambre*," he thought.

" The creature who pilfered me of the bracelet is in her service—like the gardener—like the fencing-master—and she has given me to understand that all this pretty set of people took part in the theft of the safe.   Am I to suppose that the orders came from her ? "

They crossed, without exchanging a word, a corner of the park, meeting with no one, and arrived before a door of the cottage that was unfamiliar to Maxime.   The countess conducted him through corridors and stairways to the large apartments on the first floor.   Neither Jus-tine nor the duenna who had twice introduced Maxime, were there to receive them.

Preceded by Madame Yalta, he reached the room in which he had seen her the day before in the great bed-stead with pillars and canopies.

"Mlle. Dorgères is there," she said, pointing to the doorway of Gobelin tapestry, which concealed the entrance to the boudoir. "Do you not think you would do well to speak to her first, and prepare her for what I have to say?"

"No," replied Maxime. "She thinks I have taken sides against Robert de Carnoël, and would not listen to me. She now believes only in you, and is distrustful of me."

He was still speaking when his eyes fell upon an object upon a Chinese lacquer table. It was a box of peculiar shape, widened at the top and closed with a lid.

"There, no doubt, is what Dr. Villagos has sent you," he said.

Madame Yalta opened the strange coffer which was of fir wood, quite rough, and drew from it a bouquet of immortelles.

"A singular gallantry," said Maxime.

The countess did not reply. She let fall the mournful flowers, and he saw that she turned pale.

"I expected it," she said.

"What does M. Villagos mean by this ridiculous present?"

"It signifies my sentence of death."

"Your sentence of death!" exclaimed Maxime.

"Yes; I am condemned."

"Condemned by this miserable Villagos!"

"By the Nihilists, of whom he is the chief. They accuse me of having betrayed them."

. "You ! "

" I have been allied to them. I deserve my fate."

Maxime was about to cry out, but the duenna whom he had seen before, entered suddenly, went straight to her mistress, and spoke to her in a language he did not understand. The conversation was very short, and the duenna went out on a motion from the countess. Turning toward Maxime, she said shortly :

" Do not ask for explanations. The conversation you are about to hear will tell you all. Go into the boudoir where Mlle. Dorgères is awaiting me, and beg her to listen with you. In a few moments she will have the proof that M. de Carnoël is innocent."

" Who is it you are about to receive ? "

" You will see—not a word more. Go in ; it is better we should not be surprised together."

" Swear to me that you are exposing yourself to no danger."

" None at this moment. You need not close the door, and by hiding behind the tapestry, may hear all that is said."

. "And if you should have need of assistance, I would be there," murmured Maxime.

He felt that he loved, in spite of all, this strange woman who now rose against the Nihilists after having coöperated with their dark dealings. It was time for him to disappear. The tapestry had no sooner closed on him than M. Villagos entered.

The doctor of medicine and conspiracies was grave as a justice, and his eyes shone with a deadly light.

The countess was calm, and she advanced deliberately toward him.

"What do you want with me?" she asked. "You have announced the sentence of death that has been passed upon me."

"I wish to question you."

"To what purpose, since I am already condemned?"

"You have accomplices. I wish to know them. Traitors must be punished."

"When I know of what I am accused, I will see whether it suits me to reply to you."

"You are accused of having compromised the success of our plans."

"This vague reply will not answer. Be precise."

"So be it. In the name of the Central Committee, I have forbidden you to interest yourself in a Frenchman suspected of a theft on the banker Dorgères. You paid no heed to this order. Not only have you charged another Frenchman with the recovery of M. de Carnoël, but have enlisted persons engaged in your service in this work,—subalterns whom we had initiated into all our secrets and who have long worked for us. Your fencing-master, Kardiki, and your *femme de chambre*, Justine, have taken part in an intrigue, the object of which was to deliver a stranger who, to prove his own innocence, would not fail to designate the guilty party."

" He does not know them."

" But he would know them if I let you live. You have sworn to restore him what he has lost, and you cannot reinstate him without denouncing us."

" Without denouncing myself, you mean. You have rightly guessed. I propose to recount to M. Dorgères, to his daughter, the true history of the theft. I shall tell them by whom it was committed and with what object. He will believe me, for I shall bring him an unanswerable proof. I think fit to add that I shall not mention the names of any of those who urged me to it."

" I have no longer faith in your discretion ; but I may ask why it is that you turn against us after having so well served us."

" Because I choose to have no dealings with the murderers who have just blown up the Winter Palace," replied the countess, looking fixedly at Villagos.

" Your scruples come rather late. When you took the vow to contend with us against tyranny, you were not ignorant that fire and sword would be employed to destroy it."

" I pictured to myself an insurrection against the Russian government," replied the countess, proudly. " I knew there had been murderers among you, but I believed these to be isolated acts to which those who committed them had been driven by despair. The news from St. Petersburg has opened my eyes. You may kill me ; you will not force me to remain one of you. I am the daughter of a man who died in Siberia, whither he had been exiled for taking up arms for the independence of Poland. It was to free my country that I consented to become your ally, and the brave men and women whom I have led into a complicity with you have had no other aim. Kardiki has served his country, and he believed he was serving her still in executing my orders. Justine is Prussian, but her father and her husband are Polish. Georget, the brave boy who has risked his liberty and his life for me, is the grandson of a Frenchman who died fighting in the ranks of the Polish army, and she who shared his dangers and who married him during the great insurrection of 1831 was born the Countess Wielenska. She has sacrificed everything for her country—rank, name and fortune, and during the forty years in which she has been consigned to the humble position to which our misfortunes have brought her, she has not ceased to work day and night for the deliverance of her country. Do you think this noble woman would consent to serve longer the cowardly partisans who murder?"

"She has permitted her grandson to aid them to steal," said the doctor, with a sarcastic smile.

"The permission was granted with the sole purpose of destroying papers which compromised hundreds of her compatriots. But it was I whom he obeyed; I who dedicated myself to the accomplishment of this act, which I regarded as a sacred duty, and I do not need to remind you what it cost me."

"Yes, I know that you have been heroic," said Villagos, slowly, "and I ask myself what mad inspiration led you to desert our party after having so bravely and skilfully served it. Not a trace remained of an accident that might have ruined us, when you suddenly undertake to stir up this affair, go to war with your friends, and, seeking to destroy your own work, launch all your auxiliaries into an insane enterprise, which has succeeded only too well. Could you explain to me the cause of this sudden change?"

"The cause? There was no other than the desire to save the innocent ; it was that I swore to repair the wrong unintentionally done to M. de Carnoël and to his betrothed."

"Very well. You confess that you have compromised us by your sentimental follies. It is an unpardonable crime. I may, however, take on me to pardon you on two conditions."

"Spare yourself the trouble of naming them. I shall not submit to them."

"The first," resumed the imperturbable doctor, "is that you leave France never to return. The second—your protégé, Carnoël is here, I am certain. It was to your house that Justine and Kardiki brought him last night. If you wish the Committee to overlook your faults,—if you desire to live, it is necessary to deliver up this man—to deliver him to me this day—instantly."

"To deliver M. de Carnoël to you !" said the countess,

with a contemptuous smile, "to be murdered, no doubt. And it is to me you dare to propose a cowardice."

"Do you refuse?"

The countess did not take the trouble to reply. She pulled a cord, and motioned the insolent doctor to the door.

"Very well," he said, in a rating tone; "you drive me away. I shall not return, and you will not see me again, for forty-eight hours from now you will be dead. One word only. Know that all who have aided you, all who have received your confidence, will be pitilessly struck. Your treason will not save them. Adieu, countess. I shall regret you. You might have powerfully aided our cause, and you will end like a traitor."

Having hurled this menacing farewell, Villagos turned on his heels toward the door. Kardiki, summoned by the stroke of the bell, awaited him there. The Nihilist Russian and the Pole exchanged not very amicable glances, and the faithful servant of Madame Yalta followed him to prevent an aggressive return. Scarcely had they disappeared, when Maxime raised the tapestry behind which he had been concealed during this tragic conversation. The countess approached him and found Alice standing behind her cousin. Alice, pale and trembling, had not strength to speak, but Maxime exclaimed:

"We have heard all."

"Then you know that I am to die," said the countess, with a sad smile.

"To die ! it is this wretch who will die. ˉ I charge my-self with sending him into the other world with a good sword thrust."

"No. You will not play your life against a murderer's. You can now no longer doubt that M. de Carnoël is innocent."

"Alice doubts it no more than I. And my uncle must yield to the evidence. , The time for circumspection is past. I want to lead back Robert to the house from which he came out poor and proud. ´ I wish to have him reënter it with his head erect. He is here, is he not ? "

"Yes," replied the countess, "but I claim the honor of presenting him to M. Dorgères. It is for me to repair the wrong that has been done."

"But," said Maxime, with a little embarrassment, "I do not know whether my uncle will consent—"

"To receive us ? You will tell him what you have just learned. I have nothing now to conceal. It matters little that they should know I have dishonored myself by allying myself with rascals. I forswear them and I brave their vengeance. I deny them so utterly that I shall ask M. Dorgères to publish everywhere their history and mine."

"It would be a grave imprudence, and I beg you not to do it. Why should you expose yourself to terrible dangers ? It is enough that Robert de Carnoël should be exonerated. I shall hasten to my uncle and announce your visit ; but all will be between him and me."

"Will you pardon me?" the countess said, turning toward Mlle. Dorgères, "for having caused you so much suffering."

Alice did not reply. She was weeping.

"Yes," she went on. "I was cruel. I should, when I first knew that your betrothed was accused, have said before you, before your father, that I alone was the guilty one. My silence was a crime. And this crime I am ready to expiate. I consent to declare publicly that I have been the accomplice of these wretches; that to save them I have dishonored myself."

"You, madame!" stammered the trembling Alice.

"Do you doubt it? You have not heard, then, what I said to that man? You do not know at what price I paid for my stupid devotion to an infamous cause? Well, look."

She made three steps and raised a black curtain which masked a niche in the wall. Alice uttered a cry of horror and turned away her eyes. She had already raised this curtain and knew what it concealed.

"It was you, then?" murmured Maxime.

"Have you not guessed it?" she asked, showing her left arm.

He had not guessed it, or rather, he had not wished to guess, for the conversation he had just heard should have left him no doubt. He understood all now; the sad history of the stranger contained no more mysteries for him.

"Yes," resumed Madame Yalta. "I submitted without a murmur to a horrible operation. I believed I was shedding my blood for my country, and it cost me less than to lend myself to the machinations of Villagos. It was he who devised the plan of using the marvellous beauty of Justine for the purpose of drawing you into an ambush. It was he who, after the failure of the first attempt, conceived the idea of bringing you here. He hoped I should succeed where Justine had failed. I might have perished in the attempt, for I could scarcely stand, and the part I was called upon to perform obliged me to incur the risk of a fatal relapse. What mattered my life to him, provided he could guarantee himself against your researches, for he feared if I should be detected he would be suspected of being my acomplice. He did not anticipate your speaking to me of M. de Carnoël, and could he have foreseen what has come to pass, would never have brought you here. The day on which he made the discovery that I wished to find M. de Carnoël, that day he turned against me. He declared war, secret war, for he did not yet act openly, but in the dark. He watched me, he set spies on my people. We were able to defeat his stratagems and to deliever M. de Carnoël ; and when he knew that the prisoner was free and all was about to come out, he announced to me my sentence."

"He forgot you had friends who would defend you. This condemnation is only a similar joke."

"Let us speak of yourself," resumed the countess, to Alice, "of your betrothed. I know him now. He is the noblest, the most fearless, the most generous of men. Were there no wrongs to be redressed I would gladly dedicate myself to restoring him to you. Pardon me for deferring your meeting. M. Dorgères must be present when I bring him back to you."

Alice was too much agitated to reply, but Maxime signified his approbation, and Madame Yalta said to him, quickly :

"Go, take Mlle. Dorgères back to her father, and prepare him to receive me. Do not lose a moment. What I may do to-day I may not perhaps to-morrow. My hours are numbered."

Maxime did not observe this allusion to the threats of Villagos. His mind was occupied with another idea. His countenance clouded over, and he replied, shaking his head :

"My uncle would listen to nothing so long as the fifty thousand francs found on Carnoël remains unexplained."

"They were sent by an enemy to ruin him," replied the countess, quickly. "Why may it not have been Villagos ? He has enormous sums at his disposal, and is capable of any infamy. The letter received by M. de Carnoël is perhaps in his handwriting. I shall see it. You will investigate on your part, and we will prove, I am persuaded, that the sending of the money was an atrocious plot. But act, I beg you, without delay. In two hours I shall be at M. Dorgères'," she added, extending her right hand to Alice, who melted·into tears.

Maxime understood that further words would be useless. "Come," he said to his cousin, and they left the house together.

CHAPTER XVIII.

THE MYSTERY CLEARED UP.

ON quitting the countess' house with Alice, Maxime had decided to approach his uncle frankly, and to deliver in concert with his cousin a vigorous assault. Alice, determined to sustain him, encouraged him in this bold design, and Madame Yalta had promised to appear in time to decide the victory. And still he felt doubtful of success. The fifty thousand francs found on M. de Carnoël constituted the weak point of the projected attack. There was little hope of convincing him while M. de Carnoël was not in a situation to prove that the fatal bank-notes had been sent to him by an unknown—friend or enemy.

But this was not a reason for deferring to engage in the undertaking, and Maxime experienced a lively disappointment when, arriving at the door of the house on Rue de Suresnes, he learned that M. Dorgères had gone out and would not return for an hour. However, he thought that before engaging in the affair, he had a duty to fulfil.

Vignory was in question; it was against Vignory, his

most intimate friend, that he was about to enter on a campaign.

Their friendship had been less warm of late but it subsisted still, and Maxime could not work decidedly on behalf of M. de Carnoël without forewarning Vignory.

It was an avowal painful enough to make, but Maxime hoped that a frank confession would not have the effect of estranging him entirely from his old comrade. He knew that good sense was his dominant quality; that he looked on life from a practical point of view, and he counted on making him see that an enforced marriage could not be a happy one, and that instead of incurring the risk, it would be better to renounce of his own free will the hand of Alice, and content himself with being M. Dorgères' partner.

Whilst revolving these arguments in his mind, he pursued his way to Rue d'Aguesseau.

It was Sunday, and there were chances that Vignory had not yet gone out. He had scarcely taken twenty steps when he perceived Georget coming toward him.

He had some difficulty in recognizing him, for in place of the office livery he wore an elegant jacket, velvet breeches and gray hat. He walked with his head high, and hands in his pockets; his eyes were bright and his mouth smiling.

" You are cured, then ? " said Maxime.

" So entirely that I seem never to have been ill," replied Georget. "I have already played ball with my right arm, and my memory has come back."

"Then I shall not leave you, my boy, you can tell me many things. Where were you going at this rate?"

"To tell my story to M. Dorgères."

"What story?"

"I am going to tell him that I explained to the persons who carried off M. Borisoff's casket how to open the safe."

"I suspected as much. Was it your own idea to come and confess to my uncle?"

"No, grandmother sent me."

Maxime began to understand. The countess must have gone early this morning to announce to Madame Piriac the delivery of M. de Carnoël, and to give her instructions in consequence.

"And you are not afraid that your former patron will have you arrested? I don't know how he will take your confessions. Is it to soften him that you are so dressed up?"

"Oh no, Monsieur Maxime, the countess brought me this costume. She is going to take me away and does not wish me to be groom any longer."

"To take you away! where?"

"I don't know. I only know she is going away this evening, and we are going with her,—grandmother and I. And I will be sorry, because I won't see you any more."

"Come with me. My uncle is not at home. He will return soon, and we will see him together. But I have somewhere to go in the meanwhile."

"With pleasure, Monsieur Maxime," said the child. He did not inquire where he was to be taken, and followed willingly.

Rue d'Aguesseau was not far off and they were silent during the short walk. On arriving at Vignory's house, they found the porter in conversation with a tall young man who bowed to Maxime.

"You do not know me," he said. Do you remember the cock of Rue Jouffroy ? "

"Very well," said Maxime, surprised at this meeting.

"Agénor Galopardin, book-keeper and member of the society of Enfants d'Apollon. I came to see my ex-comrade Vignory. I say *ex*, because he has dropped me for the last two months. Only think, he sends this morning a messenger begging me to call at his lodging. I sacrifice my fritters and run. No Vignory. Monsieur is gone out."

"I came to see him also, and am very much vexed at not finding him."

"You too, he has set you down too ! Ah, fortune changes men. He was not so proud two months ago, when he came after me at the café to ask me to do him a favor. He had confidence in me then, for it concerned a delicate matter, an anonymous restitution."

"What ! what do you mean ? " asked Maxime, quickly.

"Oh, it was a very simple thing. Fifty thousand francs that a client of the Dorgères' house owed to a ᵑntleman, and wished to return it without giving his name. Between ourselves, I always believed he had stolen them."

"And—Vignory charged you with remitting `this, sum?"

"*Ma foi!* yes. I am not rich, but I am honest, and I delivered the package safely to the address of the gentleman, Boulevard des Batignolles. I even wrote the letter accompanying it. It seemed the debtor didn't want his creditor to know where the bank-notes came from, and this creditor knew the handwriting of the employés of M. Dorgères, and that was why he applied to me. He even promised that his patron would make me a nice present, but it has never come."

Maxime was pale with emotion. He learned all at once that Robert de Carnoël was innocent, and that Jules Vignory had been guilty of a base act.

"Would you recognize this letter that you wrote—"

"Under Vignory's dictation? Perfectly. He would recognize it too. I didn't change a word in the copying."

"Then come with me."

"Where?"

"To M. Dorgères', my uncle's. He would like to thank you."

"I would ask nothing better. However, if it would draw on me the displeasure of Vignory—"

"Come, monsieur, come and do a good act. I swear that you shall be rewarded."

Galopardin suffered himself, to be led off by Maxime, who had taken his arm.

Georget had listened without a word, but it could be read on his face that he understood all.

Two hundred steps from the house, Maxime perceived Vignory approaching. He was hastening toward him, but Vignory also perceived Maxime and had recognized the book-keeper. He turned immediately and retraced his steps at full speed.

"Ah! that is too much!" exclaimed Galopardin. "Now this monsieur makes off when he sees me. He is afraid of being obliged to confess that he once frequented the society of a poor devil of my sort. He is ashamed of me. Very well. I will pay him back some day."

"Yes," exclaimed Maxime, "he wishes to avoid us; he has guessed all. Let us hasten, I beg. I have not a minute to lose in presenting you to my uncle."

Galopardin was not pleased with his *ci-devant* friend, and he followed Maxime without further thought of what unhappy consequences the presentation might have for the ungrateful Vignory.

Father Doulevant opened his eyes wide at seeing Georget in his new costume, but his astonishment did not prevent him from informing Maxime that M. Dorgères had returned and was awaiting him at his office.

At this moment a carriage stopped before the gateway, and his astonishment changed to stupefaction when he saw Robert de Carnoël descend from this coupé, and give his hand to the Countess Yalta to aid her to alight.

The countess leaning on the arm of M. de Carnoël, Maxime Dorgères agitated, Georget radiant and Galopardin bewildered, formed a cortège which the conçierge regarded in consternation.

Maxime bowed to the countess, pressed the hand of Robert in silence, and said in an undertone :

"My uncle will receive us. I answer for our success. And Providence has brought me face to face with a man who brings conclusive testimony," he said, designating with a glance the book-keeper leaning against the wall."

"Let us go," said Madame Yalta, simply.

She was very pale, less pale, however, than Carnoël who bore the impress of the long agony of his captivity. But she walked with a firm step, and the prisoner of Col. Borisoff had lost nothing of his pride. It was plain they had come to ask not pardon, but justice.

They met no one on the great stairway, and were conducted by Georget to the waiting-room attached to M. Dorgères' office. This hall was empty, but the banker was not alone, for through the door of the office in which he had formerly dismissed Robert de Carnoël could be heard the sound of his voice pitched in a high key. Maxime requested Galopardin to remain in the waiting-room with Georget until called for, opened the door of the office, and moving aside to allow the countess and Robert de Carnoël to pass in, entered immediately after her.

Alice, who was sobbing in the depths of an arm-chair,

sprang to her feet. M. Dorgères uttered a cry of indignation on perceiving the visitors his nephew had brought. He would certainly have burst forth if his former secretary only had been present, but he restrained himself, less out of respect for the countess than consideration for his daughter, who was in a condition of extreme nervous excitement.

To vent his anger on some one, he selected Maxime.

"Why do you undertake to bring to my house persons who have no business here?"

"My dear uncle," replied the nephew, quietly, "you will thank me presently for what I have done."

"Thank you! you are mocking me."

"Monsieur," began the countess, calmly, "I beg you to listen to me."

"It is useless, madame. I know what you are going to say. My daughter has already told me, and I do not believe a word of the romance you have invented. As for the man who dares to appear before me when I have driven him away," he added, advancing toward Carnoël, "I am determined not to suffer his presence."

The young man started, and had nearly replied in a manner to cut short all the attempts of his defenders at reconcilation, but his eyes met those of Alice and he was silent.

This proud silence only served to exasperate M. Dorgères, who resumed in a still sharper tone:

"This assurance is too much, and it is time to put an

end to it. My daughter, madame, has repeated what you have told her—that you have attempted to force the safe. You are free to boast of an action at which you should blush, but do not hope to persuade me that your protégé is not also your accomplice. I do not wish to pursue him. I even wish to forget your unjustifiable conduct ; but I have no use for your explanations. They will not exonerate the man you are bent on upholding. You wished only the papers of Borisoff, that is possible, but M. de Carnoël has taken from me fifty thousand francs. This pretended letter witnesses against him. It has been fabricated in his defence, and I would defy him to present me the so-called debtor who wrote it."

"Do you wish to see him ? " asked Maxime, approaching the door.

" To see—whom ? " exclaimed M. Dorgères

"I ask you," replied Maxime, quietly, "if you wish to see the person who wrote that letter ? "

"What stupid joke is this ? "

"Nothing is more serious. The person is there in your ante-chamber, and with or without your permission I am going to call him in."

And partly opening the door, Maxime put his head out :

"Be so good, dear monsieur, as to enter," he said to the clerk who was seated beside Georget on a bench ; " my uncle wishes to speak with you."

"No, no ; not at all," growled the banker.

Maxime took no notice of this denial, and drawing Galopardin after him, ushered him into the office.

The joyous youth, thus forced to appear before an imposing assemblage, thought no more of imitating the cock. He opened his eyes in a scared manner, bowed all around, and turned his hat awkwardly in his hands.

"Who are you?" asked M. Dorgères, roughly.

"Galopardin," stammered the employé. "Agénor Galopardin, book-keeper at M. Charoule's, wholesale charcoal merchant, Rue de Flandre. If you wished, monsieur, any information about me, my patron would tell you that."

"I know your patron, but no matter about him. What did you come here for?"

"I—I don't know—"

"But I know," said Maxime. "Come forward, monsieur. Take that paper that is on my uncle's table."

Galopardin obeyed mechanically, and as soon as he had the letter in his hands, exclaimed:

"Hold! this is the letter that I wrote."

"You!" exclaimed the banker, "you wrote that! We shall see pretty soon whether you are telling the truth. Here is a pen and ink. Copy the first sentence."

Galopardin thought perhaps the banker before offering him a situation in his banking house wanted to see if he wrote a good hand. He excused himself from taking the banker's chair, and set to work calligraphing with great pains. He had not written six words before M. Dorgères seized the paper, and designating Robert de Carnöel, said :

"Enough ! I am satisfied. It was certainly you who acted as secretary to monsieur."

"But—no—I do not know him," stammered Galopardin.

By the manner in which he and Robert de Carnöel looked at each other M. Dorgères could see that they met for the first time, and he began to change his tune.

"Then will you tell me who dictated this letter ?"

"Willingly, sir. It was M. Jules Vignory, your cashier."

"You lie !"

"I swear I do not. Vignory was my friend. He came one evening to Café Cardinet, bringing me the model of this letter and begging me to copy it—he asserted that he came from you."

"What ! he dared—it is impossible. Vignory is an honest man, and you would not repeat what you are saying in his presence."

"I beg your pardon, monsieur, I am all ready, and if you wish to send for him I answer for it, he will not give me the lie."

This answer was made so frankly and naturally that it greatly unsettled the convictions of M. Dorgères who remained very undecided and much out of countenance.

Carnöel knit his brow. He was not a man to rejoice in being betrayed by a friend, even though the treason should turn to his own profit.

But Alice who had never loved Vignory, and who saw the innocence of Robert made clear—Alice was radiant.

"What do you think now, my dear uncle?" Maxime said gently.

"I think," replied the uncle with ill-humor, "that all this is perhaps a play that has been gotten up, and until I have questioned Vignory—"

"He did not finish the sentence."

The door opened, and Georget entered just in time to draw on himself M. Dorgères' ill-temper.

"You rascal! what did you come here for?"

"Why do you come before I called?" asked Maxime, who wished to reserve for the end of the interview the appearance of the groom.

"Do you know, wretched child," resumed the banker, "that I might have you sent to prison? My daughter has told me that you have aided rogues to open my safe with a false key.

"You are a thief."

"Yes," replied the boy tranquilly, "if to be a thief is to assist brave people to recover papers that a police spy wanted to make use of to their hurt. Have me arrested if you think I deserve it."

"All very well," said Maxime, impatiently, "but I forbade you to come in till I called."

"M. Maxime, you need not be angry with me. It was M. Vignory who sent me."

"M. Vignory! Have you lost your mind?"

"He arrived like some one mad. He asked if M. Dorgères was in the office. I told him that he was with you, with Mlle. Alice, with Madame the Countess, and M. Robert; then he gave me this letter and told me to bring it immediately to the patron, and he has fled."

"A letter!" exclaimed M. Dorgères, "a letter from Vignory. Give it to me, boy."

Georget handed it to his patron who broke the seal nervously. Each one present understood that the dénouement of this family drama was imminent and there was a profound silence.

The banker read, and they could follow on his face the impressions that were created. He turned pale, his features contracted, and soon two big tears rolled down his cheeks.

At length he raised his head and said in a husky voice : "Listen."

"Monsieur," wrote Jules Vignory, "this is my confession. You doubtless know already the unworthy act of which I have been guilty, for I have just met the friend who unconsciously aided me in it. I understood that you were about to be informed of what I had done, and that I was lost. There remains nothing for me but to quit France never to return. I have deserved my fate; I do not complain, and if I write it is not in the hope to justify myself. But, perhaps, when you have read my full confession you will judge me less severely. The day M. Borisoff came to claim his casket, I arrived

at the office several minutes before him and found the
safe open. I had to reproach myself with not having
warned you of the first attempt at theft. When I saw
that the thieves had begun again, and this time had
succeeded, I lost my senses to that degree that on as-
certaining the deficit of the fifty thousand francs I forgot
entirely that the evening before I had put aside these
five packages of notes prepared by me to pay a draft.
They were in my table drawer, where I found them
several days after. At this moment you were accusing
M. de Carnoël, and M. Borisoff was engaged in pursuing
him to recover his casket. I did not accuse Robert, who
honored me with his friendship, but I suspected him.
When I placed my hand on the missing sum my first
feeling was one of joy. I was happy to be able to prove
that my friend had been calumniated, and to do that I
only needed to bring you this money. Unfortunately,
you had gone out. I did not succeed in getting an
interview with you during the evening and was compelled to defer the restitution till the next day. It cost
me much to take this step, for you would naturally reproach my heedlessness. A cashier who forgets fifty
thousand francs in a drawer is guilty of culpable negligence. I was, however, resolved to confront a blame I
deserved only too well, but an evil thought occurred to
me. I had sometimes dared to dream of becoming your
partner and son-in-law. It was a dream, but you had
shown so much interest in me that it did not seem one

impossible to realize. However, I spoke to no one of
these chimeras which I secretly caressed, and would
never have permitted any one to see that I entertained
the shadow of such a hope. I resigned myself to love
Mlle. Dorgères in silence, for I did love her with a disinterested love, and would have wished she were poor
that I might aspire openly to her hand. I suffered the
more since she did not—she could not—love me because
she was betrothed to Robert de Carnoël, my comrade,
my friend. And Robert, wounded by the repulse he had
just met with, had gone away swearing that he meant to
expatriate himself—that he would never return. The
obstacle which rose up between Mlle. Dorgères and me
had disappeared. I carried my delusion so far as to believe the day would come when she would forget the
absent one and would come at length to perceive that I
adored her.

"But the day after I discovered the missing sum I received from Carnoël a letter, through which I learned
that after a short journey to Brittany he had returned to
Paris ; that he would remain there some days in the
hope of making arrangements for going to America, and
meant to attempt a meeting with Mlle. Dorgères. He
gave me his address and asked to see me. This letter
overwhelmed me. All my plans crumbled away, for I
felt that Carnoël could easily justify himself if he was in
a situation to make explanations. Then despair seized
me and jealousy suggested an infernal thought. This

money, which I should have reported to you, I would
not keep it, and dreaded, in returning it, well-merited reproaches.   The loss of fifty thousand francs affected you
very little and you had ceased to think of it. It occurred to me to send it to Carnoël, feigning an anonymous restitution.   I said to myself that this money
would enable him to live in foreign parts and even make
his fortune there ; that in sending it to him without his
suspecting whence it came, I should accomplish a reparation in saving from poverty the friend whose flight left
the field open to my ambition.

"I said this, but I lied to myself ; I forced myself to
hide from my own eyes the base feeling which prompted
me, and I begin to-day to expiate my crime by confessing the truth.   At heart I had only one object. To
ruin Robert de Carnoël forever if he should venture to
reappear. I knew M. Borisoff was searching for him ;
that if he succeeded in discovering him he would find on
him the missing sum ; that you would be informed of
this discovery, and that Mlle. Dorgères could never marry
a dishonored man.   It was an odious calculation—cowardly, infamous, and I thank God that he has baffled it
by means of your nephew. Now you know all. I am
ignorant what has become of M. de Carnoël, and I earnestly hope my confession will arrive in time to prevent
an atrocious injustice. I have done. There only remains for me to ask, not that you will pardon, but that
you will forget me. Adieu, you who have overwhelmed

me with benefits. Adieu all you whom I have loved. I go, and you shall never hear of me again. Adieu, and pray God for one who is desperate."

It was all, and it was enough. Maxime wept, he who never shed tears, and looked at the Countess Yalta.

Georget bounded with joy. Galopardin smiled to keep himself in countenance.

Suddenly the countess turned pale and staggered. Maxime came forward to support her.

"It is over," she murmured. "The wretch has poisoned me."

And she fell. They all rushed to her relief. Their cares were unavailing. Her beautiful eyes opened no more. She was dead.

＊　＊　＊　＊　＊　＊　＊

A month has passed since the catastrophe which closed so gloomily this strange history. Alice and Robert are not yet married. They wear mourning for the noble woman who reunited them. But their marriage is arranged; and is to take place in May.

The death of the countess has never been avenged, and it is probable never will be, for Villagos disappeared the day of the crime, and all trace of him was lost. He had fled to some land frequented by the rascals whose chief he was,—bandits who prepare their crimes in darkness, profiting for concealment by the criminal toleration of governments.

The Nihilists abuse what is most sacred. They dishonor the right of asylum.

It was not Maxime's fault if the infamous doctor was not punished as he deserved. He pursued him without losing a minute, but the cowardly knave had taken his precautions in advance, and was not to be found. It was known that poison had been mixed by him in a glass of water prepared for the countess, who foresaw, doubtless, her approaching end, for the evening before she had written her will.

She had forgotten no one who had served her faithfully or who had loved her.

Madame Piriac, Georget, Kardiki, Justine and her husband inherited large sums, to be deducted before the succession of Robert de Carnoël, who was made universal legatee. And Madame Yalta left Maxime Dorgères a bracelet and a ring, more precious to him than all the riches of the world ; it was all that remained to him of a woman slightly known, but passionately loved.

The countess passed into his life like a meteor which blazes for an instant and disappears, leaving a luminous track in the firmament.

The memory of this extinguished star will never be effaced from the heart of Maxime, who is not yet consoled, and who, to recover from so violent a shock, is projecting a voyage round the world.

Perhaps in some far-off country he will meet Jules Vignory, expiating, by a life of toil, a moment of shameful weakness.

Robert de Carnoël only accepted the heritage of Madame Yalta to bestow it upon the poor. The Avenue de Friedland house is for sale, and the proceeds of the sale are to be devoted to a hospital for those disabled by accident. The workman mutilated in a factory will owe an asylum to the woman of the severed hand.

The servants and allies of the countess have all left Paris. Justine has gone with her husband to Algeria; Kardiki has taken refuge in Constantinople, and gives fencing lessons to the subjects of the Sultan; Georget has entered a ship-boy's school, and Madame Piriac is established at Brest.

But Galopardin has remained. M. Dorgères has taken him for cashier, and the safe is well guarded.

THE END.

CPSIA information can be obtained
at www.ICGtesting.com
Printed in the USA
LVHW080112131222
734902LV00031B/373

9 781340 988272